D0753207

F
1414.2   Duncan, Walter Ray-
•D86   mond

        Latin American
        politics

DATE DUE

OCT 25 '81			
DEC 7 '81			

COLLEGE OF MARIN LIBRARY
COLLEGE AVENUE
KENTFIELD, CA 94904

IVC

Latin American Politics

Latin American Politics

A Developmental Approach

W. Raymond Duncan

State University of New York at Brockport

Praeger Publishers New York

Map 1 is from John Rothchild, ed., *Latin America Yesterday and Today* (New York: Praeger, 1973). Maps 2–7, prepared by Eileen James, are from Preston James, *Introduction to Latin America* (New York: Odyssey Press, 1965). Copyright © 1965 by Odyssey Press, Inc., and reprinted by permission of The Bobbs-Merrill Company, Inc.

Published in the United States of America in 1976
by Praeger Publishers, Inc.
111 Fourth Avenue, New York, N.Y. 10003

© 1976 by Praeger Publishers, Inc.
All rights reserved

Library of Congress Cataloging in Publication Data

Duncan, Walter Raymond, 1936–
    Latin American politics.

    Bibliography: p.
    Includes index.
    1. Latin America—Politics and government—
1948–   1. Title.
F1414.2.D86   320.9′8′03   73-6496
ISBN 0-275-22120-2
ISBN 0-275-85300-4 pbk.

Printed in the United States of America

To my family,
Ute, Erik, and Christopher

Preface

As Latin America enters the late 1970s, the spirit dominating the region is that of development—an imperative spawned by post-World War II events that affected less developed countries everywhere and a vision that motivates most political leaders south of the Rio Grande. The postwar years brought a plethora of complex and interrelated problems—urban growth, unemployment, population explosion, malnutrition, and increasing income inequalities; at the same time, foreign-aid programs and the creation of United Nations development agencies suggested that these problems might be solvable and generated a search to improve the standard of living of the average citizen. Different political models of change resulted from the interaction of these forces: revolution in Cuba, an elected Marxist president in Chile, military reformism in Brazil and Peru, continued institutionalized reforms in Mexico, a new Canal policy in Panama, and oil power in Venezuela are some cases in point.

Yet change is no easy matter. Resistance comes in both material and human forms. Geography—the towering Andes, equatorial jungles, vast desert wastes—tends to divide Latin America into relatively prosperous coastal areas and isolated impoverished hinterlands. Combined with unequal resource distribution, this division impedes economic growth

and greater agricultural productivity. To these physical factors must be
added the intransigence of wealthy elites, the conservatism of the
military, outside economic pressures from foreign investors, and closed
authoritarian social systems. The clash of change and tradition often
produces open conflict and repression.

The Latin American political terrain is complex, for the variety of
developmental problems to be solved is immense, and the rates and
types of change range greatly from Mexico to Argentina. This book undoubtedly raises as many questions as it attempts to answer in regard
to that complexity. But if it stimulates its readers to think more deeply
about the links among politics, economics, and society, as well as the
uniqueness of the major forces at work in different Latin American
countries, it will have achieved its purpose.

Many individuals helped in clarifying the concepts and in producing
the pages that follow. Special thanks go to Manuel Alguero, Dieter
Zschock, and Robert Arnove for reading carefully and criticizing the
early drafts of the manuscript. I am also indebted to my friend and
colleague Walker Connor, who stimulated the work on ethnicity and
national identity which appears in Chapters 5, 6, and 7. Denise Rathbun,
Praeger's gracious and thought-provoking editor, made incisive observations on the manuscript throughout its production, for which I am
most grateful. The SUNY Research Foundation provided me with the
time and funding to develop several relationships between ethnicity
and politics in Latin America that are probed in following chapters.
Sylvia Colburn, Adele Catlin, Joni Anderson, and Roxanne Cifaldi were
dedicated typists, whose help I deeply appreciate. Finally, my students
in Latin American and Third World Politics at Brockport College deserve credit for their continuing interest in the subjects of this book.

W.R.D.

Contents

Part 4 Political Patterns

Part 5 Prime Development Problems

1
The
Setting

One

Introduction

Latin America is a vast world region, extending from the Rio Grande River in the north to Tierra del Fuego in the south. The population exceeds 315,000,000, compared to Anglo-America's 214,000,000, and the total land size is far greater than the continental United States. Brazil alone is larger than the forty-eight contiguous states in North America. Latin America's inhabitants include people of widely diverse origins, ranging from European ancestry (Spanish, Portuguese, French, British, Italian, German, Polish, Dutch, among others) to descendants of ancient Indian civilizations and the African continent. While Spanish and (in Brazil) Portuguese are the principal languages used by the educated public, much of Latin America's population does not speak them, using instead one of the numerous Indian dialects or, as in the case of tiny Haiti, Creole. Life styles vary from those of members of jungle tribes and small Indian villages to the dwellers in modern coastal cities. A traveler arriving in Buenos Aires from Mexico City has passed through thousands of miles and many ways of life.

Despite its great size and diversity, Latin America's common features are sufficiently similar to distinguish it from such other world regions as Africa, Asia, and the Middle East. It reflects the cultural patterns of southern Europe and exposure to common colonial experiences and early settlement patterns. These produced a dominating Church and Crown, and a small upper class of educated, European, and wealthy ancestry who controlled the land, the military, and the Church. This entrenched elite impeded the development of self-government even after independence had been won. Most of the countries in the region separated from Spain early in the nineteenth century through violent struggle. Brazil's break with Portugal was admittedly more peaceful, but also occurred in the early 1800s, giving the Latin American countries a period of independent rule much longer than other Third World, formerly colonized areas. The population, predominantly Roman Catholic in religion, young, and rapidly urbanizing, is, at about 3.0 percent annually, growing faster than any other in the world. These conditions, in addition to the region's common political, economic, and social problems and its distinctness from the industrialized, Protestant-Catholic, Anglo-Saxon northern zone, make it a unique world area meriting separate study by scholars and policy makers.

THE FIVE LATIN AMERICAS

Latin America's total area can be viewed as five separate subregions, each with its unique physical and historical characteristics: Mexico and the Caribbean republics; the Central American countries; the Andean states; the Atlantic area; and a fifth subregion comprising foreign-held, or recently independent territories, including French Guiana, Belize, Surinam, Guyana, Trinidad, Barbados, and a large number of other islands. We exclude the fifth region here because it is more amenable to separate treatment, given its disparate geography, territorial status, and cultural patterns.

Mexico and the Caribbean republics of Cuba, Haiti, and the Dominican Republic form the subregion that is closest to the United States. Its history includes past military interventions by the United States, with the most disastrous results in Mexico, which lost about half its domain to North America in the mid-1800s. Two of the countries—Mexico and Cuba, those most geographically proximate to North America—have experienced violent revolutions that radically restructured their political, social, and economic systems toward serving more people. Mexico today is a relatively industrialized country, with steel mills, textiles, petroleum refineries, and factories, while Cuba attempted with less success to move from dependence on sugar exports to a diversified economy after its 1959 revolution. Haiti and the Dominican Republic are by contrast underdeveloped. Mexico, the only country in Latin

America sharing a common border with the United States, is the largest of the four republics, with a population of sixty million, compared to the next largest, Cuba, with about ten million; Haiti and the Dominican Republic have six and five million people. The populations in these four countries are mixed; Mexico's mestizo people reflect Spanish and Aztec Indian mixture, while the other three countries are of Spanish and African ancestry, the mixture called mulatto.

The second major subregion is Central America. This narrow and curving zone, extending from Guatemala through Honduras, El Salvador, Nicaragua, Costa Rica, and Panama, is the isthmus connecting Mexico with South America. Once separated from Spain in 1821, the countries of Central America (except Panama, part of Colombia until 1903) attempted early unity through their United Provinces of Central America (1823-38), a political federation based in large part on the Constitution of the United States. This failed, due to internal factionalism and localism, and Central America split into separate independent republics in 1838. Today, however, some mutual benefits are derived from the Organization of Central American States (formed in 1951) and from the Central American Common Market (1960), the latter stressing cooperative trade policies.

Unlike Mexico and Cuba, no country in this subregion has experienced a sociopolitical revolution. These tropical, small countries (averaging about three million population) are less economically developed than Mexico and Cuba. Their mixed peoples of pronounced Mayan and other Indian ancestry, except in more European Costa Rica, rely principally upon single exports of raw materials, such as bananas, coffee, cotton, or forest products. But like their northern neighbors, they have experienced North American influence, the most notable example being Panama with its United States-controlled sea canal. Their diverse political systems include democratic Costa Rica, one-family rule (the Somozas) in Nicaragua, and the military-influenced governments of Guatemala, Honduras, El Salvador, and Panama.

A third subregion, much larger in size and population than Central America (seventy-six million compared to Central America's twenty million), is the Andean zone. It includes Venezuela, Colombia, Ecuador, Peru, Bolivia, and Chile—all countries that have largely escaped the direct effects of United States military intervention so strongly felt more to the north, although certainly not the influence of trade and corporate business. A common geographical feature within these countries is the Andes mountains, which extend along the west coast of South America from Venezuela through Chile. These Andean countries, whose pronounced Inca Indian and mestizo populations and natural resources are divided by the huge mountains, are trying to progress economically, as demonstrated by their organization known as the Andean Pact, formed in 1969. Yet their political styles are as different as their types and rates of change. Colombia and Venezuela are reasonably open political systems, and both are attempting to work out progressive social and economic policies. Venezuela's oil wealth gives it more promise in these efforts than Colombia. Peru is moving forward in the economic and social spheres, but unlike Colombia and Venezuela, under military guidance. Landlocked Bolivia, the smallest country with about five million people, is governed by the military, yet is moving much more slowly in reform directions and with less political freedom and participation than Colombia and Venezuela. Ecuador's leaders speak of economic and social progress, but frequently seem more interested in order and discipline. Chile, meanwhile, started out with great hopes for economic and social change in the mid-1960s, but began to look like a nineteenth-century military dictatorship, complete with repression and military torture, after the coup of September, 1973—leading to a life style sharply unlike its democratic self before the coup.

The fourth major part of Latin America is the Atlantic area, comprised of Brazil, Argentina, Paraguay, and Uruguay. Its hundred and forty million people make it the largest of the four regions, with Brazil's population alone amounting to about a hundred and ten million, followed by Argentina's twenty-five million. Gigantic Brazil thus dominates this part of Latin America, as Mexico and Cuba dominate the far north. Brazil in fact began to attain world-recognized economic growth in the early 1970s, even compared to that of Germany and Japan, although its political system came in for criticism for its undemocratic methods, strong military centralization, and subversion of human rights and freedoms. Argentina's situation by contrast is one of great political disorder (kidnapings, urban violence) and continued economic difficulties (inflation, excessive wage demands compared to productivity), in spite of the country's plentiful natural resources. Uruguay fell under military domination during 1973, a surprising turn of events since that country had long been known for its political freedoms, combined, it must be said, with severe economic problems generated by a heavily social-welfare-oriented economic sector unable to support its payments. Paraguay, by far the least well-known and studied country of this region, is a landlocked republic like its Andean neighbor Bolivia, and hard pressed for economic development and representative government. Brazil's population is of European-mulatto-African mixture, while Argentina and Uruguay are about 90 percent European. Paraguay, by contrast, is approximately 98 percent mestizo, many people being descendants of Spanish settlers and Guaraní Indian tribes.

THE CHANGING POLITICAL ENVIRONMENT

How does one begin to study the politics of this vast and complex world region? An appropriate beginning is to understand the forces affecting significant changes within the political environment. Latin America is caught up in the same forces that have been at work in many areas of the globe since World War II. It is experiencing the impact of industrialization, expanded communications, urban growth, and increased social mobility, but it is particularly affected by the population explosion. The population, growing annually at about 3.0 percent, doubled between the early 1930s and the 1960s. Future population projections estimate six hundred million people by the year 2000, thanks to high fertility rates, the effects of Hispanic culture, public-health campaigns, and a decline in the mortality rate. Latin America's twenty-two largest cities tripled in population between 1930 and 1960, and the urban sector is projected to be 60 to 70 percent of the total population by the year 2000, because its industrialized life and assumed employment opportunities act as a magnet attracting rural folk seeking a better life. But the rural to urban migration is in fact producing enormous poverty belts around the large cities, with thirty million people (more than 20 percent of the population), many of whom are unemployed, living in urban slums. As cities enlarge, the demands on government for public policies dealing with employment, health, education, transportation, welfare, economic development, and respect for human dignity continually grow.

The urban problem is only one of many pressures demanding a better life for the population as a whole and creating a new political environment in which many political leaders throughout Latin America are taking the lead in pressing for broad-range improvement in living conditions for much of Latin America's impoverished millions. The political accent is now distinctly on development, a process of many different political patterns, each with its unique style of trying to restructure the old order and each with different degrees of success in doing so.

The political will to move Latin America out of economic underdevelopment has multiple dimensions. It means asserting independent solutions to its problems and reaffirming the sovereign independence of Latin American states vis-à-vis traditional United States influence in various parts of the region. This determination has led to increased criticism of United States policies toward Latin America (such as quota restrictions and other trade relations), and to nationalization of American businesses by various governments. At the same time there is a growing sense of urgency to cooperate among the Latin American countries, matched by an identity of interest with the under-developed Third World of Africa, Asia, and the Middle East. In pursuit of these new interests, Latin America has joined in Third World programs for development (such as Venezuela and Ecuador's participation in OPEC—the Organization of Petroleum Exporting Countries), while expanding its trade outlets beyond the North American sphere into the Soviet Union, East Europe, and mainland China. The overall result of these growing commitments to development is an enlarged role of the state, and therefore the capabilities and effectiveness of Latin American political systems take on special importance.

Decline of the Western Hemispheric Community Idea

One major dimension of the new political will in Latin America is the decline of the Western Hemispheric Community idea. This is the notion, largely stressed by United States diplomats from the early nineteenth century onward, but also adopted by a number of Latin American leaders in the newly independent republics, that Latin America and the United States are two sister areas of the world which could and should cooperate together in moving toward a common future. The Western Hemispheric Community idea assumed that a special relationship existed among the Western Hemisphere countries, forged by their common revolutionary experiences with old Europe, their geographical ties, and the promise of republican ideals by independent countries in the new world setting. This concept lay behind the varied forms of inter-American relations from the nineteenth century onward, including the Monroe Doctrine, Pan Americanism, the Good Neighbor Policy, and the Alliance for Progress.

The Western Hemispheric Community idea in fact was built on sand from the outset. Geography per se does not mean solidarity of geographically contiguous people. Moreover, the revolutions in North and South America stemmed from different cultural and political pasts. Latin America emerged from the Hispano-Catholic culture in which the institutions of self-government did not exist; the North American variant grew out of a tradition of self-government and Protestant culture. Nor were the political systems comparable, the north being more equalitarian in orientation, the south authoritarian. Finally, the sense of community of states sharing together in the decision-making process was eroded by enormous disparity in size, power, and policies of North America. In terms of power and international politics, the Latin American countries always occupied a subordinate position vis-à-vis the United States, as the practice of direct and indirect United States intervention over the years demonstrated. North America consistently overwhelmed the Latin American states in terms of modernization, material successes, technology, and military power. This difference in power and influence meant that inferiority-superiority relationships were built into the structure of inter-American relations, notwithstanding the Western Hemispheric idea.

United States-Latin American relations in the post-World War II era are marked by the near abandonment of the Western Hemispheric concept. Some would say that its demise is long overdue, since it created a whole range of false promises that could lead only to disappointment and confusion. The new psychological perspectives within Latin America accentuate differences, not similarities, between the two continents. The Latin American countries, strongly affected by the postwar anticolonialism among all developing countries, now identify more closely with the southern portions of the globe, Africa and Asia, than northward with the more developed United States. Joining the anticolonial neutral and nonaligned Third World countries, Mexican President Luis Echeverría opened the Hemispheric Foreign Minister's Conference in Mexico in February, 1974, by stressing that:

> Even the best doctrines and programs of Pan-Americanism, those which were inspired by the Bolivian ideal, have been frustrated by the effects of the balance of real forces in the hemisphere. Territorial plundering, armed aggression, intervention in the political affairs of our people and in their processes of democratic liberation, restrictions on the exercise of sovereignty over our natural resources, as well as obstacles placed in the way of our active participation in world affairs—all these have meant, on one degree or another, a geographical and economic program of continental domination. . . . Latin America is part of the Third World. Its struggles coincide with those waged by other nations against colonialism, modern attempts of subjugation, injustice in international transactions and the concentration of the political power of wealth and its methods of growth.[1]

The energy crisis, stimulated by the Arab states' cut-back in oil supplies to the Western World in 1973, is a recent visible symbol of decline in the Western Hemispheric idea. Venezuela's president-elect at that time, Carlos Andrés Pérez, warned that Venezuela would use oil both as a political lever to get more capital and technology and as a voice for Latin America in international trade and monetary policy. Meanwhile, the Latin American states had been insisting for some time that the developed countries, particularly the U.S., had a special obligation to the less developed areas in terms of export-import policies and access to U.S. capital. The oil crisis put new and forceful pressure on this subject, since many Latin American states depend on oil imports, including Brazil which imported more than 50 percent of its oil from the Arabs. Prices also would be forced up on imported capital goods using oil inputs. At a time of development consciousness and an energy crisis, the Western Hemispheric Community idea faded.

Energy crisis pressures impelled U.S. Secretary of State Henry Kissinger to travel to Mexico City in February, 1974, to try "Super Henry" personal diplomacy, the first major positive step in U.S. diplomacy toward Latin America for some time, and one that had a soothing effect. Yet the Latin American leaders had arrived in Mexico City before Kissinger to try to hammer out a common policy, indicating their separate identity from Washington. Later, accentuating the decline in shared harmony, when the General Assembly of the Organization of American States met in Atlanta, Georgia, in May, 1974, it criticized the unregulated activities of U.S.–based multinational corporations, the presence of the United States in the Canal Zone, and the determination of the Latin American members that in OAS the United States is simply one among equals. The foreign ministers of all hemispheric countries then agreed that Cuba would be invited to the hemispheric foreign ministerial meetings of March, 1975, in Buenos Aires, against strong U.S. resistance.

The present epoch is looked upon by many in U.S. governmental and academic circles with deep frustration, given the profound deterioration in United States–Latin American relations in the 1960s. The United States and Latin America, to be sure, have experienced frictions since the first days of their independence, but in the period since World War II, and particularly the late 1960s and early 1970s, the going was particularly tough. Different perceptions of Castro's revolution and Chile's Marxist road, Latin American nationalization of United States business properties, a conflict over payments for nationalized industries, the "tuna war" involving the capture of U.S. fishermen off the west coasts of those Latin American countries claiming a 200-mile territorial sea, and access to U.S. markets are only some of the problems that sharply divide the Hemisphere today.

A Latin American Identity of Interests

When Fidel Castro Ruz visited Chile in November, 1971, he made an important speech in the Sotomayor Plaza at Valparaiso. Castro stressed the solidarity of Latin American interests, the joining of Latin Americans in brotherhood and the common struggles for progress, and of a "community of 600 million inhabitants which will be a united Latin America."[2] In this and in other speeches during that tour Castro linked up loyalty to one's "fatherland" (e.g., Cuba or Chile) with broader solidarity with Latin America, an identity he often termed as *Nuestra America* (Our America)."[3] He also emphasized the return to the "will of Bolívar, San Martín, Sucre, O'Higgings, and other patriots who made possible the independence of Mexico and Central America, and those who fought for Cuban independence."[4]

This leitmotif meshes with the domestic- and foreign-policy positions developing in Latin American politics throughout the 1960s and 1970s. They demonstrate an increasing Latin American identity of interests, which has a number of dimensions. *Etatisme* (statism), a first aspect, is the commitment on the part of state leaders to regain control over such state resources as oil, copper, and tin in order to stimulate economic development and restore a measure of dignity to the state. Most Latin American leaders, secondly, insist on the duty and commitment to conduct programs of economic development. These commitments are found in numerous statements, including the joint-policy declarations at Viña del Mar, Chile (1969) and Lima, Peru (1971).

New regional trading groups also are being formed to stimulate internal trade and domestic economic development, such as the Andean Pact of Bolivia, Chile, Colombia, Ecuador, Peru, and Venezuela. In addition to regional trading groups, new technological agreements among the Latin American countries emphasize their common development interests. These include new gas pipeline construction between Bolivia's Santa Cruz province and Brazil; and hydroelectric, bridge, road, and railroad building between Argentina and Paraguay.

Other elements in the Latin American identity of interests should be cited. These are the rapidly expanding diplomatic, trade, and aid links with the Soviet Union, Eastern Europe, and China. Finally, the ending of Castro's isolation in the Western Hemisphere sharply accentuates the differences between the United States and at least several Latin American countries on the Cuban revolution. In the early 1970s, Fidel Castro made two long and significant trips abroad (Chile, Peru, and Ecuador in November-December, 1971; Africa, Eastern Europe, and Russia in May–July, 1972). Cuba also enjoyed favorable diplomatic ties with Argentina, Chile, Peru, Mexico, Barbados, Guyana, Jamaica, Trinidad, and Tobago. The Cuban government increasingly aligned itself with positions taken by those spokesmen in Latin America and the Organization of American States who condemned the inequality in development between the U.S. and Latin American countries. Bending to these pressures, the U.S. State Department allowed Argentine subsidiaries of Detroit car makers to sell vehicles to Cuba in April, 1974—a beginning of the thaw in the economic blockade against Cuba. The thaw eventually led to the Organization of American States' vote in July, 1975, to end the political and economic sanctions imposed against Cuba in 1964 for fostering Communist guerrilla activities in the hemisphere. The United States approved the decision.

TRADITIONAL IMPEDIMENTS TO CHANGE

Understanding Latin American politics requires more than a focus on today's changing political environment, for tradition is equally strong. Its presence permeates society and politics, and includes both human and material elements. The political will to change is conditioned by equally powerful forces of tradition from geography to the traditional power holders, and underlying cultural attitudes and values.

Across the vastness of Latin America, for example, the imprint of geography is pronounced, from the desert areas of Mexico, Peru, Chile, and Brazil, to the Andes Mountains of South America, to the sweltering equatorial jungles. These geographic pressures perpetuate the gap between coastal cities and hinterland villages, impeding each country's total integration, and leaving thousands of square miles over which governments exercise no effective sovereignty. Geographic barriers restrict communication and transportation, and impede access to arable land as well as to mineral resources. This results typically in centers of economic and political life lying near the coasts, separated from their interior regions. Droughts, earthquakes, and hurricanes plague many countries' development potential, as in Mexico, Haiti, Nicaragua, Cuba, and parts of South America. Natural resources are frequently inadequate, such as the general shortage of coal or the low fertility of tropical soils. These geographic constraints are difficult to alter.

Human obstacles equally hinder development throughout Latin America. Older power holders, dating back to colonial times when early settlement patterns spawned political power, frequently resist change. These traditional power elites—principally the Church, military, and landed aristocracy—may be seen even today in the operation of politics. Latin America, moreover, does not have a tradition of self-government. Its inheritance is rather that of rule from above over those below—a result of Church and Crown domination during colonial times—called *patrimonialism*. This historical legacy places importance on strong people, rather than strong laws or institutions, and is known as *personalism* in Latin America. Still another force is the tendency toward dominant-submissive interpersonal relations, *authoritarianism*, that spills over into politics. Nor do many of the Latin American countries have a powerful national identity (like Bolivian, Guatemalan, Peruvian, or Nicaraguan) to unify their disparate populations, most of which remain divided along regional, cultural, ethnic, linguistic, and class lines—as well as into "haves" and "have-nots" in the economic sense. Guatemala, for example, the cradle of Mayan civilization, is fragmented by a population more than 50 percent Indian, speaking many dialects and living in villages that are worlds apart from their countrymen in Guatemala City.

These conditions cause great difficulty in reaching easy consensus over political issues, the questions of who gets what, when, and how. Political instability often results, and politics tends to be that of people in conflict rather than of institutions resolving conflict. New demands must be accommodated within Latin America's political systems as change occurs, but older power holders and life styles do not give way easily. The results are often headline news—riots, strikes, street demonstrations, kidnapings, peasant land-seizures, and other forms of civil disorder. Political patterns spawned by the ferment vary greatly, from Marxist-Leninist Cuba under Fidel Castro's personalist rule, to Brazil and Peru under sharply different military governments, to a declared state of siege in Colombia. In other cases, the older power holders effectively control the status quo, as in Chile since President Salvadore Allende's overthrow in 1973, and in much of Central America. Then there are the in-between countries, like Argentina, where the mixture of demands for change versus tradition churns on but real development seems far off, notwithstanding plentiful natural resources and a favorable geographic setting.

Each subregion of Latin America is coping with the conflict generated by change and tradition. Some countries fare much better than others in accommodating change. Mexico and Cuba stand out in their region, compared to Haiti and the Dominican Republic. Costa Rica and Panama show a progressive blend of political order and economic development, contrasting with El Salvador, Guatemala, Honduras, and Nicaragua. Colombia, Peru, and Venezuela are modernizing leaders in their subregion, with Bolivia, Chile, and Ecuador lagging behind. Brazil is clearly the dominant leader among the Atlantic area countries, although its political repression to attain economic improvements is a qualifying factor. To examine Latin America is to examine the political dynamics of this conflict.

Latin American politics varies from country to country, a point illustrated in more detail later, but nevertheless entails general characteristics that can be identified. The future course of politics in Latin America's development will be shaped by these traditional patterns, which differ sharply from those in the United States. As we shall see, limitations in the scope and effectiveness of governmental institutions, a political culture dominated by parochial rather than universal norms, and problems of absent national identity are only a few of the obstacles that must be overcome by Latin America's leaders as they attempt to bring about change in the face of strong traditional forces, change that involves not simply the political system but the interaction of social forces with politics and the interface of politics and economics.

NOTES

1. Mexico City Radio Broadcast in Spanish, February 21, 1974.
2. Chilean Radio Broadcast in Spanish, November 30, 1974.
3. Castro's Speech in Concepción, Chilean Radio Broadcast, November 18, 1971.
4. *Ibid.*

Suggested Readings

Alba, Victor. *The Latin Americans.* New York: Praeger, 1969.

Burnett, Ben G. and Kenneth F. Johnson. *Political Forces in Latin America; Dimensions of the Quest for Stability.* Belmont, Calif.: Wadsworth, 1968.

Clissold, Stephen. *Latin America, New World, Third World.* New York: Praeger, 1972.

Connell-Smith, Gordon. *The Inter-American System.* New York: Oxford University Press, 1966.

Dozer, Donald M. *Latin America; An Interpretive History.* New York: McGraw-Hill, 1962.

Edelmann, Alexander T. *Latin American Government and Politics,* 2d ed. Homewood, Ill.: The Dorsey Press, 1969.

Hirschman, Albert O. *Journeys Toward Progress.* New York: Twentieth Century Fund, 1963.

Lambert, Jacques. *Latin America: Social Structures and Political Institutions.* Berkeley and Los Angeles: University of California Press, 1967.

Ranis, Peter. *Five Latin American Nations; A Comparative Political Study.* New York: Macmillan, 1971.

United States Government. House Committee on Foreign Affairs. *Inter-American Relations.* A collection of documents, legislation, descriptions of inter-American organizations, and other material pertaining to inter-American affairs. November, 1973.

Two

Political Development in Latin America

A developmental approach is appropriate for the study of politics in Latin America since World War II. The stress of political development is on the process of Latin America's people becoming more integrated within polity—putting demands into government and the government responding (or not responding!) with a more equitable allocation of the country's valued resources. As a method of analysis, it takes us beyond the standard description of a government's main features, like its electoral system or constitution. Rather, it makes us think about how the political system interacts with society and the economy, under the pressures of change versus tradition, either becoming more effective in meeting modern public needs or falling apart in the effort. Politics—the study of who gets what, when, and how—by this analysis is put into a framework of probing the conditions under which more people come to share in a country's valued goods, e.g., employment, money, education, health care, social welfare, status, prestige, and so on.

When a political system (the government and its underlying political dynamics) evolves to meet public needs, it tends to change in specific ways. For one thing, it increasingly mobilizes and integrates the human and material resources of the country to benefit the population as a whole, as has occurred in Mexico and Cuba. This means the weakening of traditional elites (the Church, landed aristocracy, old-line military rulers), who, because of their very privileged high standards of living, typically do not wish to alter the status quo to their disadvantage, and the coming to power of new leaders committed to change. For another thing, the political system becomes more adept at controlling society and the economy in peaceful ways. This means evolving institutions and organizations for the expression and accommodation of new demands on the system, as with Mexico's Institutional Revolutionary Party (PRI) or Cuba's grass-roots organizations, rather than allowing these pressures to erupt in insurrections, coups d'etat, and other forms of civil disorder.

A developing political system, then, is increasingly able to cope with the stresses released by economic and social change. It channels these into peaceful outlets, while mobilizing society's human and material resources for the public good. Mexico, Brazil, Cuba, and Peru, by these criteria, would be rapidly developing countries, while Haiti, Guatemala, and Nicaragua would not.

With development comes the transformation of old political structures into more sophisticated ones. Government begins to move away from one-man rule, where a single individual tends to be not only the executive, but the legislative and judiciary branches as well, as with the Dominican Republic under Rafael Trujillo (1930-61) or Mexico under Porfirio Díaz (1876-1910). Instead of one man or group dominating the political and governmental apparatus, more interest groups and political parties become involved, and popular participation in national life expands. Political development brings with it new political leaders who seek power on behalf of new interests ranging from those of the working classes and peasants to middle sectors (small businessmen, clerks, white-collar workers, teachers, students, and others), as well as new industrial and commercial groups. Political power, to put it simply, begins to be more equalized throughout a country (at least as far as its *own* past is concerned), more people actually share in the process of and benefits provided by government, and the political system as a whole begins to disseminate the resources of the country that matter so much in everyday life, such as income, health, education, housing, and social security. The dynamics of politics involves how the new and older contenders for power try to influence each other in this process of change, what means they use to do so, and the effects of the overall interaction within society, the economy, and government.

POLITICAL DEVELOPMENT IN LATIN AMERICA

As a preliminary comment on political development in Latin America, one may observe two basic transformations since World War II. In fact, two totally separate periods can be distinguished, one from the early nineteenth century until the War, the other thereafter. The major changes have occurred in the *structure* of politics and in the *ideological goals* of policy makers. Structure and ideology have changed, while much of the *culture* of politics has changed only marginally. By culture of politics is meant the underlying attitudes toward authority and legitimacy which affect the way people "see" other people in politics, how they interact within the governmental framework, and what they consider to be legitimate behavior on the part of the government, that is, behavior they will accept without coercion. The degrees to which this observation applies depend upon the country, for the changes have not been of the same rate, degree, and kind everywhere.

Political Development in the Nineteenth Century

The nineteenth century can be characterized as a period—when measured against the present day—of little political development. The wars of independence during the early 1800s did not change the social or economic situations of the masses. One set of political elites, the upper-class white Creoles, born in the new country, replaced those from Spain (the *Peninsulares*), and the dominant pillars of power became the large landowners, the military, and the Hispanic Catholic Church. Society and politics remained a basically closed system, with little fluidity or movement outside the ascriptive patterns of prestige, status, and power, based upon birth and family name. Traditional elites in society were those in politics.

In terms of political structures, Latin America at this time was underdeveloped. Political structures were not highly diversified by functions, very little decentralized, and not open to mass popular participation. Few checks operated on elite political actors; political control was typically oligarchical in nature. Strong-man rule by *caudillos* and *caciques*—both in capital cities and isolated regions—was the rule rather than the exception. Extensive political-party and interest-group representation did not exist, although two parties, typically Liberal and Conservative, usually represented upper-class interests. The political culture remained basically authoritarian, and large numbers of people were not socialized to believe that there should be popular participation in choosing leaders or national policies.

Another major indicator of political underdevelopment in the early nineteenth century is the low degree of, and concern with, national identity. One is hard pressed to find strong evidence of a sense of widespread national consciousness on the part of people in various regions, territories, and states. The wars of independence were based neither upon a deeply felt attachment to "homeland" or "fatherland" nor to perceived notions of "a people" in the national sense, struggling against an outside enemy, or for a better life in the material sense. The wars of independence in Latin America must be distinguished from such struggles as those of Biafra, Bangladesh, or other self-determination movements of the mid-twentieth century. They were elite struggles of Peninsulares versus Creoles, essentially struggles for power where Creoles refused to be dominated by Spanish-born Peninsulares. They were not wars of ethnic nations seeking an independent state and a chance for economic development.

Following the wars of independence, much of Latin America became plagued by the so-called legitimacy vacuum. The wars destroyed the legitimate authority of the Spanish Crown, but since the paternalist Spanish colonialists had not trained people in the arts and attitudes of self-government, no accepted institutions of popular self-rule developed to replace the Crown. The result was typically either anarchy or authoritarian rule by a combined military, Church, and landholding power elite, many times headed by the military. Certainly the distribution and control of political resources (money, jobs, the legal right to exercise power, and other such devices used in a society to exercise power) was greatly unequal, affected by the small upper-class versus large lower-class patterns of society and economics. A few people owned much of the choicest land (called *latifundias*) and the economy was primarily agricultural.

Characterized in other terms, much of nineteenth-century Latin America was a period of low rates of development. The traditional elites were strong, and stagnation in society and the economy conditioned perpetuation of traditional power groups in politics. The central administrative apparatus of the state and its political activities were not wide in scope, as reflected in the power of regional bosses, large landowners on their *latifundias,* and the isolation from contact with the central government of villages, farms, and outlying regions.

Latin America Since World War II

Latin America since World War II, in contrast to its counterpart in the early nineteenth century, shows considerable political development. Certainly the political structures of many Latin American countries are remarkably transformed. The ideological goals reflect new policy objectives more relevant to the countries' masses, and several leaders stressed a common national consciousness, such as Mexican or Cuban, as a key prerequisite to legitimize state political endeavors, and to tap and mobilize the human energy required for sustained economic and social change. The Bolivian, Cuban, and Mexican revolutions are cases in point. The extent to which these propositions hold, as well as their specific nature, naturally depends upon the particular country.

Structural Change

Changes in political structures between the nineteenth century and World War II in Latin America are sharp. Popular participation increased as is shown by the growth and variety of political parties and interest groups over the years that helped to aggregate popular demands and to propel them into the marketplace of competing political policies, alternatives, and decisions. Greater checks and balances on one-man centralized control developed through these mechanisms, which included the rise of labor unions into organized political power, and juntas (groups of officers) rather than dictators in military rule.

Structural changes were spawned in part by the postwar forces in Latin America. Industrialization, urbanization, and the spread of mass transportation and communication media, commerce, industry, and percent of the labor force in secondary and tertiary levels of employment (manufacturing and services) are relevant. The demands created by this economic development pushed political structures toward increased functional differentiation and spread potential political power to wider groups in society. As broad middle-sector groups were spawned and labor diversified away from a primarily agricultural base, the traditional bases of power and influence—military, Church, and large landowners—began to erode somewhat. We probe the status of these groups later.

Ideology is another aspect of basic evolution. Latin American leaders in several countries showed less concern about narrow, personal aggrandizement, and more commitment to improve the material plight of their country's people, during the period following World War II. Given continuing economic problems, attention turned toward how to develop with an emphasis in many cases on expanded governmental responsibilities in the public sector. The postwar period is in this sense one of ideological modernity, where the goals sought and policies pursued were those of making the government an engine and source of public benefits.

Political Culture: The Least-Developed Sphere

An abiding curiosity and fascination of Latin American politics is that while structural and ideological change occurred, political cultures changed only very little. To understand much of contemporary Latin American politics—the factions, cliques, personalism, continuing military intervention, violence, emotionalism, and instability—it is imperative to understand the culture of politics and the still low levels of national identity, notwithstanding leadership goals.

Limited studies of Latin American culture show a persistence of traditional attitudes in spite of development elsewhere. These attitudes and values, which we will consider in detail later, include personalism, paternalism, transcendentalism, fatalism, the importance of social hierarchy, stress on emotion as fulfillment of self, and *machismo* (male virility and power), and they tend to produce authoritarian political systems. The typical characteristic is the importance of individual human beings—their personality and charisma—and the emotions of dominant-submissive attitudes between leaders and led. They also condition the expectation of individuals in lower strata of society that they are to be protected and cared for by those in higher.

These sets of attitudes and values tend to stress people rather than nonpersonal, problem-solving institutions. They help to explain the strong-man rule in many Latin American countries and continued executive predominance in political life despite constitutional provisions for separation of powers and checks and balances among executive, legislature, and judiciary.

Continuity in political culture—attitudes toward authority and interpersonal behavior within the political system—suggests that as time marches on in Latin America, development will be sui generis, that is, uniquely conditioned by Latin American attitudes and values. Equalitarianism in the North American sense does not permeate the social structure nor will it likely be a part of political decision making in the near future. Traditional attitudes and values continue to condition authoritarian interaction of people within the changed political structures, although many policies pursued have developed toward expanding the state's capacity to serve its people and to improve their well-being. Meanwhile, the obstacles to a common national consciousness, which is important in helping to stimulate new political orientations and to legitimize state leaders and institutions, remain tenacious. But it is also true that new political leaders and institutions may have a remarkable impact on transforming traditional attitudes and values. Cuba is a case in point where Castro, the Cuban Communist Party, and new organizations stress achievement, personal work, and love of Cuba by all Cubans.

A Warning on the Use of the Political Development Framework

Any discussion of political development in Latin America requires certain warnings.

First, traditional obstacles should not be underestimated in evaluating political development, for it conditions the rates, degrees, and kinds of change. One should not assume, for example, that as industrialization, urbanization, and communications expand, a given Latin American society is automatically moving toward equalitarian, interpersonal relations and democratic government as we know it. All Latin American political systems continue to evince traditional patterns of political rule, even though they may be moving simultaneously toward greater capacity to meet public needs. Castro's personalist power in socialist Cuba, the military-led public policies in Peru since 1968, and the economic programs of Brazil's military-dominated government since 1964 are all examples of political development, and all show the face of old patterns of authority under new direction. Indeed, the imprint of one-man rule was so strong in Cuba by January, 1959, that when Fidel Castro rode in victory parades, the standard joke was that if someone pulled off his beard, underneath would be Fulgencio Batista, the dictator Castro had overthrown.

Secondly, each country in Latin America is unique. Wide ranges in social and economic transition exist. These include literacy (from 10 percent in Haiti to 91 percent in Argentina), urbanization (from 17 percent in Haiti to 81 percent in Uruguay), per capita income (from $72.00 in Haiti to $934.00 in Venezuela), and in the percentage of the labor force in agriculture (93 percent in Honduras to 22 percent in Uruguay). Therefore, even though we can learn much about the scope and range of political systems in Latin America through a developmental overview of the area, each country merits study in depth to understand its peculiar history and political style.

LATIN AMERICAN POLITICS IN A NEW ERA

The new era of Latin American politics is one of great attention to economic development by styles that vary from the Marxism of Cuba to the militarism of Peru and Brazil. The essence of the times is the attempt to use government to diversify economies, increase economic growth rates, and more equitably distribute income among the population. The process is carried on differently according to each country's political elite's perceptions and its political traditions, so the policies vary widely. But given the attempts of political leaders to alter economic conditions toward a wider sharing by society within an industrialized setting, development is indeed an appropriate framework to study the region.

Certainly the fact of poverty and under-industrialization in much of Latin America is indisputable. Income distribution, to illustrate the point, is vastly unequal. The average per capita personal income is only about four hundred and ten dollars per year. Yet, for about half the population the per capita average is approximately one hundred twenty dollars, while for the upper strata, representing about 5 percent of the population, it is twenty-six hundred dollars. Consumption in the low-income strata, representing 50 percent of the population, accounts for only two-tenths of the total consumption, while three-tenths are absorbed by the upper 5 percent. A small percentage of Latin America's population manages a life style similar to (perhaps far better than) those of high-income countries, while millions barely subsist. The marginal hand-to-mouth existence of Latin America's poor must be seen to be fully realized, as a visit to the urban slum areas of most capital cities will quickly attest.

Latin American leaders, of course, face enormous obstacles in their attempts to alter conditions in the economic sphere through government policy. A pattern of exporting raw materials and importing manufactured goods—the latter's costs often rising more rapidly than price of raw-material exports—is strongly operative in Latin America dating back to the colonial period. In addition, large areas of the region are dependent upon single exports, such as sugar, coffee, bananas, beef, wool, copper, tin, or petroleum. The drive to industrialize through government efforts is also hindered by insufficient land suitable for modern agriculture—so very important in the process of economic growth—proportionately less than in Europe or the United States, and much of the land that is available still remains in a few hands even after years of attempted land reforms. Shortage of skilled workers, scarcity of capital, backward taxation policies, the flight of private profits abroad (rather than reinvestment), and heavy debt financing on former loans are additional problems faced by modernizing political leaders. Not surprisingly, then, land reform, nationalization of foreign businesses, and employment practices are rallying points of *political* action in postwar Latin America.

The claims on which many political leaders ran for Latin American presidencies during 1973-74 rested upon the growing attention to economic development through progressive governmental action. Alfonso López Michelsen roundly defeated the conservative candidate, Gómez Hurtado, in Colombia in April, 1974, campaigning on a platform of *desarrollismo* (development reformism). This campaign was very much in tune with that of Carlos Andrés Pérez, who won the Venezuelan presidential elections in December, 1973. While the Colombian president spoke of agrarian reform and a better distribution of wealth, his "friend," the new dynamic Venezuelan president, strongly emphasized a development orientation through nationalization of oil and new domestic use of oil revenues.

Meanwhile, the new president of Costa Rica, Daniel Oduber Quiros (elected in February, 1974), stressed the task of closing the gap between the rich and poor. Brazil, still under military rule since 1964 "elected" a new president, Ernesto Geisel, in January, 1974, and he too stressed developmental reformism under Brazil's controlled conditions.

Not all elections stressed reformism and development, to be sure, as seen from the Guatemalan presidential election of March, 1974. This resulted in election fraud and the "victory" of General Eugenio Kjell Laugerud García, representing conservative military and large landholding interests. But in Brazil, Colombia, Costa Rica, and Venezuela, new presidents stressed economic and social reforms to match the thrust of economic and social developments in Cuba, Mexico, Panama (under General Omar Torrijos who pressed for agrarian reform and stronger Panamanian control over the Canal), and Peru. Chile experienced a radical approach to development under its Marxist president, Salvador Allende, between 1970 and September, 1973. But the country fell under conservative military rule after Allende's overthrow.

PROBLEMS OF POLITICAL DEVELOPMENT

The process of political development in Latin America is fraught with uncertainty, given the stresses released by change and tradition. No single answer explains the high prevalence of political instability in Latin America, but a number of reasons have been suggested which seem to get at the heart of the matter. A brief look at these explanations is useful in understanding the postwar ferment in Latin America, and can serve as a fruitful introduction to the politics of the region.

The "Legitimacy Vacuum" Theory

One central thesis about political instability in Latin America is that the wars of independence swept away a colonial political system based upon legitimate authority from above, expressed through royal succession authorized by the grace of God. The new system advanced a concept of legitimate authority based upon the principle of equality and popular will from below.[1] But in effect a "legitimacy vacuum" resulted. The legitimacy vacuum is the reality that no single compelling source of legitimacy behind public office replaced the colonial system. Post-independence leaders in Latin America thus face the problem of building legitimate authority, and the obstacles they encounter are great. Legitimate democratic institutions are lacking, and popular experience with self-government is slim. Chief executives find that when they fail to consolidate their power through force or by delicate and shrewd balancing of competing interests, they lose power and are out.[2] Instability, then, is a natural corollary to political rule when the leader's source of legitimate authority rests more upon personalist criteria, force, or his political skill in balancing and regulating a host of competing power contenders.

Corporate Politics and the Competition for Limited Resources

When we speak of corporate interests (*intereses*) in Latin America, we are not referring to organizationally or politically cohesive pressure groups, like those common in the United States. Although *intereses* have a self-conscious sense of their sociopolitical role, their psychological roots are in the traditional hierarchical model of society as made up of corporate elements which intervened between the state and individual. Against this background, new, and relatively more differentiated and programmatic, interests have come into being, but their effectiveness is hampered by both the culture and the political systems in which they operate.

The corporate political model helps explain the instability in at least two major ways. First, new corporate interests, such as organized labor and peasants, mass-based political parties, more professionalized and development-oriented militaries, a new Church, or middle-sector groups, must demonstrate their power capability before they are accepted as legitimate parts of the corporate state by older elites. *Intereses* can be termed "power contenders";[3] they demonstrate a variety of power capabilities such as the demonstration, "manifestation," general strike, coup d'etat, or other forms of violence. Their gradual admittance into the corporate pool has evolved throughout the twentieth century, and brought with it a great amount of political instability.

A key point to remember in this process of acquiring elite status is that both violent and nonviolent political resources are appropriate and legitimate for mobilizing power. This situation arises from political culture and the state's low level of peaceful, institutionalized politics. Instability is produced by the variety of political resources used in a typically violent or quasi-violent setting.

Second, the combination of newer and older *intereses* within the corporate state structure is extremely difficult to manage and regulate by chief executives. The political power of the corporate elites is unequal, the life styles of the members are highly incompatible (conservative landowners versus organized peasants), and their objectives are typically at odds with one another. Old elites are not eliminated and their objectives pertain to different historical epochs from which they emerged compared to the newer interests.[4] The combined demands and expectations exerted upon the president by competing corporate interests are frequently too complex for him to manage, particularly given the increased amount of political participation in the twentieth compared to the nineteenth century, and the limited supply of resources which can be allocated. As older groups attempt to cling to their power and status while newer groups press for wider income distribution and increased power, political instability naturally results. One can imagine the difficulty of coordinating the complex network of corporate interests in a system of limited resources.

Participation versus Institutionalization

A more simplified, but equally useful explanation centers on the two issues of rate of participation versus rate of institutionalization. One observer argues that instability results from a rate of participation that exceeds the rate of political institutionalization.[5] When political participation increases, as it has in Latin America, and with it the number and scope of popular demands, the complexity, adaptability, and effectiveness of the state's political institutions must increase if political stability is to be maintained. Since the level of governmental outputs has usually not kept pace with increased demands, instability has resulted.

A classic example would be Salvador Allende's Chile, when new labor and peasant groups swelled the arena of participation between 1970 and 1973, while institutional means of incorporating these groups did not evolve. The result was increased political instability throughout 1972 and 1973, with illegal land seizures and factory takeovers occurring from the left, along with violence and terrorism from the right.

Participation-Economic Development

Political instability, it can also be stressed, results from rates of political participation exceeding the increasing level of economic development.[6] The economy must develop in order to provide a higher level of welfare and other economic resources in order to match the increased level of political demands. When it does not, again the result is political instability, or political order maintained by physical force. Much evidence in Latin American politics suggests the credibility of this thesis, such as the increased political stability of Mexico after the 1930s, matched with higher economic performance or, conversely, the great instability and resort to physical force coupled with low economic development, in Bolivia.

Two additional economic interpretations of political instability in Latin America can be identified. One is simply that industrialization generates new bases of power and new power contenders to check the power of the older elites. Industrialization, by this analysis, plays the role of diffusing power, by building separate power centers, and creates a system of group checks and balances. Low industrialization, as in Bolivia, means that no new power groups emerge to check the military and landed interests. They, along with their families, patrons, and clients, continue to squabble exclusively among themselves, which results in a sort of game of military musical chairs.

A variant of this interpretation is that low economic development means the general absence of new sources of power and upward political mobility. This situation means that a prime avenue to power is control of the government itself. The government remains the one certain means of rapid wealth and power as demonstrated by the fact that more than one dictator left office far more wealthy than when he entered. But unlike the traditional bases of power—agrarian wealth and religious influence—the government is subject to takeover, as different groups become eager to take the risk involved in a revolt or coup d'etat. The upshot is chronic instability in many Latin American countries.[7]

Cultural Explanations

A wide range of cultural explanations for Latin American political instability exists. Wide acceptance of violence may make it a power source partially responsible for the region's unrest.[8] Ethnic and racial differences undoubtedly explain in part the frequency of political instability, since those states high in ethnic and racial differences are also states high in political coups d'etat.[9] The absence of a national community is also closely related to these mixed ethnic perceptions in Latin America. These cultural forces, as we will see, inhibit the formation of organization men and of rules, regulations, and political institutions operating through rational procedures rather than personalist emotions.

A Military Thesis

A key aspect of political instability in Latin America involves the high rate of military intervention. How does one account for this, beyond the explanation that military groups have traditionally played a prestigious and powerful role in Latin American politics dating back to the colonial period and even before, to Iberian experiences expelling the Moors.

One helpful hypothesis is suggested by Samuel P. Huntington.[10] The central thesis is that the role of the reforming military varies with the development of society. When society is backward, the reforming military can afford to be more progressive and radical, since they have nothing to fear from other reforming political groups. Peru is an example. But the more advanced a society becomes, the more conservative and reactionary its military becomes. When society moves into mass participation in government and politics in the absence of effective political institutions, the military begins increasingly to play the role of protector of the existing system against lower-class incursions. The military become, in Huntington's words, "guardians of the existing middle class order."[11] The essential point is that between 1935 and 1964, as popular lower-class reform movements came to power through elections, the military increasingly engaged in efforts to maintain the status quo; depose legally elected presidents; intervene to forestall the election of reforming presidents; and openly fought reforming groups through the use of the coup d'etat.[12]

These six explanations offer fascinating insight into Latin America's political difficulties. Exceptions to political instability of course exist, such as Mexico and Costa Rica. But even in these states, political instability seems at times to lurk just below the political surface. During the mid-1960s, moreover, who would have thought that bloodshed, violence, and a coup d'etat would erupt in Chile, a country so often cited as advanced in democracy and high in political stability? An understanding of Latin American politics requires, therefore, insight into the combined forces of economics, society, and politics that erode the building of accepted legitimate authority and institutionalized political procedures.

THE PROBLEM OF LEGITIMATE AUTHORITY

The legitimacy vacuum discussed above is in one sense misleading. It suggests the absence of legitimate power and authority in Latin American politics after independence compared to the colonial period. But we have seen that various forms of mobilizing political power *do* exist in Latin America and that each appears to be perceived as legitimate as the next, whether constitutional or not, peaceful or violent. The problem, then, is that no consensus exists on the ultimate accepted form, which makes political development a difficult task.

Each of these power-mobilizing methods requires effective personalist leadership—a combination of political skill and charisma that typically activates and plays upon mass emotions. Each suggests the impact of personalist forces in Latin America, which are obstacles to, and carry much more political weight than, impersonal problem-solving institutions. The state's jurisprudential and legal system, electoral procedures, political parties, and bureaucratic organizations operate in Latin American government, but they are dominated by *personalismo* when it comes to the question of legitimate power.

The fact is that legitimate authority is not missing in Latin America. It is simply fragmented into different sets of patron-client relations, extended family units, charismatic leaders, regional bosses, and corporate elites. Its fragmentation is one way of explaining the difficulty of building state-wide political institutions carrying the same commitments and loyalties.

A fascinating aspect of the Latin American political drama is the continuation of personal rulership into the modern era, even in those countries where the development of modern political institutions has experienced greater success than in others. Mexico illustrates the point. The PRI is a highly institutionalized, state-wide political party that links popular participation through party institutions into government policy making. Yet personal rulership prevails in that country. The boss of a small community might be the man with some education who controls the post office, the only telephone, and/or has gunmen on his payroll. The ability to speak, read, and write Spanish can mean power (the power to be the *cacique*) in many Indian communities. Powerful families also dominate in other areas, as they have since the last century.

Caciquismo—strong individual power over a territorial group; a powerful autocratic leader in local and regional politics—exists as much in rural Mexico as in other Latin American countries. It represents a kind of government-within-a-government, controlled by a single dominant individual who is not formally accountable either to those residing in the community under his control or to external political and governmental authorities.[13] *Caciquismo*, moreover, prevails within the slum areas of Mexico City just as it does in rural areas.

Legitimate authority is segmented, then, by personalist loyalties and followings in Latin America. This situation is produced by cultural norms such as the corporate concept of society and personality features that accentuate the worth of people, emotion, charisma, and social hierarchy. Personalist forces, of course, operate in all countries, including the United States, where charisma is not at all an unfamiliar factor in politics. The difference between the United States and Latin America on this matter is not one of kind as much as it is one of degree. Personalism and personal rulership are simply more pervasive and influential in the Latin American region, promoting different types of political instability.

Conclusion

With its emphasis on how a country's political system evolves to incorporate more people in sharing the society's valued resources, political development "fits" the publicized concerns of many modern leaders in Latin America today. In studying Latin American politics and government, it is helpful to think of them as operating within a larger social system, in which politics, society, and the economy are parts of the whole so that what happens in one part will interact with and affect what happens in the others. Political decisions on how to industrialize, for example, affect the economy, and conversely, a process of industrialization spawns new political groups like labor unions and corporate business interests. Society, in turn, has a class structure, and value, ethnic, kinship, and attitude characteristics which affect both the drama of politics and the achievement of economic goals.

As elsewhere, in Latin America, the state's political system is the largest and most universal, and commands final allegiance if not by other forms of legitimacy, then by its command over physical force. The state's government has final power, sovereignty, to make authoritative decisions affecting all the inhabitants of the state. However, in studying Latin American politics, one must also analyze other power and influence networks that lie at the substate level. These power centers are not necessarily legally or formally sanctioned by the state and may not be connected with the state's legal—constitutional or governmental—system. They operate because the state's central administrative structure may not have expanded to include all sectors of the territorial unit within its de facto control. Furthermore, allegiance to the state's governmental system, which can be termed the *public* political system, is not well developed throughout the population of many Latin American countries. Ultimate loyalty on the part of large numbers of people may instead be oriented to their kinship group along ethnocentric lines, local *latifundia,* community, village, or a specific charismatic and personalist leader with whom they identify. Where this traditional loyalty supersedes loyalty to the larger, more abstract and less familiar state, with its rational institutions and organizations, we must look below the surface of the state's formal-legal constitutional system to understand the dynamics of politics. Frequent coups, corruption, instability, and violence, for example, suggest the absence of state-wide, civic-public perceptions and low regard for the legitimacy of the state's governmental institutions. Operative loyalty and legitimacy may lie elsewhere and, hence, with them, operative power and influence.

NOTES

1. See Martin Needler, *Latin American Politics in Perspective* (New York: Van Nostrand, 1963), p. 37ff.
2. On the fascinating problem of building legitimate authority which political leaders in the Third World commonly face, see Norman H. Keehn, "Building Authority; A Return to Fundamentals," *World Politics* 26 (April 1974): 331-52.
3. Charles W. Anderson, in John D. Martz, ed., *The Dynamics of Change in Latin America*, 2d ed. (Englewood Cliffs, N.J.: Prentice-Hall, 1971, p. 292.
4. Howard J. Wiarda, "Toward a Framework for the Study of Political Change in the Iberic-Latin Tradition: The Corporative Model," *World Politics* 25 (January 1973): 227.
5. Samuel P. Huntington, *Political Order in Changing Societies* (New Haven: Yale University Press, 1968), pp. 78ff.
6. Martin Needler, "Political Development and Socio-Economic Development; The Case of Latin America," *The American Political Science Review* 62 (September 1968): 889-98.
7. Merle Kling, "Toward a Theory of Power and Political Instability in Latin America," *Western Political Quarterly* 9 (March 1956): 21-35; and James F. Torres, "Concentration of Political Power and Levels of Economic Development in Latin American Countries," *The Journal of Developing Areas* 7 (April 1973): 397-410.
8. William S. Stokes, "Violence as a Power Factor in Latin American Politics," *Western Political Quarterly* 5 (September 1952): 445-69.
9. See Martin Needler, *The Causality of the Latin American Coups d'Etat: Some Numbers, Some Speculations*. A paper presented to the American Political Science Association Meeting, September 19, 1972.
10. Huntington, *op. cit.*, pp. 221ff.
11. *Ibid.*, p. 222.
12. Martin C. Needler, "Political Development and Military Intervention in Latin America," *The American Political Science Review* 60 (September 1966): 616-26.
13. Wayne A. Cornelius, "A Structural Analysis of Urban Caciquismo in Mexico," *Urban Anthropology* 1 (Fall 1972): 234-61; and John Duncan Powell, "Peasant Society and Clientelist Politics," *The American Political Science Review* 64 (June 1970): 411-25.

Suggested Readings

Almond, Gabriel and G. Bingham Powell. *Comparative Politics: A Developmental Approach*. Boston: Little, Brown, 1966.

Anderson, Charles W. *Politics and Economic Change in Latin America*. New York: Van Nostrand Reinhold, 1967.

Einandi, Luigi R. (ed.). *Beyond Cuba: Latin America Takes Charge of Its Future*. New York: Crane, Russak, 1969.

Fagen, Richard R. and Wayne A. Cornelius. *Political Power in Latin America: Seven Confrontations*. Englewood Cliffs, N.J.: Prentice-Hall, 1970.

Heeger, Gerald A. *The Politics of Underdevelopment*. London: Macmillan, 1974.

Horowitz, Irving Louis, et al. (eds.). *Latin American Radicalism*. New York: Vintage, 1969.

Huntington, Samuel. *Political Order in Changing Societies*. New Haven: Yale University Press, 1968.

Lipset, Seymour Martin and Aldo Solari (eds.). *Elites in Latin America*. New York: Oxford University Press, 1967.

Mander, John. *The Unrevolutionary Society: The Power of Latin American Conservatism in a Changing World*. New York: Knopf, 1969.

Martz, John D. (ed.). *The Dynamics of Change in Latin American Politics*. Englewood Cliffs, N.J.: Prentice-Hall, 1965.

Needler, Martin C. *Political Development in Latin America: Instability, Violence, and Evolutionary Change*. New York: Random House, 1968.

Stepan, Alfred. "Political Development Theory: The Latin American Experience," *Journal of International Affairs:* 20 (1966).

Veliz, Claudio (ed.). *The Politics of Conformity in Latin America*. New York: Oxford University Press, 1967.

Von Lazar, Arpad and Robert R. Kaufman. *Reform and Revolution*. Boston: Allyn & Bacon, 1969.

2
The
Countries

Three

Mexico, the Caribbean, and Central America

A look at the newspaper headlines of the early 1970s creates a number of impressions about political life in Latin America—that the United States Central Intelligence Agency (CIA) controls internal politics through outside funding, that foreign companies pull the strings of politics by financial means, that urban and rural guerrillas threaten to overthrow governments at every turn, that military regimes are the only form of rule. Just how accurate is this picture?

The answer is that Latin American politics vary sharply from country to country, and reflect in widely differing manners the extent and effects of external influences and guerrilla activities. To depict Latin American politics as simply the product of United States or other foreign control, including, for example, Soviet influence over Cuba, overlooks the heart of politics, which beats from within. The region is rich in a complicated diversity of political styles that do not lend themselves to any simple explication, including the sometimes popular notion that Washington or American business governs everything south of the Rio Grande. To begin to appreciate this diversity, we must turn to the countries themselves.

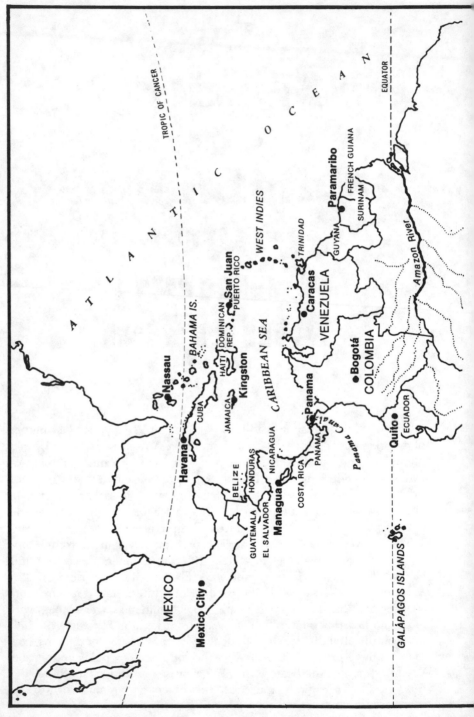

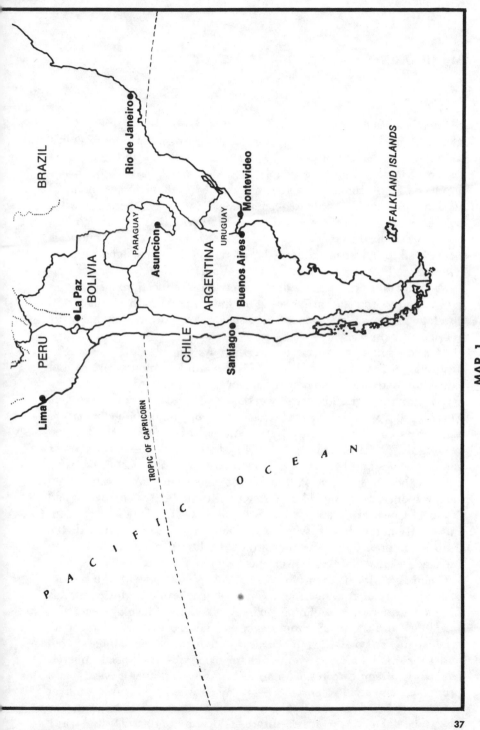

BRAZIL

Rio de Janeiro●

PARAGUAY

Asuncion●

●La Paz

BOLIVIA

PERU

ARGENTINA

URUGUAY

Montevideo●

Buenos Aires●

CHILE

Santiago●

Lima●

TROPIC OF CAPRICORN

FALKLAND ISLANDS

P A C I F I C   O C E A N

MAP 1

MEXICO AND THE CARIBBEAN REPUBLICS

Mexico

Mexico is unique at least in part because of the relative stability it has enjoyed since the revolution of 1910. That enormous social and political upheaval, the first of its kind in Latin America, began the incorporation of large numbers of people into Mexican national life. It also produced a governmental system dedicated to economic and political development and one able to accommodate conflicting demands without excessive use of force. By the end of World War II, Mexico had evolved a stabilizing single-party system as well as government policies committed to industrialization, education, and labor and land reforms. These were backed by a Mexican revolutionary national identity channelled into the arts, public media, and mass education. Mexico, in addition, took the lead in pursuing an independent path of change in the late 1930s under President Lázaro Cárdenas by nationalizing its foreign oil industries.

Mexico's single-party system overshadows the political scene. The Institutional Revolutionary Party (PRI) controls communications and education and incorporates as its major subdivisions Mexico's key interest groups: agrarian farm workers (CNC); blue-collar workers (CTM); and white-collar teachers, clerks, and others who belong to the Party's Popular Sector (CNOP). All major administrative decision making is generally a part of the PRI system as is the determination of public policies at all levels of government. Opposition parties do exist, such as the Conservative Party of National Action (PAN), and so do nonparty interest groups like the Mexican Catholic Action Society and National Union of Parents. Both of the latter would like to see a restoration of Church power, which was substantially weakened with the 1910 revolution. But opposition groups traditionally are little able to influence events in Mexico, given the power of the PRI.

Compared with its own nineteenth-century past or with the politics of many Central American and Caribbean neighbors, Mexico stands out as a leader in formulating policies of national development. The revolution and the many programs it engendered stimulated the government toward a deliberate Mexicanization of the economic system and aggressive state intervention into economic and social spheres, backed by attempts to forge a national consensus for the government's programs. The results can be seen today in Mexico's central banking system, its social security programs and welfare services, its heavy governmental outlays in agriculture, education, railroads, highways, and irrigation projects, and in the state-controlled monopolies in petroleum, natural gas, and electric power. While Mexico has in fact a mixed economy, one that allows both private business and foreign investment under controlled conditions, the government regulates the credit extended to private enterprise, controls import licenses, and maintains other economic policies aimed at giving maximum encouragement to Mexican interests.

Mexico's development-oriented domestic politics are mirrored in its foreign policy. The country is a leader in emphasizing Latin America's mutual interest with other developing countries on such matters as control over natural resources and multinational corporations. President Luis Echeverría Alvarez, who began his six-year presidential term in 1970, also openly supported Chile's Marxist president Salvadore Allende, and campaigned strongly for Cuba's reintegration in the inter-American community. Echeverría also supported the idea of cartels among producers of raw materials as an economic weapon against developed countries.

Tradition, however, still conditions Mexican political development. Authoritarianism is strong, and some would say that the PRI system is, even with its positive attributes, a patrimonial system simply replacing the Church and Crown of yesteryear. Patron-client relations continue to operate, for who one knows is very important in civil-service appointments, and regional and local bosses (*caudillos* and *caciques*) continue their reign. Mexico, moreover, is still a pluralist society, even after years of revolutionary programs designed to integrate the population. Several million Indians, for example, estimated at 10 to 25 percent of the total population, do not identify as "Mexicans," live outside Mexican national life, and are subject to both economic and social discrimination. Income, furthermore, has not been equitably redistributed since 1910, for the official calculation is that 10 percent of the population owns more than 50 percent of the nation's wealth. And indeed some states of Mexico continue to suffer official violence and political corruption.

A number of development problems face Mexico. Land redistribution, a basic tenet of the revolution, is hampered as the amount of arable land available declines in relation to the increasing population. Urban poverty and unemployment plague the government. They are stimulated in part by a 3.3 percent annual population increase, a serious annual inflation running about 20 percent in the mid-1970s, an increasing trade deficit, and problems in food production. Population pressures also impede the country's educational efforts. To the Indian and other lower-class peoples, both rural and urban, the government is frequently little more than an abstract idea.

These mounting difficulties began to produce a politics of confrontation rather than conciliation starting in the late 1960s. Those seeking more rapid social and economic reforms began to take sharp issue with conservative interests, which in turn blamed the Government for its objectives of redistributing income and making political overtures to the politically disenchanted. This has culminated in assaults, kidnappings, demonstrations, rural and urban guerrilla violence, right-wing terrorism, and mutual recriminations between businessmen and government officials. President Luis Echeverría, for example, made overtures to the poor and released scores of students and intellectuals imprisoned after student riots in 1968, encouraging them to form a legal opposition. The highly conservative business community has criticized these moves, blaming them for the growth of extreme leftist activity, including the kidnapping of the president's own father-in-law in August, 1974. But on the whole, compared with its prerevolutionary past and with many of its neighbors, Mexico stands out not only as a country attempting to cope with problems of development but also as one that is notably independent of the United States. The recent discovery of large oil reserves in southeast Mexico may serve as a shot in the arm for the government's development efforts. These will be under the direction of a new president in 1977, undoubtedly López Portillo, the candidate of PRI, selected in late 1975 by the government party.

Cuba

Cuba began to attract worldwide attention in January, 1959, with the fall of its longtime dictator, Fulgencio Batista, and the coming to power of Fidel Castro Ruz. Like the Mexican, the Cuban revolution stressed massive social, economic, and political restructuring of old conditions, aiming at incorporating more people into a modern national life. Also like the Mexican, the Cuban revolution spawned a single-party system, government intervention in the economic and social spheres, independence from former outside influences, and the forging of a distinctly Cuban national identity. But unlike Mexico, Cuba did not produce a new constitution, regular and frequent elections, nor a constitutionally required rotation of the country's presidents each six years. Instead the political system became dominated by the personality of one man, Fidel Castro, who grafted Communism onto Cuban nationalism.

Castro's forceful personal leadership is easily seen in Cuban politics. He is a highly charismatic socialist *caudillo*, the *líder máximo*, who is Prime Minister of the Republic and First Secretary of the Communist Party—an organization that gradually extended its scope under Castro's leadership during the fifteen years after he assumed power. Leading members of the Cuban Communist Party, ipso facto the official heads of the Cuban hierarchy, are essentially *fidelistas*—former associates of Castro in his earlier campaigns against Batista's regime, whose loyalty, typical of Latin America, is personalist rather than Marxist. Castro is the central decision maker, a circumstance that became obvious as the government extended its control over the economy and society and began to mobilize the masses in such areas as bolstering national defense, improving literacy, initiating public-health campaigns, and bringing in the annual sugar harvest. Castro's personal dominance over both party and government apparatus since 1959 clearly reflects traditional Cuban political culture; despite its new guise, this undoubtedly helps to make the system work.

Under Castro's leadership, Cuba experienced vast changes throughout the 1960s and 1970s. The middle and upper classes virtually disappeared as the state began to expropriate private domestic and foreign property and formulate new programs in agriculture, health, education, housing, and welfare. Many members of the old order, which had been closely interlocked with American business interests especially in sugar and public utilities, simply fled the island as Castro turned increasingly toward Communist prescriptions for change. Communism and a militant brand of Cuban nationalism became the order of the day, leading toward a host of new grass-roots political organizations accompanied by exhortations to work for the new order. Many people found Castro's policies unbearable, but many more, formerly on the periphery of sharing in the state's goods and services, found themselves much better off, particularly in respect to health, education, and welfare benefits, and general participation in the country's future. By the mid-1970s, moreover, the country's economic and social transformation, including the new emphasis on a common *Cubanidad* taught in the classroom and urged in mass-communication media, had gone far toward ending the racism of former days.

A major issue in Cuban politics is the extent of Soviet control over Cuban affairs once Castro began to link Cuban nationalism with Russian Communism. Some observers feel that by the mid-1970s, after several shifts and turns, Cuba had become little more than a Soviet satellite in the Western Hemisphere. Their argument hinges upon Soviet aid running at about two million dollars per day, Cuba's four billion dollar debt to the Soviets, and the island's admittance to the Soviet-controlled council for Mutual Economic Assistance (COMECON). Others argue that Cuba still remained a very independent government—far more so than the old Cuba, where Americans first intervened regularly in political affairs and later, through business interests, in gambling casinos, public utilities, sugar plantations, and other commercial interests. The Soviets—so it is argued—came generally as technical advisers.

Cuba's relations with the United States and Latin America are a part of this question. By late 1974, visits to Cuba by members of the United States Senate Foreign Relations Committee gave clear indications that Cuba and the United States were leaning toward renewed diplomatic relations, severed in 1961 when Castro adopted attitudes favoring the USSR. And by the 1970s many members of the Organization of American States (OAS), Latin America's regional organization, were advocating the lifting of the political and economic sanctions that had been imposed in 1964 because of Havana's alleged attempts to interfere in the internal affairs of Latin American countries by aiding guerrilla movements. Since then Castro's regime has become increasingly moderate in its dealings with established Latin American governments, thereby encouraging such countries as Argentina, Costa Rica, Colombia, Mexico, Panama, Peru, and Venezuela to press for abolishing the OAS sanctions. Reestablishment of normal relations with the Latin American countries and with the United States would certainly counterbalance the assumed influence of Moscow in Cuba's domestic politics. Another step in this direction occurred in July, 1975, with the formal ending of the 1964 OAS embargo.

Cuba's potential for future development turns upon several major questions. The amount of participation by workers instead of bureaucrats in planning and production in factories and on farms, if increased, would go far toward increasing productivity and do so along socialist lines, a fact now recognized by Castro. Increased material incentives are also receiving more attention, since Castro's former stress on moral incentives had not satisfactorily increased productivity, and worker absenteeism was high. There are still insufficient numbers of skilled workers and professional people, especially given the exodus of thousands of skilled people during the 1960s, but the government hopes to fill this gap through mass education. A host of other problems arises in the management of a socialist economy, such as systems control, socializing the population, shoring up flagging revolutionary élan, and balancing the need for advanced education with the need for workers. How to diversify the economy while maintaining productivity when sugar is still the island's economic mainstay is another key problem. All these issues raise questions where Fidel's personal rulership ends and where institution building begins in the management of economic and social change.

Questions of a more purely political nature also face Cuba. Political dissent is not possible and the number of political prisoners is high. Political power, not widely distributed, centers on the rather small *fidelista* group. Even constructive criticism of the revolution has become increasingly disallowed as society has become more and more militarized and regimentized. Thus, while the government has expanded its capacity to meet public needs, it has done so under extremely restricted conditions accompanied by limited political rights, far more circumscribed than in revolutionary Mexico next door. Whether the political system will "loosen up" in the future remains to be seen. As Castro grows older and the revolution wears on, however, problems of institutionalizing the revolution and establishing a stable political succession in leadership must be met. Undoubtedly, innovative methods must also be devised to avoid alienating Cuba's new generations from the political system.

Haiti and the Dominican Republic

Haiti and the Dominican Republic, occupying the island of Hispaniola, sharply contrast with Mexico and Cuba. Neither country has experienced a revolution in the recent past—outside of the perpetual game of musical chairs among their strongmen rulers—nor are their economic, social, or political systems changing rapidly today. Both lands are noted for recent dictatorships, Francois "Papa Doc" Duvalier (1957-71) in Haiti and Rafael Trujillo (1930-61) in the Dominican Republic. Neither one did much to foster viable civic institutions, given their absolute ruthlessness and systematic repression. Furthermore, both Haiti and the Dominican Republic sustained occupation by the United States: Haiti from 1915 to 1934 and the Dominican Republic from 1916 to 1924 and again in 1965. The latter raised severe strains within the OAS, as had Washington's earlier Bay of Pigs invasion of Cuba in 1961. Yet, of the two, the Dominican Republic's record contains at least a spark of hope for political development.

This observation is based upon the different political, economic, and social settings of the two countries. Haiti, separated from France in 1804, the first Negro republic in the Americas, is greatly restricted by its meager endowment of resources and its tradition of violence, fear, and suspicion growing from past politics. The country is 90 percent illiterate and the great majority of the population is rural. Only one-third of the country is arable. The population concentration per acre in the rural areas is extremely high, a circumstance that hinders economic development. Haiti has had thirty-six heads of state since independence, twenty-four of whom were forced to resign and seven killed in office. The present national palace is the fourth of its kind; the other three were blown up by basement explosions. Francois Duvalier was noted for his use of repression, murder, imprisonment, nighttime raids on opposition offices, torture, mysterious abductions, and his elaborate network of security forces, called the *tonton macoute* (Creole for "bagmen" or "bogeymen").

Upon Duvalier's death, political power passed to his son, nineteen-year-old Jean Claude who, like his father, became President for Life. Political competition then began to center within the palace itself, since the country had not been industrialized to the point of producing other competing groups. Jean Claude has made gestures toward economic development, but existing conditions make rapid change difficult.

The chances of development in the Dominican Republic, by contrast, began to rise with the assassination of Trujillo in 1961. The first free elections in thirty-eight years were held in 1962 and Juan Bosch was elected president on a platform of reform. Bosch's policies, which included reduction of military perquisites, proved too liberal for the entrenched right, however, and Bosch was overthrown in 1963. His regime was replaced by a military group which, in turn, was challenged by followers of Bosch and others in April, 1965. Fearing Communist activity and the rise of another Cuba, President Lyndon B. Johnson sent in the United States Marines to "protect American and other lives." The upshot was still another election in 1966, won by Joaquín Balaguer who has ruled since then with military support. Balaguer was elected to his third consecutive term in August, 1974.

Given the Dominican Republic's resources, in addition to Trujillo's ending of the country's foreign debt and his building of public services, the potential for development is present although unfulfilled. The land is fertile, sugar is exported under government management, and a land-reform program has been legislated. Its other resources include cocoa, coffee, tobacco, nickel, and bauxite. Among the country's major problems are a continuing single-export economy (sugar), lack of business confidence due to continuous political upheavals, and the high cost of supporting the military. Political violence is high and is frequently aimed at left-wing opponents of the government, and the nation's newspapers are filled with alleged plots against the government and right-wing activities against the extreme left.

THE CENTRAL AMERICAN STATES

A close look at the Central American lands is surprising. These are not, as commonly assumed, "look-alike" countries steaming under the noonday sun. Their commonalities—economic and social structures, predominance of the Roman Catholic religion, Spanish language, Hispanic culture, and nearly 300 years of colonial rule under the Captaincy General of Guatemala—conceal unique differences. Their ethnic composition ranges from 90 percent white in Costa Rica to 55 percent Indian in Guatemala and mixed Indian and Negro in Nicaragua. Guatemala is 38 percent literate compared to 85 percent in Costa Rica. Rates of political violence are high in several Central American countries, but low in Costa Rica. While Roman Catholicism is the predominant religion, much of Central America's Indian population lives untouched by the Christian faith.

Nor are these six countries hopelessly adrift in terms of trying to restructure their social and economic systems. Their governments are, in varying degrees, pressing for agricultural and industrial growth through a variety of programs. A host of agencies have been established during the period since World War II to promote agricultural and industrial development in the related fields of planning, agrarian reform, education, technical aid, and credit facilities. Not least among the indications of a desire for development is the Central American Common Market (CACM), which seeks the eventual economic unification of the region.

A balanced view of Central America is of course not completely rosy. Political and economic power remains in a few hands, and there is a real question as to whether "development" of the public economic sector will benefit the large landowners or the ordinary peasants. The landholding structure is notoriously lopsided in most of Central America, as indicated by the one-tenth of 1 percent of total farms in Guatemala comprising 5000 acres or more but occupying 41 percent of the farming land, or the 4 percent of farms in Honduras being more than 100 acres, but accounting for 50 percent of all farmland.

Additional pressures against development were added in the late 1960s and early 1970s. El Salvador and Honduras went to war, thus undermining the region's Central American Common Market.* World inflation pressures and the rising price of petroleum and petroleum products, as fertilizers and chemicals, added to Central America's burdens. The estimated inflation figures, for example, ran at a low of 10-15 percent in Honduras to a high of 30 percent in Costa Rica during 1974. Moreover, when the Central American countries tried to impose a one-dollar-per-crate banana tax on the exports of the foreign-owned Standard Fruit Company and United Brands of Boston—a major initiative of Central America's fledgling Union of Banana Exporting Countries (UPEB)—they found stiff opposition from the multinational corporations. Indeed, President Oswaldo López Arellano of Honduras is alleged to have received an immense bribe (one and a quarter million dollars) from United Brands to lower the banana export tax in 1974.

Yet efforts to underwrite development are stronger than a quick look

* The war erupted in July 1969 ostensibly over ill feelings generated during the eliminating round of the 1970 World Cub Association soccer competition. Behind these tensions were disagreements over boundary definitions, Salvadorian immigration into Honduras, and rising nationalist feelings in both countries.

at the area would indicate. The establishment of UPEB is one indication. Another is the continuing attempts to make CACM a truly effective organization after the Honduran-El Salvador disagreements of late 1969. Meanwhile, Venezuela agreed in January, 1975, to supply financial aid and investment to the six Central American countries to offset their heavy oil import bills. All these efforts, in addition to government programs in investment, education, research, and planning cannot be discounted.

Guatemala

Guatemala, the cradle of Mayan Indian civilization, is different from other Central American countries. It has the highest concentration of Indians, about 55 percent of the population, who live fragmented in self-contained villages with their own dialects, customs, and clothing. Indians rarely marry outside their village, and although the winds of European civilization have been beating against them for 400 years, these people of ancient Mayan stock live much as did their ancestors before the Spanish conquest. Certainly they feel no "Guatemalan" identity. About 45 percent of the population are *ladinos,* of Indian and white stock, while the rest are Spanish, German, or black. Guatemala is the most populous Central American country, the most northerly, ranks first in foreign trade, and its industry accounts for the highest percentage (15 percent) of gross national product (GNP) in Central America.

Political violence is high in Guatemala, owing to highly polarized bitterness between the extremes of left and right. This stems from a tradition of despotic rule that left little experience with democratic government, from the demands for change that emerged after World War II versus entrenched opposition from landowners and rightist military officers, and from the partial reforms begun immediately after World War II but suddenly reversed in the mid-1950s. The upshot has been killings and tortures of extreme leftists, rightists, and even moderates. At least a thousand persons were killed in 1970-71 alone.

A brief political record puts these events into perspective. Juan José Arévalo, Guatemala's first democratically elected president, supported by young teachers, professionals, intellectuals and leftist army officers, assumed power in 1945, hoping to develop Guatemala somewhat along the lines of Mexico. Arévalo completed his term in 1951 without having translated his ideals into programs, owing largely to the lack of an organized political base and to continuous opposition from the country's traditional oligarchy. Jacobo Arbenz Guzmán followed in the presidency, putting into operation an agrarian reform that expropriated a million and a half acres of land, which was allotted to some hundred thousand peasants. Insofar as food imports are necessary in Guatemala, owing partly to the idleness of much of the private land, the agrarian reform was a step in the right direction. But this kind of reform was not to last.

Fears of Communist penetration into the Arbenz government, coupled with growing intransigence from the right, led to the overthrow of Arbenz in 1954 by Colonel Carlos Castillo Armas with, many students argue, the help of the United States Central Intelligence Agency. Armas in turn ruled as a dictator and dissolved all political parties and trade unions, although he did try to stimulate the economic development of the country. He was assassinated in 1957, and the next years saw military rule without substantial progress in agrarian reform, but with moderate rates of industrialization. The left and right became increasingly antagonistic, which escalated political violence. General Carlos Arana Osorio, coming to the presidency in 1970 in a continuing climate of violence, showed himself aware of Guatemala's need for development by proclaiming the country's first five year development plan. By 1974, when General Eugenio Kjell Laugerud García became president, Arana had also pacified the country by bringing both left and right more or less under control. But the roots of violence are still there, and Guatemala's future will not be easy.

Honduras

Honduras is generally considered the poorest and least industrialized of the Central American countries. Its people are a mixture of Indian, Negro, and Spanish, with the mixed-blooded mestizo predominating. Agriculture is the mainstay of the economy, bananas—produced chiefly by United Brands—being its principal export. Regional rivalries are high in Honduras; the military exercises a major force in politics, and the country has experienced a number of clashes with its neighbors (Guatemala, El Salvador, Nicaragua, Costa Rica) in the past over various political disputes and boundary issues. Seventy percent of the population live in the countryside, and about one million of these people earn less than thirty dollars a year.

While these conditions do not augur well for development, Honduras recently began to show signs of progress. General Oswaldo López Arellano came to power in 1972, and after much acrimony pushed through an agrarian reform bill, coupled with the publication of a national development plan to change the tax system, promote industrial development, and increase the share of the state in economic enterprises. These moves were undoubtedly stimulated by Hurricane Fifi in 1974, which almost totally destroyed agriculture, industry, and communications in the northern coastal belt—Honduras' biggest producer of wealth. Honduras' withdrawal from the Central American Common Market following the war with El Salvador, however, did not help the government's economic efforts.

The Honduran picture by mid-1975 was mixed. President Lopez Arellano was replaced by Colonel Juan Alberto Melgar Castro in mid-1975, partly resulting from the bribe scandal with United Brands. Colonel Melgar is noted to have connections with conservative landowners and the business community. But the ouster of López Arellano was also supported by determined young army officers with recognized reformist leanings. Meanwhile, more than a hundred peasant league leaders had been jailed as a result of land invasions in May, 1975, and conservative landowners were denouncing the technical training being given to the peasants as Marxist, even though the foreign technicians brought in to accomplish that training were financed by international agencies. The summer of 1975 found a strong peasant movement underway headed by the thirty-eight thousand member National Peasant Union, growing resistance from the powerful Cattle Farmers Federation, land invasions by peasants, and a number of killings in the countryside.

El Salvador

El Salvador, the smallest and most densely populated of the Latin American republics, is dominated by a small and wealthy oligarchy often designated as the "fourteen families" exercising suzerainty over a rural population of landless peasant mestizos. Politics is the domain of the oligarchy and the army; eight of the nine presidents between 1931 and 1970 were military men. Outside of the economic oligarchy and the military there are no significant pressure groups, although popular unrest is possible. In fact, by late 1974, a number of nascent leftist groups, such as the Revolutionary Army of the People, had initiated a wave of bombings directed against government buildings and the government of Colonel Arturo Molina. One would not expect to find attention being given to social reform and economic development under these conditions.

Yet even tiny El Salvador shows some signs of development. The government has increased state investments for social and economic reforms, economic development agencies have been set up, and a National Council for Planning and Coordination was established in 1970. While little serious attention has been given to land reform—one of the reasons for peasant unrest, but a real problem given the power of the large landowners—the country's overall economy was given a tremendous boost by entry into the Central American Common Market. The output of light industries, for example, doubled in the 1960s. Unfortunately the war with Honduras almost paralyzed the Central American Common Market, causing El Salvador to find new markets for its exports. By early 1975, it appeared that difficulties between Honduras and El Salvador might be resolved, thus stimulating internal economic growth again. One of the remaining question marks is the degree to which people from El Salvador will be attracted to emigrate illegally into neighboring Honduras as in the past, given the much larger territory and smaller population of Honduras, thereby generating new tensions between the two nations.

Nicaragua

Nicaragua, the largest in area and next to the smallest in population among the Central American republics, unfortunately does not show as many signs of political development as do its neighbors on the isthmus. The country admittedly has made some progress in reducing illiteracy, stimulating some trade, and reducing the annual death rate since World War II. Much of the country's marginal economic growth owes to the increased sales of cotton, coffee, beef, and sugar, plus material assistance from the United States and new developments in the mining of copper. The problem in Nicaragua is that much of the material benefits from these economic improvements go not to the public at large, but to the traditional elite of landowners, military hierarchy, and Church, and in particular to the ruling dynasty—the Somoza family. Farms with more than 864 acres constitute 1.5 percent of the total number, but more than 40 percent of the land in use—an indication of gross inequality in land ownership. The Somozas meanwhile own an extensive commercial empire in real estate, sugar and banana plantations, cattle ranches, shipping, lumber, textiles, distilleries, and cement and other booming businesses.

The Somoza regime has ruled in Nicaragua almost continually since 1937. It maintained law and order through control of the National Guard, a well-trained force thanks to the occupation of the United States Marines earlier in the twentieth century. The Somozas also count upon the material assistance of the United States, forthcoming in part from the stake of American business concerns in this land. The Somozas also promote public-works projects, though for whose benefit there is considerable debate. The modest economic progress attained by Nicaragua by the early 1970s was severely undermined in 1972 when Managua, the capital city, was struck by a devastating earthquake. It destroyed much of the country's manufacturing and commerce, thereby causing a major decline in the republic's economic growth rate. To this tragedy was added the loss of sales to Honduras following that country's withdrawal from the Central American Common Market. Nicaragua was thus forced to look for new markets, as were the Market's other members. Meanwhile, Nicaragua goes on, without the visible growing peasant unrest found in Guatemala or Honduras.

Costa Rica

Costa Rica is the most socially and politically advanced of the Central American countries and indeed of all the Southern Hemisphere Americas. Its literacy rate is the fourth highest in Latin America; it has one of the lowest rates of coups d'etat and political violence; and its land and wealth are more evenly distributed than is generally true of Central America. Costa Rica is well known for political stability and the peaceful transition of political power, due largely to the lack of military involvement in political affairs. The *latifundia* system of a small, dominating white oligarchy over mixed-blooded peasants did not develop in Costa Rica, which, when coupled with a homogeneous white population, produced a community of small landholders predisposed to a democratic way of life. Costa Ricans, not unreasonably, feel superior to their Central American neighbors.

Costa Rica has other positive assets when it comes to existing and future political development. Domestic and foreign investments, plus a high rate of foreign aid, contribute to a solid rate of growth in both agriculture and industry. The government set up a national planning office in 1963 and is active in planning, regional development programs, and financing. The government is also highly conscious of the need to continue economic diversification, expand markets, and industrialize. Costa Rica is likely to be more successful than other Central American lands given the lack of economic waste in a heavy spending military establishment added to the country's political stability and the high degree of national identity as "Costa Ricans," so helpful in legitimizing government programs.

Costa Rica of course has its difficulties. It is not rich in such natural resources as petroleum, coal, and iron. It developed a high rate of inflation in the early 1970s, triggered by the rising cost of oil and oil-related goods. But it is increasing its trade goods—coffee, bananas, beef, sugar, and cocoa—and the future is definitely hopeful. In the peaceful elections of February, 1974, the presidency passed from José Figueres Ferrer—one of the best-known architects of modern Costa Rica—to Daniel Oduber Quiros.

Panama

If one believes that geography determines politics, then Panama makes a classic study. Its independence and subsequent political dynamics arose from the narrowness of its land, making it the easiest route from the Atlantic to the Pacific, and from the construction of a sea canal between the two oceans. A 1903 treaty gave the United States sovereignty over the Canal Zone—the Canal and a ten-mile wide, forty-mile long zone—that cut Panama in two and dominated its political and economic life. These circumstances have caused bitterness among Panamanians for virtually the entire seven decades of the Canal's existence, in spite of the economic prosperity the Canal has brought to Panama.

Before Panama's independence it was a geographical appendage of Colombia, and separatist leaders had long opposed Bogotá's distant political rule. Their chance for independence came in 1903 when the American president, Theodore Roosevelt, resolved to support a move for Panama's separation from Colombia, thus allowing him to conclude a canal treaty with Panama instead of Colombia, which had been less enthusiastic in the matter. Panama declared its independence, American warships neutralized Colombia's reactions, and a treaty was concluded between the United States and newly independent Panama.

Over the years, notwithstanding an annual rent payment of $1.9 million dollars by 1955, Panamanian resentment kindled out of opposition to the United States presence. Riots and loss of life occurred in 1964, resulting in a rupture of diplomatic relations between the U.S. and Panama. President Lyndon Johnson then began negotiations for an essentially new treaty, the principles of which were worked out by May, 1974. These principles included the surrendering of United States "sovereignty in perpetuity" over the Panama Canal Zone, as in the original treaty. Remaining questions by mid-1975 included the U.S. military role in the Canal Zone, the location of the headquarters of the U.S. Southern Command, if and where to build a new canal to meet the increased size of ships and volume of shipping, and arrangements for turning over jurisdiction of the Canal to the Panamanians.

Panama is the youngest and least populated of the Central American countries. Its population is predominantly the mixed-blooded mulatto of white and black ancestry. Literacy is approximately 78 percent, about sixth highest in Latin America, roughly equal to that of Mexico. A small number of families dominate the country's economy and politics as in other Central American states, while the rural population is scattered. The economy is growing at about 8 percent per annum—good in Latin America—and output of bananas, cattle, and citrus fruit is up.

A coup d'etat in 1968 brought General Omar Torrijos Herrera to power, a man committed to asserting Panama's independence from United States control, and to raising Panama's standard of living. Thus he pressed for the new Canal treaty negotiations, was active in the "banana tax" policy against the multinational corporations, advocated the return of Cuba to the Latin American family against United States pressure, and shows strong concern for improving Panama's agricultural productivity. The future success of Torrijos and other Panamanian leaders in developing their country will turn largely on the status and use of the Canal.

Suggested Readings

Fagen, Richard. *The Transformation of Political Culture in Cuba*. Stanford, Calif.: Stanford University Press, 1969.

Goldrich, Daniel. *Sons of the Establishment; Elite Youth in Panama and Costa Rica*. Chicago: Rand McNally, 1966.

Gonzalez, Edward. *Cuba Under Castro: The Limits of Charisma*. Boston: Houghton Mifflin, 1974.

Horowitz, Michael M. *Peoples and Cultures of the Caribbean*. Garden City, N.Y.: National History Press, 1971.

Johnson, Kenneth F. *Mexican Democracy: A Critical View*. Boston: Allyn & Bacon, 1971.

Mesa Lago, Carmelo (ed.). *Revolutionary Change in Cuba*. Pittsburgh, Pa.: University of Pittsburgh Press, 1971.

Schneider, Ronald. *Communism in Guatemala, 1944-1954*. New York: Praeger, 1959.

Scott, Robert. *Mexican Government in Transition*. Urbana: University of Illinois Press, 1964.

Suchlicki, Jaime. *Cuba, Castro, and Communism*. Coral Gables, Fla.: University of Miami Press, 1972.

Four

The Andean and Atlantic Countries

THE ANDEAN AREA

The Andean countries—Venezuela, Colombia, Ecuador, Peru, Bolivia, and Chile—are larger in size and population than the Central American lands, tend to have higher rates of literacy, and have political systems that are on the whole more sophisticated. By this is meant that since World War II their political parties have shown interest in progressive development of their economy and they manifest a greater variety of interest groups and a wider spread of political opinion and power. The Andean countries also tend to be more developed in terms of distribution of population into more than one major city, and in the percentage of their working force in nonagricultural employment. In 1969 they formed the Andean Group to foster a common policy toward foreign investment and to encourage wider internal markets. They all have declared their intention to limit armaments and stop acquiring offensive weapons, an agreement reached in December, 1974.

Yet much variety exists among the Andean republics. The ethnic distribution ranges from 70 percent Indian in Bolivia, to 97 percent white in Chile. Per capita incomes vary between a high of over $1,260 in oil-rich Venezuela to around $185 in Bolivia, and the population size runs from twenty-six million in Colombia to Bolivia's five million.

Not all the political systems are well developed, as the rather conservative military rule in Bolivia attests, and even progressive governments at one moment in history can succumb to political reaction, as in Chile after the fall of President Salvadore Allende in 1973. Venezuela and Colombia by contrast have competitive party systems and, by Latin American standards, are democratically representative governments. Moreover, there are disagreements and frictions within the region, as between Colombia and Venezuela over the disputed continental shelf and territorial waters in the Gulf of Venezuela, and continuing friction between Bolivia and Chile dating back to the 1879 War of the Pacific when Bolivia lost its access to the sea. The rich variety of countries within the Andean region can be seen by looking briefly at each one.

Venezuela

Venezuela, with its twelve million people, predominantly mixed-blooded mestizos, recently emerged as the leading advocate of the economic independence of Latin America. As one of the world's leading oil producers, it is an active member of the powerful Overseas Petroleum Export Countries (OPEC) in which it strongly defends the high price of oil and other raw materials, and has attacked the industrialized countries for using "economic totalitarianism" against developing countries. In advocating Latin America's economic independence, Carlos Andrés Pérez, elected president in December, 1973, quickly began to nationalize Venezuela's oil industries, headed by Exxon, Shell, and Gulf, and iron-ore companies, United States Steel and Bethlehem Steel. Pérez showed a determination to make good his campaign pledges to use energy money—oil revenues jumping from three billion dollars in 1973 to ten billion dollars in 1974—to advance Venezuela's independent development; "democracy with energy" was his campaign pledge, and the Venezuelan congress approved a bill in August, 1975, allowing total state takeover of the oil industry. Venezuela also publicly opposed the United States Foreign Trade Act of January, 1975, which denied preferential tariff treatment to members of OPEC.

Venezuela has far to go to improve material standards of living for all its people. Urbanization is extremely high, producing great poverty belts around Caracas and other cities due to unemployment, insufficient housing, and inadequate school, sanitary, and transport facilities. While its per capita income is the highest in Latin America, in actual fact 3 percent of the population owns 30 percent of the country's wealth, a quarter of the labor force is unemployed or underemployed, and nearly five million rural people and migrants live a bare subsistence life. But Venezuela is an open society with great physical and social mobility and a large middle class. Furthermore, since the end of the last dictatorship in 1959, successive governments have poured money into agricultural programs as well as into health, education, and housing. Lack of qualified manpower, organizational bottlenecks, and administrative difficulties have hampered some of these massive efforts.

This fascinating country had experienced sixteen years of democratic representative government by 1975. Following the dictatorship (1952-58) of Marcos Pérez Jiménez, the reformist political party of Acción Democrática (AD) came to power under the energetic leadership (1959-64) of President Rómulo Betancourt. He was followed by a second AD veteran, Raúl Leoni (1964-69), after whom government power passed to another reform party, the Christian Democrats (COPEI), as Rafael Caldera assumed the presidency (1969-74). In the peaceful elections of December, 1973, in which Venezuela's 4.6 million voters could choose from among thirteen presidential candidates representing parties from the far left to the far right, the Acción Democrática candidate, Carlos Andrés Pérez won. These sixteen years of democratic and development-oriented government are remarkable, not only because of recovery from the dictatorship of Pérez Jiménez and that of Juan Vicente Gómez (1908-35), but because the system also withstood extreme left-wing violence in the 1960s without reverting to military government.

Colombia

Colombia, the third largest in population and fifth largest in area of the Latin American countries, is impeded in its development by several obstacles. Mountain barriers make communication and transportation among regions difficult and reinforce regional differences—and even antagonisms. Colombia's history of Conservatives and Liberals engaging in fierce competition, rather than offering democratic alternatives, has culminated in a polarization of political positions even to the point of armed conflict. Unlike Peru and Brazil, Colombia has not seen the military emerge with a coordinated policy of modernization, but rather remains divided between the law-and-order "Brazilian" school and a reformist "Peruvian" school. A culture of violence is rooted in the regional rivalries and political feuds that erupted between 1948 and 1953, a period called *la violencia,* in which an estimated three hundred thousand men, women, and children were brutally massacred. Continuing unresolved problems of population growth, urban and rural poverty, unemployment, and soaring inflation are sources of deep discontent. Sixty percent of Colombia's people are estimated to be suffering from malnutrition.

Colombia's political system is largely controlled by a traditional elite composed of a landholding oligarchy, the military, and the Church, and a more up-to-date group of industrialists and leaders of commerce and the professions. They tend to support either the Liberal or Conservative parties—the two traditionally dominant parties of Colombian politics. After the violence from 1948 to 1953 followed the authoritarian rule of General Rojas Pinilla (1953-57). The Liberals and Conservatives then decided to share power in a National Front in order to give the country's passions a time to cool down. Neither Conservative nor Liberal administrations between 1958 and 1974, however, were able to make substantive progress in the country's development, although the Liberals tried to cope with economic and social problems through modest agrarian reform and economic diversification. Industrial growth has in fact proceeded in the areas of Medellín and Cali, but on the whole Colombia's governmental reforms pale when compared to those of Venezuela.

The Colombian elections of April, 1974, seemed to herald a new era for Colombia. The electorate chose Alfonso López Michelsen, a liberal law professor with a major program for broad social and economic reforms within a democratic system. But by mid-1975 little change had come to the country's poor majority, many of whom were illegally moving into neighboring Venezuela, just as El Salvador's population is attracted to Honduras. A rise in kidnappings of wealthy people or their children by guerrilla groups—either the Army of National Liberation (ELN) or the Revolutionary Armed Forces of Colombia (FARC) —in addition to student unrest and workers' strikes prompted the new president to return to past "law-and-order" policies by imposing a state of siege. This gives the military the right to intervene on matters relating to public safety, such as strikes, student demonstrations, and peasant unrest.

Ecuador

Ecuador, the smallest of the Andean lands, lags in its development. Its population of four million includes a large Indian element, about 40 percent of the total, who live mostly in the temperate valleys of the *sierra* (mountains) as linguistically and culturally divided communities. Guayaquil is the country's principal port and commercial entrepôt, while Quito is the staunch colonial and conservative center of the hinterland. The sierra landowners are determined to oppose any significant land reform, and although the more open-minded progressive elite of Guayaquil talk of reform, in truth they form a financial and commercial oligarchy of their own. The middle class is weak, the masses backward and apathetic, and politics tends to be highly personal rather than organized toward reform.

The military in Ecuador, as in Colombia, are affected by the positive roles of their counterparts in Brazil and Peru, and may be the catalyst for change in the future. President José María Velasco Ibarra, five times called to the presidency and four times deposed, a charismatic individual who puts into practice his idea of "give me a balcony and the country is mine!," was last deposed in 1972 by General Rodríguez Lara. The military then published a development plan for 1973-77 in which they recognized that Ecuador's problems lay in the countryside, noting that 1.8 percent of Ecuador's population controlled 24 percent of its wealth. While no significant progress had been made in the military's objectives by mid-1975, at least attention to Ecuador's problems existed. Ecuador's Amazonian oil deposits, moreover, might provide new capital for development in the future. Ecuador, a member of OPEC with Venezuela, is determined to keep oil prices up. Meanwhile, the country claims total sovereignty of 200 nautical miles, and continues to fine United States tuna boats in what it considers Ecuadorian waters, another source of income that could be used for development projects. But Ecuador's obstacles to change are great, and the mid-1975 inflation rate of 30 percent does not bode well for the immediate future.

Peru

Peru, home of Cuzco—capital of the vast Inca Empire—and the famous Inca mountaintop city of Machu Picchu, is one of the most fascinating lands of contemporary Latin America. A 1968 military coup deposed president Fernando Belaúnde, an avowed reform leader but one having difficulty in maintaining public support for his programs. Instead of just another round of military intervention, for which Peru had become famous, the new military leaders launched the country on a road of dramatic social and economic transformation.

The post-1969 policies are particularly interesting since Peru's social, political, and economic structures were much like the others in Latin America. An oligarchy of landowners, industrialists, bankers, and businessmen ruled over the Indians and mixed-blooded *cholos* of the mountainous regions, the poverty-stricken people of Peru's shantytowns, and the growing middle class in urban areas. Only 47 percent of the population claimed Spanish as their natural tongue in 1940, although 60 percent did so by 1961. Yet in 1961, 35 percent of the population still claimed the Indian tongue of Quechua as their maternal language and some regions of the mountains—the high mountain plateau called the *altiplano*—still were up to 95 percent Quechua-speaking. Meanwhile, about 2 percent of Peru's population owned more than 90 percent of the farmland before the 1968 reforms. Out of this backward, nationally unintegrated situation came a military corps dedicated to changes nearly as dramatic as those in Mexico and Cuba.

Peru admittedly has a long tradition of reform-oriented movements and leaders. The Popular Alliance for Revolutionary Action (APRA) emerged in the 1920s under the leadership of Víctor Raúl Haya de la Torre. APRA attacked the oligarchy, opposed "Yankee Imperialism," and advocated internationalizing the Panama Canal. But APRA was continually up against the power of the oligarchy and the military, which over the years caused it to modify its position considerably, leading many former *Apristas* to become disillusioned. Later, during the 1950s, another reformist movement emerged, called *Acción Popular*, which assumed power in 1963 when its leader, Fernando Belaúnde, became president. Belaúnde's programs included (as had APRA in its early stages) reincorporating Indians into national life, plus constructing irrigation canals, schools, and clinics, and generally assisting local initiatives with funds and technical advice from the central government. Financial scandals, a growing public debt, and problems with left-wing guerrillas eroded public confidence in Acción Popular, bringing in the military in 1968. Thus, the reformers of Peru's past could not effectively organize for change, nor could they forge the needed consensus to push ahead with their programs.

What has the Peruvian military accomplished since 1968? It has nationalized a number of foreign concerns, including the International Petroleum Company, owned by Standard Oil of New Jersey, in 1968 and the giant United States-owned mining complex of Cerro de Pasco in 1974. It passed a law calling for the participation of workers in ownership and administration of industrial concerns, called the "industrial community" concept, and by 1973 more than 3,300 enterprises had begun to put the program into effect. Perhaps most significant is its agrarian-reform program, one of the most intensive in Latin America, under which more than 170,000 families have received land. This occurred without the sudden production declines experienced in neighboring Chile under the government (1970-73) of President Salvador Allende or in Cuba during the early 1960s. Finally, the Peruvian military government has taken up the cause of the Indian by recognizing Quechua as the official second language of Peru and by passing a Jungle Law establishing the legal existence of tribal societies, guaranteeing their territorial rights, and protecting their property and tribal justice—in addition to providing training and technical assistance.

Naturally Peru is not without its problems. More than a million families still remain landless or have just enough property for a marginal existence. The majority of the population is still poor and as desperate as they always were. About two-thirds of the people, including small peasants, petty traders, artisans, casual workers, and other members of the middle class, have yet to benefit tangibly from the military reforms. The conservative elite is also unhappy, as they showed by their sharp reaction to the military takeover of Lima's daily newspapers in 1974. The troubled situation has produced strikes and disturbances in industry, mining, and agriculture during the early 1970s, fueled, it must be said, by a 30 percent inflation rate in 1974. Nor has the government's attempts to mobilize the masses in support of the revolution through mass organizations worked, whereas opposition movements emerged in the 1970s. The military, moreover, is not completely unified in its policies of drastic reform. But on the whole, the military president, General Juan Velasco Alvarado, showed himself to be a remarkable leader during a time of revolutionary change. New oil discoveries in the Amazon should aid the government's activities, and the country receives income from the United States for fines levied against tuna boats encroaching on the 200-mile jurisdiction claimed by Peru, as is also true of Ecuador and Brazil. President Velasco's fellow generals staged a bloodless coup in August, 1975, removing Velasco, who had been ailing since undergoing a knee operation in 1973. Observers saw this as a lessening of the dictatorial tendencies shown by Velasco in his later years, but emphasizing a continuation of the "socialist revolution." The military commanders named the prime minister, General Francisco Morales Bermudez, to be Peru's new president.

Chile

Chile, that narrow country 2,700 miles long with a population of ten million on South America's eastern seaboard, is a tragic case of frustrated reforms. Its future looked bright in the mid-1960s when the Christian Democratic reform government of President Eduardo Frei (1964-70) began to nationalize Chile's foreign-owned copper industry, at the same time putting into effect extensive agrarian-reform and housing programs. Set against a long history of commitments to fundamental social and economic reforms, stable democratic government, a nonpolitical military establishment, and a political culture of constitutional legality, Frei's approach to needed change had all the markings of a success story. But it was not to be. Despite a population that is 95 percent white and 85 percent literate with a strong sense of national identity, and despite highly developed transportation and communication facilities, this land had by mid-1975 become a repressive military dictatorship, following a blood bath in which more than 2,500 people died. Among the dead was the president, Dr. Salvadore Allende, who by "official" statements had committed suicide rather than surrender.

President Allende (1970-73), Latin America's first democratically elected Marxist president, attempted to carry Chilean reforms much further than past administrations, moving Chile from capitalism to socialism through Chile's traditional legal route. Allende's socialist program of total copper nationalization, sweeping agrarian reform, state control of the banks, and income redistribution initially met with some success, but eventually precipitated extensive economic dislocations, such as rising food imports, a fall in copper production, long lines waiting for food in the cities, and polarized political opinion. Like other reform presidents, Allende faced the traditional Chilean impediments of inflation, legislative obstructionism in Chile's multiparty legislature, resistance from foreign entrepreneurs, and divisions within his own party when things did not go as easily as predicted. But in Allende's case these forces combined to produce a 700 percent inflation rate in 1973 and escalated urban violence, illegal factory and land seizures, and strikes by copper workers, truckers, shop owners, and women, and provoked growing military dissatisfaction. The result was a military coup in September, 1973.

After the 1973 coup, a number of developments began to come to light. The director of the United States Central Intelligence Agency, William E. Colby, told Congress that the Nixon Administration had authorized more than eight million dollars for covert activities in Chile between 1970 and 1973 to make it impossible for Allende to govern. Part of this money was used to provide benefits for anti-Allende strikers in 1972 and 1973, with funds winding up in the hands of individuals, political parties, trade unions, and media outlets in Chile opposed to Allende. At their peak, in 1973, these strikes involved more than 250,000 truckdrivers, shopkeepers, and professionals and made many analysts conclude that violent overthrow of Allende was inevitable. Needless to say, these revelations raise the question of whether Allende's efforts at reform—which included the nationalization of United States business holdings—collapsed from external intervention or from the dynamics of change inside Chile. Proponents of both views can be easily found.

Since the 1973 coup, the clock has turned backward in Chile. The new junta, headed by General Augusto Pinochet Ugarte, closed Congress, shackled the press, forbade political party activity, and repeatedly violated civil liberties. Thousands of students and professors were expelled from the universities and the military began a campaign to revise texts in elementary and secondary education that had allegedly been infiltrated by Marxist ideology. The Human Rights Commission of the Organization of American States (OAS) estimated that Chile had incarcerated 5,500 political prisoners in August, 1974, although Interior Ministry spokesmen claimed that the actual number was 8,000. Chile's international reputation fell as embassies filled with exiles and reports of severe repression flooded out of the country. By mid-1975, the Chilean Church and Eduardo Frei's Christian Democratic Party were strongly attacking the military, but with little indication of changing its directions. Meanwhile, the shantytowns remained intact, working-class income fell to below subsistence levels, and civil liberties disappeared.

Bolivia

Bolivia, like Chile, has a past record of government efforts to stimulate development, but like Chile in the mid-1970s had become more the home of conservative military rule. Of all Andean lands, Bolivia has the smallest population and the highest concentration of Indians. The country experienced a revolution in 1952 led by the progressive National Revolutionary Movement (MNR), which for twelve years ruled Bolivia under Víctor Paz Estenssoro (1952-56 and 1960-64) and Hernán Siles Zuazo (1956-60). These governments brought transformation so vast as to rank Bolivia with Mexico and Cuba as sites of Latin America's twentieth-century revolutions. The MNR nationalized the great tin holdings and initiated agrarian reforms (under simultaneous pressure from the Indian peasantry itself), leading to millions of acres of arable and grazing land being distributed to thousands of rural families. It also extended the franchise to the 70 percent of the population classified as "Indian." Thenceforth "Indians" were known as campesinos.

While these twelve years of reform truly changed the face of Bolivia, the pace of change gradually died out of the revolution in the late 1960s—indeed the direction of reform had itself begun to change under the MNR administrations. The MNR and subsequent governments increasingly relied on massive foreign aid and private foreign capital to diversify their economy, including such private oil concerns as the American-owned Bolivian Gulf Oil Company—a subsidiary of the company that paid out at least four million dollars in bribes to government officials in 1966 and 1970, with Bolivian officials being likely candidates. Thus, the "anti-imperialism" of the MNR changed, causing a decline in popular support.

Paz was reelected in 1965, but deposed five months later by a popular Air Force Colonel, René Barrientos, who in fact had peasant support. Barrientos, who ruled until his death in 1969 in a helicopter accident, did not turn back earlier MNR reforms, but revolutionary momentum ebbed and private foreign investment became the emphasis of government policy. His death was followed by a series of coups and counter-coups, from General Alfredo Ovando Candia, who nationalized the Bolivian Gulf Oil Company, through General Juan José Torres, who continued the leftward trend by nationalizing the American-owned Maltide zinc mines, to the right-wing reaction of Colonel Hugo Bánzer Súarez in August, 1971, who still rules at this writing.

Bolivia is a highly unstable country, owing partly to factionalism within the military and partly to the various domestic movements that must be coped with. Left-wing militancy is periodically high, as during the ill-fated attempts of former Castro aide Ernesto "Che" Guevara to spark a rural guerrilla uprising in eastern Bolivia in 1967. The principal left-wing group, the National Liberation Army (ELN) now forms part of a movement called the Junta of Revolutionary Coordination (JCR) set up in Argentina in 1974 by four extremist movements in neighboring South American countries. Meanwhile, organized labor is almost congenitally hostile to the government, as tin miners' strikes show, and the Church began to condemn the Bolivian government's abuses of human rights in 1973. Peasant revolts (there was a severe one near Cochabamba in January, 1973) are other sources of tension between the people and the government. Bolivia's military regime, under Bánzer is not in the same league as those of Peru or Brazil when it comes to military-led development. Yet it is not as harsh as neighboring Chile after Allende's deposition.

The Bolivian military government is attempting to make some headway in economic development. It is trying to diversify its economy and escape its reliance on tin by exploiting other resources such as zinc, antimony, petroleum, and natural gas. The Soviet bloc is providing technical aid and credit to Bolivia, and China began to show an interest in the country in 1974. The government signed an important long-term agreement on industrial cooperation with Brazil in May, 1974, under which the countries will build a pipeline from the more dynamic Santa Cruz province to São Paulo. Bolivia will then deliver an average of 240 million cubic feet of natural gas per day for twenty years, using the profits to establish an industrial development complex, including an iron-and-steel-plant in eastern Bolivia where iron-ore deposits are rich. Meanwhile, the government continues to try to negotiate a route to the sea with Chile, but efforts to date are unsuccessful.

Bolivia remains a landlocked country, geographically fragmented, with much extreme poverty. The annual per capita income is about two hundred dollars, half of all Indians die before their fifth year, 40 percent of the population suffers from tuberculosis and other diseases, illiteracy is about 70 percent, and nearer 80 percent in rural areas. Much remains to be done in the development of Bolivia.

THE ATLANTIC AREA

The Atlantic Area, as the Andean region, shows remarkable diversity in the make-up of individual countries: Brazil, Argentina, Paraguay, and Uruguay. Land size varies from the overwhelming mass of Brazil to diminutive Paraguay and Uruguay. Brazil's population of 110 million far exceeds Paraguay's 2.5 million or Uruguay's 3 million. Brazil has a large mulatto population, while Argentina and Uruguay are 90 percent white and Paraguay is 98 percent mestizo. Three of the four Atlantic countries—Brazil, Paraguay, and Uruguay—are under military rule, but with sharply diverging results. Brazil is experiencing what many observers call an "economic miracle," while Uruguay and Paraguay lag in economic development. But all three of these military regimes severely curtail individual rights and political liberties. Argentina, the single civilian regime in mid-1975, was in economic chaos. Morcover, with the rise of civil disorders, political violence, the death of popular President Juan D. Perón, and the illness of his widow and successor, Isabel Perón, the country seemed destined for a military takeover soon. These Atlantic countries, like the rest of Latin America, deserve careful individual study to appreciate their differences in political and economic dynamics.

Brazil

Perhaps the most exciting of Latin American countries, and certainly the one destined to become a major world power according to many Latin America "watchers," is Brazil. Under military rule since 1964, this giant has undergone economic growth rates comparing favorably with such industrial powers as Germany and Japan after World War II. Brazil's per capita income increased from three hundred dollars a year in 1964 to almost eight hundred dollars in 1975; its rate of inflation declined from 87 percent in 1964 to 14 percent in 1973; and its gross national product grew at a rate of 10 percent in 1974 compared to a rate of only 3 percent when the military assumed power ten years earlier.

Many elements account for this remarkable economic record. Brazil is rich in natural resources, including hundreds of thousands of square miles of arable land, enjoys a mild climate, and is innocent of the earthquakes, hurricanes, and tidal waves that plague the Central

American and Caribbean countries. Brazil is a leading world producer of sugar, coffee, soybeans, cocoa, and cotton. It has enormous iron-ore deposits and is preparing for large-scale mining of bauxite, tin, manganese, nickel, and uranium. The country has an immense nuclear-energy program and is cooperating with West Germany in developing the peaceful uses of such energy. The state operates oil refining, railroads, telecommunications, and steel production—much as Socialist countries do. But foreign money and technical investment is welcome under the identical rules that apply to local capital. Thus multinational corporations play a big role in Brazil, unlike Peru, with the United States investment of about 3.5 billion dollars being the largest.

Even with Brazil's phenomenal economic growth since 1964, many problems remain. About forty million adult Brazilians still live a marginal existence, with about twenty million of these living in the big city slums, while the rest are subsistence farmers. Population statistics also indicate that the richest 40 percent of the population increased its actual wealth more than twice as much as the poorest 40 percent between 1960 and 1970. The country also registered a 4.7 billion dollar trade deficit in 1974, the worst in its history, due largely to costly oil imports. Meanwhile, the foreign debt rose to 17 billion dollars. But the economy is basically sound, and most foreign bankers agree that Brazil will continue to prosper.

The government is beginning to invest money in health, education, and urban services, but much needs to be done. Literacy hovers only around 60 percent, life expectancy is about fifty-seven years compared to seventy-one in the United States, infant mortality averages 92 per 1,000, but up to 180 per 1,000 in the northeast, compared to 22 in the United States, and there are 2,530 inhabitants per physician compared to 650 in the United States. The 1975 budget calls for increased spending in these areas, with only 10 percent of the budget going into the expensive armed forces that run the country. The government is also beginning the first tentative steps toward land reforms, calling for expropriation and redistribution.

What bothers many people about Brazil is that the economic gains have come under a harsh authoritarian regime. Brazil is by no means a democratic government. Old political parties were dissolved after 1964 and replaced by two artificial ones—a government party (ARENA) and its opposition, called MDB. A representative congress thus ceased to operate. Nor do autonomous trade unions channel worker grievances into the government, although it is the working class that has been forced to work the hardest to earn enough to buy basic necessities. Church and state relations were not good in the mid-1970s, for the Church had begun to criticize such constant government violations of human rights as arrests without habeas corpus, disappearing political prisoners, and extreme press censorship. The Church also castigated the government for closing rural and urban workers' unions, persecuting workers, peasants, and intellectuals, and harassing priests and militant clergy by imprisonment, tortures, and assassinations. Other critics of the government were discontented with the treatment of Brazil's indigenous Indian population.

Economic growth with political restraint under military rule is a new combination of forces in Brazil's twentieth-century life. Getúlio Vargas, who ruled as dictator from 1930 until 1945, introduced an *Estado Novo* (New State) program of state-financed and directed industrialization. Vargas incorporated the working class into Brazilian politics, and encouraged both light and heavy industry, but economic growth was not so spectacular as after 1964. The administration of Eurico Gaspar Dutra (1945-50) began to restore democratic processes, but the economic situation worsened. Vargas' second term as president (1951-54) was weak and dilatory. Under post-Vargas civilian leaders—Juscelino Kubitschek, Jânio Quadros, and João Goulart—Brazil experienced the introduction of economic planning, the construction of a new capital, and some economic growth in the industrial sector. But a population increase of 3.0 annually, continuing high inflation, the rise of left-wing (including Communist) militancy and right-wing opposition to needed social reforms—often from conservative state governors who were traditionally strong in Brazilian politics—the country was becoming increasingly polarized. When the governors of all the major states, together with the military commanders of São Paulo and Minas Gerais, were in opposition to the central government under President Goulart, who seemed unable to manage political order, the military stepped in.

From then on, the military was determined that economic growth was needed, but that it should occur without political anarchy and under conditions of maximum national security. By mid-1975 Brazil's formula was working, in sharp contrast with neighboring Argentina's civilian political rule, high political violence, and economic chaos. President (General) Ernesto Geisel, assuming power in March, 1974, affirmed his intention to follow the same path as his predecessors since the 1964 coup.

Argentina

Argentina is an absolute paradox. It appears to have all the basic requisites for development, but cannot put them together under any consensus on who or how to govern the country. The largest of the Spanish-speaking countries, it boasts 91 percent literacy, a 90 percent white population of European stock, is situated at the mouth of a great

river system, and has vast agricultural potential in its pampas.* Its resources include lead, zinc, iron, sulphur, silver, copper, gold, and oil;
it admittedly lacks iron and coal. It is the world's fourth-largest meat
exporter, one of the world's largest exporters of food and other agricultural products, and has more manufacturing than any other South
American country except Brazil. Compared to Peru, on the other side
of the Andes, this land seems aptly suited for phenomenal economic
growth and political development, but by the mid-1970s seemed to be
going nowhere fast.

Since the days of the popular—at least among the working classes—
dictator, Juan D. Perón, who, many students argue, ruined the Argentine economy, the country has not been able to combine economic
growth with democratic representative government. Perón ruled from
the end of World War II until deposed by the military in 1955, and
during this time he built a base of power on organized labor through
wage increases (eaten up by inflation) and extensive social benefits.
His wife, the attractive Eva Duarte, aided him in this effort to court
the laboring groups, called the *descamisados* (shirtless ones). Thenceforth labor became a major interest group in Argentine politics, one
frequently at odds with the military, employers, big business, and
landed interests—and one persistently dreaming of the good old days
under Perón. After successive administrations, including several military interventions, none of which could produce sustained economic
growth and long-range political development, Juan Perón returned to
become president again in 1973.

The new Perón was extremely different from the older version, owing
in part to changed conditions in Argentina. Symbolic of what was to
come during his new presidency, more than a million people gathered
at the Buenos Aires airport to glimpse Perón on his return from exile
in Spain, but were dispersed after a gun battle among rival Perónist
factions that left more than a hundred dead and several hundred
wounded. The Perón government, in short, was going to be plagued by
severe political discontent, much of it among his own followers, now
divided between leftist and rightist factions. Perón was to support the
latter and shun the former, unlike the old days.

Perón accepted the backing of the armed forces, who had deposed
him in 1955, and the large landholders, the Roman Catholic hierarchy,
and big businessmen—all groups he had formerly opposed. But it was
a happy combination in 1973 since Perón wanted power and the others
wanted stability. Meanwhile, Perón installed his third wife, Isabel

---

* The heart of Argentina and its most productive region is the Pampa, a broad
fertile plain that spans out from Buenos Aires. It comprises about one-fourth of the
country. More than two-thirds of Argentina's population lives there, and it is the
region of much of the land's wealth.

Martínez de Perón, a former cabaret dancer with no political experience, as his vice-president—an appointment that certainly did not please everybody. Perón's conservative shift embittered his leftist followers, but not to a formal breaking point, and pleased his conservative supporters. This caused violent political infighting between right-wing and left-wing Perónists during the nine months of his rule, intensified by guerrilla violence in both rural and urban areas.

Perón's economic policies found rough going in the country he had returned to. Black marketeering, labor unrest, and strikes by dissident labor unions shook his wage-price freeze, and businessmen blamed price ceilings for shortages of spare parts and food. A wave of kidnappings by guerrillas helped to slow down the infusion of badly needed foreign and domestic capital, and meanwhile inflation was running close to 100 percent. Juan D. Perón, one of Latin America's most famous leaders, died on July 1, 1974, at the age of seventy-eight, and the inexperienced Isabel became president of Argentina.

Political violence and economic difficulties continued to plague Mrs. Perón, and by mid-1975 it appeared that a military take-over was imminent. Within five months after she assumed power, 138 people had been killed in acts of political violence, and she found it necessary to invoke a state of siege empowering security forces not only to search and detain without warrant, but to hold those detained without charges. By July, 1975, her chief adviser, a controversial astrologer by the name of José López Rega who dominated Mrs. Perón, was forced into exile, and Mrs. Perón was in virtual seclusion.

Argentina's future prospects for development, despite all its natural endowments, are simply not as bright as are those of Brazil, Peru, Mexico, Venezuela, Costa Rica, or Cuba. It lacks national unity and national identity and has not forged the institutions necessary for long-range political stability coupled with economic development. Nor does its military show the qualities found in Brazil and Peru.

Uruguay

Studying Uruguay just after World War II, one would have said that it was a model country not only within the Atlantic region but in Latin America as a whole. It then had, and continued to have for some years, the reputation of one of Latin America's most democratic and progressive countries. With an effective two-party system—the *Colorados* (reds, but not Communist) and *Blancos* (whites)—in addition to regular elections and a nonpolitical armed forces, Uruguay had little history of military intervention or dictatorship and a high regard for individual rights and representative government. Equally important, it had evolved a tradition of social services as comprehensive as found anywhere, supported by a flourishing foreign trade and an agricultural base producing wool, meat, corn, flaxseed, citrus fruits, and other important products. The smallest country in South America, with a 90 percent white population that was also 90 percent literate, Uruguay was recognized for a standard of living equal to that of such small but prosperous countries as Denmark or New Zealand.

Thirty years later, in 1975, Uruguay had become a different land indeed. The once-quiescent military had erupted to enforce the closure of congress, censorship of the press, suspension of civil rights, and dissolution of striking trade unions. The parliamentary system was in fact suspended on June 27, 1973, and the military intervened directly in the government of the country for the first time in the history of Uruguay, whose democratic traditions went back to 1830, when the first free elections were held. The military was induced to take this action largely as a result of their suppression of the left-wing *Tupamaro* guerrilla movement which had itself revealed the presence of extensive corruption and injustices in the country. The question, of course, is whether the military remedy to "injustice" was worse or better than the disease.

The truth is that Uruguay's economic situation had deteriorated badly in the 1960s, owing to the extremely costly social services on top of an increasingly weak economy. Not only was inflation running high, but Uruguay was still essentially a pastoral economy, so that when wool prices fell after World War II, the Uruguayan economy suffered. Uruguay's lack of economic diversification was reflected, in part, in the division of the country into a densely populated capital city, Montevideo, and a sparsely settled rural hinterland. Uruguay was nearly bankrupt toward the end of the 1960s, and a wave of strikes and extremist militant activity began to rock this once-envied land.

Toward the latter half of the 1970s, Uruguay had become quiet thanks to the tactical defeat of the notorious *Tupamaros*. But its basic economic and political problems were far from being solved, and the Uruguayan military looked more like that of Argentina or Chile, rather than Brazil or Peru, in terms of economic know-how or commitments.

Paraguay

Paraguay is a landlocked country about the size of California deep in the heart of South America, and is the personal fiefdom of its dictator-president, General Alfredo Stroessner, who has ruled since 1954. It is linked to the Atlantic seaboard by a thousand miles of riverway, most of which passes through Argentine territory, and by a road running overland through Brazil. Its small population of two and a half million is predominantly mestizo, a strong fusion of Spanish and Guaraní Indian people. The Guaraní ancestry is a source of pride among Paraguayans, most of whom speak *Guaraní* as well as Spanish. (Being "Paraguayan" may not be a source of pride for many others, for about a third of the population has chosen to leave the country to live elsewhere.) Paraguay, in contrast to neighboring Argentina and Brazil, is very underdeveloped and underindustrialized and, in comparison to Uruguay, has not experienced much in the way of civil liberties or representative democracy.

General Stroessner rules with an iron hand. By the mid-1970s, many reporters were comparing Paraguay to the extremely repressive era in Haiti under "Papa Doc" Duvalier. In an alleged plot against the general in 1975, for example, hundreds of officials were questioned under torture by interrogation teams using the latest drugs and psychological techniques in their zeal to extract "the truth." From 1969 onward a serious confrontation developed with the Church, which attacked the government's censorship of news, imprisonment without bringing prisoners to trial, and other infringements of civil rights.

If the country is not evolving toward a more representative government, as did Venezuela during the 1960s, neither is it making much economic progress. Fifty percent of the country's arable land is said to be owned by 145 families; smuggling is rife; corruption in government is notorious; agricultural productivity is stagnating; and inflation continues to be high. The regime is preoccupied with political stability, not with development. It is as if Paraguay's geographic isolation has secluded it against the quest for development that dominates much of Latin America today.

Suggested Readings

Alexander, Robert J. *The Bolivian National Revolution.* New Brunswick, N.J.: Rutgers University Press, 1958.
———. *The Venezuelan Democratic Revolution.* New Brunswick, N.J.: Rutgers University Press, 1964.
Astiz, Carlos A. *Pressure Groups and Power Elites in Peruvian Politics.* Ithaca, N.Y.: Cornell University Press, 1969.
Blanksten, George L. *Perón's Argentina.* Chicago: University of Chicago Press, 1953.
Fals Borda, Orlando. *Subversion and Social Change in Colombia.* New York: Columbia University Press, 1969.
Feinberg, Richard E. *The Triumph of Allende: Chile's Legal Revolution.* New York: Mentor Books, 1972.

Gil, Federico. *The Political System of Chile.* Boston: Houghton Mifflin, 1966.

Martz, John. *Colombia: A Contemporary Political Survey.* Chapel Hill: University of North Carolina Press, 1962.

Smith, T. Lynn. *Brazil: People and Institutions.* Baton Rouge: Louisiana State University Press, 1963.

3

Culture
and
Society

Five

A
Continent
of
Absent
Nations

Political studies of Latin American countries are filled with references to "nation," "nation-state," and "nationalism." While these are extremely important postulates about the setting and effect of the political world, the perceptive student is bound to experience confusion in many of the ways these terms are used. If any concepts were to be identified as the most frequently ill used in the literature of recent political studies, those associated with the "nation" would rank high on the list. A first order of priority, then, is to get these terms straight, and secondly, to use them to assess Latin America's situation.

NATION AND STATE

A nation is a group of people bound by and aware of a common cultural, historic, and ethnic background, projected into the present and future. The binding elements of the nation include, in various combinations, a common language, culture, assumed blood ties, religion, and custom. The nation may exist as a historical community and cultural unit without political autonomy, or statehood.

A state is a purely political entity, possessing sovereignty, boundaries, a government, a population, and an economy. The state's government represents and acts for all the people within its domain regardless of their national identity. The state's population, however, may be relatively homogeneous, as are Germans in Germany, or may be composed of two or more separate nations, as are Shans, Karens, and Burmese in Burma. The nation may also spill across state boundaries, as was the case of Germans in Germany and Czechoslovakia during the period between the two world wars. Or the state may contain a great many people who possess little or no national identity, as is the case in Central and South America, with their Indian populations spread among small villages and isolated enclaves. When it exists, the nation helps foster strong state governmental institutions, as can be shown by Germans identifying with Germany and Japanese with Japan. Similarly, national feeling can weaken a state when more than one loyalty affects the population, as is the case throughout much of modern Africa and Asia. Where national loyalty does not exist, as in much of Latin America, political unity and consensus are made difficult.

A nation and a self-identifying ethnic group may be treated quite properly as interchangeable.[1] National and self-consciously ethnic identity are personal and subjective states, a consciousness of belonging to a sui generis people symbolized by a name, historic language, and culture. Personal and subjective identity with such a group, once formed, does not easily disappear. This is true even if most daily experiences fail to reinforce traditional, culturally distinct patterns of behavior. The cases of continued ethnic identity in multinational urban settings throughout Africa, Asia, and Latin America, and after migration to new countries, are relevant examples.

One important way to examine the nation is in terms of nation-building. This process is occurring in various degrees throughout Latin America, albeit not in identical forms nor with uniform success. By it is meant the attempt to stimulate a common national identity with the entire population of the state becoming sufficiently strong to override any other preexisting ethnic or national consciousness. The process is extraordinarily difficult, and includes experiences that range from intensive governmental indoctrination (being "Cuban" in Castro's Cuba) to partial emphasis on a common heritage (as in Peru after 1968). Other experiences are exemplified by the Mexican revolution after 1910, resulting in a country under single-party control with stress on common *Mexicanidad* in communications and education. The essence of nation-building, to create a common national identity overriding all other loyalties, is an extremely important task for governmental leaders. It helps to legitimize their power, institutionalize change, and create a popular and accepted consciousness for the whole population that eases the task of imposing needed economic and social development.

Nationality and Political Consciousness

It can be argued that national consciousness is the precondition for the willingness and desire to engage in statewide governmental activities or to feel allegiance to state leaders and institutions. A number of political theorists have discussed this point. John Stuart Mill argued that nationality provides "a consequent community of recollections, collective pride and humiliation, pleasure and regret, connected with the same incidents of the past," which could be viewed logically as a key source of allegiance to a state's political system.[2] Lord Acton also concluded that the great importance of nationality is that it constitutes "the basis of political capacity."[3] In short, the notion of being a *public citizen of a state*, owing obligations to and feeling commitments toward it and its people, seems to arise from the sentiments of men banding together into the myth of national unity and sharing. This does not solve the political problems created by multinational states, where nations are frequently in conflict with each other. But it does suggest a connection between national identity and corresponding perceptions of politics, in terms of the legal, formal, and constitutional state.

Conversely, to paraphrase Lord Acton, the absence of national identity—single or several—within a state's population weakens the psychological conditions for an institutionalized state political system. It is, of course, logically imprecise to argue that the absence of something causes something else. Yet one is struck by the pronounced absence of any national groups in many of Latin America's states, coupled with high rates of political instability, extraconstitutional assumptions of power, and the domination of government by cliques, factions, such interest groups as Church, military, or landowners, and myriad abuses of privileges. To be sure, these latter political phenomena can be explained as part of the Iberic-Latin tradition of how society is politically organized, a point examined in detail later. At the same time, the absence of a single national identity means that much of Latin America's people are not bound by a common identity with past, present, and future. They tend rather to be extremely fragmented societies. This lack of feeling of nationality and its concomitant fragmentation causes civic consciousness, or "citizenship" feelings, within the state in Latin America to be very weak.

Major obstacles to creating a common national consciousness and nation-building within Latin America's states lie in its geographic and ethnic settings.

GEOGRAPHY: A DIVIDING FACTOR

In looking at a map of Latin America, the first thing that strikes one is the *isolation* of its states. This is isolation in terms of separation not only from the rest of the world but from each other, and embraces sharp internal divisions within the states themselves. South America, for example, faces Africa, not Europe. It thus faces another underdeveloped area. To be sure, its isolation from the rest of the world changed substantially with the coming of the transportation facilities of the late nineteenth century; but for a long time, South America was virtually cut off from the rest of the developed world and its events. Its extreme southerly position is conducive to an isolationism brought about because the main routes of commerce are east and west rather than north and south. Even today the location of the Latin American states breeds a strong sense of separation from the world. One has the feeling in many Central and South American cities that events that are world-shaking elsewhere simply do not carry the same impact.

Latin America is not, however, isolated simply from the rest of the world. Internal isolation between and within states is also a dominant feature of the region. Size, shape, and topography operate to produce this phenomenon. The three obvious geographic configurations are the Andes Mountains, lowland jungle basins—particularly in the Amazonian region, much of which is still unexplored even today—and desert areas (see Map 2). All of these are tremendous barriers to internal unity. The Andes separate the east coast from the west and divide people within states. They separate, isolate, and fragment whole peoples, leaving vast numbers pocketed in valleys six to fourteen thousand feet above sea level. With few (and extremely difficult) passes, the Andes stretch the length of the continent rising three to four miles high. Central America replicates this setting in miniature (see Map 3). It contains two mountain regions separated by a low depression across Nicaragua. While neither mountain region is continuous or exactly clear-cut structurally, both are formidable barriers to movement between the two coasts. Like the valleys between the lofty peaks of the Andes, these ranges contain valleys and basins running roughly from fifteen hundred to seven thousand feet high, where many of the inhabitants reside. Nicaragua and Panama, with their lowland populations, are exceptions.

The Amazonian basin lies on the eastern side of the Andes. It covers half, and in some cases more, of the territory of Brazil, Venezuela, Colombia, Ecuador, Peru, Bolivia, and Paraguay. Estimated at two million square miles, or approximately as large as the continental United

SOUTH AMERICA

ATLANTIC OCEAN

R. Orinoco

Negro

Madeira

Amazon River

EQUATOR

Xingu

São Francisco

CABO SÃO ROQUE

CABO BRANCO

CAPRICORN

PACIFIC OCEAN

R. Paraná

CABO FRIO

SURFACE FEATURES

- Intermont Basins
- Tabular Uplands
- Diabase Area
- Plains
- High Mountains and Marginal Ranges
- Hilly Uplands and Low Mountains
- Great Escarpment

0   200   600   800 Miles
  200   800   12,000 Km

CAPE HORN

MAP 2

States, it is a major obstacle to the development of interior South America. The Andes fringe it on the west, and the Brazilian Highlands—a steep mountain range rising to ten thousand feet, with an average height of four thousand feet—on the east. Given the Amazonian rain forest, high temperatures, and soil problems, the area is unappealing to human habitation and unproductive agriculturally.

The desert areas of Chile, Peru, and northeast Brazil are another major land form. Their impact on human life again is striking. When onè arrives by air in Antofagasta, Chile, en route to Santiago, the first impression is of landing in the Sahara Desert. The hot, dry wind blows across a treeless horizon, marked by little vegetation of any kind as well as sparse settlement. It is not difficult to imagine that coastal Peru and the Atacama Desert of northern Chile are among the driest places on earth.

These three key geographic barriers make political unification and common national identity extremely difficult in the Latin American states. Their territorial domain consists of populations divided into a number of clusters isolated from each other. Not only has this physical setting imposed its pattern of settlement since colonialization; but it has also made fusion of the settled groups into nationally integrated states extremely difficult to this day.

The juxtaposition of state boundaries and internal physical settings clearly are not conducive to easy national unity. Latin American states are typically not cases of single "natural regions" enclosed by a legal territorial boundary; population concentrations are in effect cut off from each other. As J. P. Cole, the British geographer, describes the setting, Latin American populations are divided into:

> a number of clusters, like islands separated by sea, or by large stretches of virtually uninhabited forest or desert. All other things being equal, the inhabitants of these clusters of population might be expected to be more closely related economically and socially with one another than with people in other clusters. Such a situation can only be expected to occur in an area in which population is very unevenly distributed.[4]

Analogously, in the words of another geographer, Robert S. Platt, writing in 1942:

> People are intensely and irregularly concentrated in clusters that do not resemble the divisions of any of the maps of major natural regions . . . in form or distribution. Additional complexity is suggested by the fact that there is no obvious similarity between the distributions of population and the mosaic of countries . . . the pattern of countries tends to disagree with that of natural regions, and boundaries between countries tend to cut across regions.[5]

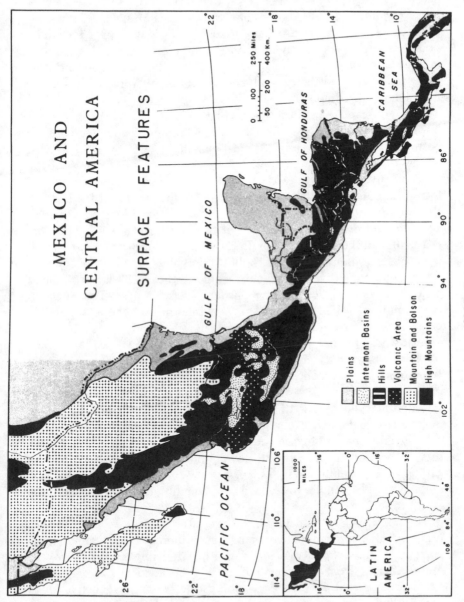

MEXICO AND
CENTRAL AMERICA

SURFACE FEATURES

GULF OF MEXICO

GULF OF HONDURAS

CARIBBEAN SEA

PACIFIC OCEAN

250 Miles
400 Km.
100 200
50 100

Plains
Intermont Basins
Hills
Volcanic Area
Mountain and Bolson
High Mountains

LATIN AMERICA

1000 MILES

MAP 3

79

The problems of national identity and political unification are intensified by yet other effects of geography. The largest concentration of people within separate states is typically in the large cities, usually located within two hundred miles of the coast (see Map 4). By the early 1960s there were, to be sure, more than 227 towns with over fifty thousand inhabitants each, having a total population of nearly sixty-two million. Some of these of course lie inland. But the urban concentration along the coasts and the general lack of large population centers in the deep interior predominate.

This geographic pattern means that a network of interior cities linked by integrated transportation and communication systems—as between Chicago, Denver, St. Louis, or Salt Lake City in the United States—is not to be found south of Texas. Indeed, the whole of the Amazonian basin has only two cities—Belém with two hundred and thirty thousand inhabitants, and Manaus, with a hundred thousand, a thousand miles farther upriver. Partly as a result of the pattern of colonization, and partly because much of the best farmland lies along the coast, the southern portions of Latin America form, from the standpoint of inhabitants, a kind of "hollow continent." In Central America, the population is divided into clusters along the Pacific coast, isolated generally from smaller, interior clusters (see Map 5). These capital cities might be called the "core" areas, while the rest of the population clusters might be termed "peripheral."

Inland populations tend to cluster in isolated towns, villages, *latifundias* (or large farms and ranches), and *communidades* (Indian communities). The contrasting coastal and inland population centers produced a wide variety of lifestyles based on culture, language, and self-identity, noted by Platt's field studies in the 1930s and by subsequent investigation by other scholars. These variations reinforce local or regional pride and hinder the evolution of a common national identity. They tend to concentrate power, influence, and wealth first in capital cities, usually along the coast but sometimes in the highlands too, followed by smaller towns, villages, communities, and large landed estates.

The range of local and provincial identities is wide in Latin America. Peruvians in Arequipa have long been different from their counterparts in Lima. Colombians from Cali and Medellín see themselves as quite different from those residing in Bogotá. Mexicans from Mérida, Villahermosa, and Hermosillo have distinct identities compared to those living in Mexico City. Bolivians in Cochabamba or Santa Cruz look with disdain at those living in La Paz. And lowland and highland Indians live in entirely different worlds.

Beyond these obstacles to political integration are the self-contained worlds of Indian communities and *latifundias*. Closed, as well as more

BASIC SETTLEMENT PATTERNS

ATLANTIC OCEAN

PACIFIC OCEAN

SOUTH AMERICA

```
0        600 Miles
         800 Kilometers
```

◇ Industrial City
◎ Capital
■ Areas of Concentrated Settlement
▨ Effectively Occupied Areas
▨ Outside The Effective National Territory

MAP 4

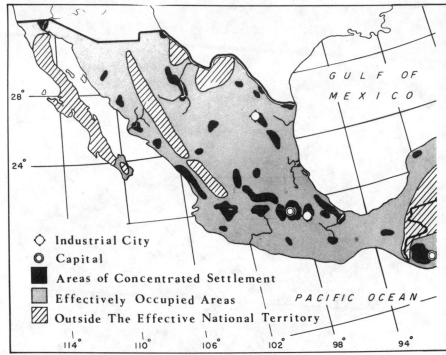

GULF OF MEXICO

28°

24°

◇ Industrial City
◎ Capital
■ Areas of Concentrated Settlement
▨ Effectively Occupied Areas
▨ Outside The Effective National Territory

PACIFIC OCEAN

114°   110°   106°   102°   98°   94°

MAP 5

open, Indian communities abound. The lifestyle of each closed community is reinforced through rigorous rules and regulations that include growing of traditional Indian subsistence crops, keeping land in
control of community members, regulating marriages, worshiping community Catholic saints (regarded as different from saints of neighboring communities), and generally preventing "outsiders" from entering
the life of the community. Just as Indian communities form self-
contained units of people, the *latifundias* operate as autonomous enclaves with their own inner identity, social relationships, and power
structure. While land-reform programs progressed in several countries
during the 1960s, the *latifundia* remained entrenched in many countries as a major institutional barrier to national integration, based on
a pattern of hierarchy, patron-peon relationships, a caste-system, and
social stratification.

The picture of geographically reinforced localism and provincialism
briefly underlines one dimension of the obstacles to common national
identity and political unity. Much of the effective life of the state lies
outside of the government located in the state's capital city. Indeed,
in some countries it is more accurate to equate the state's "national"
political system with the capital city, and perhaps one or two lesser
towns. In the rural areas, patterns of political rule, legitimate author-

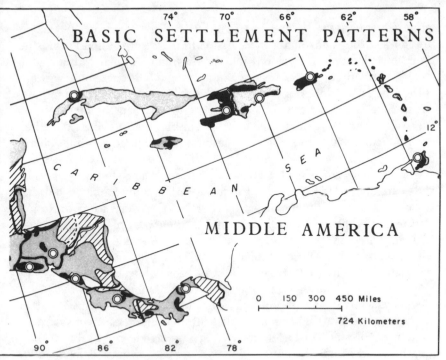

ity, and influence are interlocked in corresponding local ethnic and economic systems. To put this point another way, the core of the politically organized area of the state that is amenable to nation-building is located where the population has tended to concentrate—geographically the most highly favored areas, which became the capital cities. These areas have been traditionally isolated from much of the rest of the state's territory and population. The result has been slow development of a distinctive body of traditions, culture, and institutions, associated with all the people of the state, coupled with slow development of political unity between capital cities and outlying areas. It results in slowness in nation-building and political development.

Transportation and Communications

Transportation and communication difficulties arise as a by-product of Latin America's contrasting geographic configurations. They in turn reinforce demographic isolation, problems of common national unity and integration, the tendency toward regional and provincial self-identity of people, the absence of truly functioning nations, and the subsequent concentration of political power in certain areas. Navigable waterways, for example, are not plentiful. Many of the major branches of the Amazon are inaccessible to large ships due to rapids in their lower courses just before joining the main Amazon stream and the Paraná-Paraguay river system can accommodate only shallow-draft ships. The steep slopes of the Andes are drained by rushing, jumping streams only portions of which are navigable between the piedmont of the Andes and the sea in Ecuador, Colombia, and Venezuela. Other such difficulties as rapids and fluctuating levels plague Central American waterways.

Even in the absence of waterways, railroads and highways inside states are characterized by short mileage rather than sophisticated, integrated networks linking communities. Nearly every form of transport used in the world is still important in some part of Latin America, including human transportation—as a visit to many areas in Latin America quickly verifies—human back, pack animal, canoe, raft, wheeled cart, internal stream, railway, coastal traders, oceangoing ship, motor vehicle, pipeline, electricity, air. Almost all railroads are single track, slow, and irregular. They tend to connect internal centers to ports (for exports), but not to other internal markets. A considerable portion of all roads in Latin America are unpaved, impassable in bad weather, and insufficiently wide for two vehicles to pass conveniently. The result is that, in some Andean areas, a traffic arrangement is worked out to go different ways on alternate days. Many a North American traveler in Andean countries has a hair-raising tale about the bus, truck, or railroad trip out of the capital city back into the hinterland. While conditions are changing, the long-term effect of such primitive transport systems on isolating peoples and politically fragmenting the Latin American states is still distinct.

THE ETHNIC FACTOR IN LATIN AMERICA'S MISSING NATIONS

Ethnicity and Nationality

Understanding nationality requires understanding of ethnic identity, since ethnic perceptions lie at the heart of nationality. Ethnic identity, long considered as an obstacle to nationality, can rather be viewed as a base of nationality. Where ethnicity is in fact "apprehended as an idea," to use Sir Ernest Barker's term,[6] and is transformed into the notion of a mythical common past, present, and future, it is the very essence of nationality. This thesis helps to probe the origins and effects of social fragmentation on Latin American politics, and merits additional comment.

Ethnic Identity

"Ethnic" refers to a population group, especially to a linguistic, cultural, or racial group. Hence, an ethnic group is a people racially or historically related, having a distinctive culture. Its membership can be identified by trained outside observers as constituting a sui generis people. Identity of ethnic status takes various forms, depending upon geographical, historical, social, economic, and political forces. The possibilities include (1) unawareness of belonging to a larger ethnic unit, where one's primary loyalty is to family, kinship, or village, as occurs in various places in the Third World among ethnically unselfconscious people; (2) personal awareness of linguistic, cultural, and racial differentiations within society and its bearing upon class, status, and political power, but only weak unity along ethnic lines, as typifies many Latin Americans; (3) sharp ethnic perceptions among a people, with politics conducted along clear ethnic, rather than broad civic, dimensions, as in Africa, and South and Southeast Asia; and (4) intense perception of ethnicity as a tie so strong as to lead to extreme interethnic conflict and establishment of an independent state, as in the Bengali uprising leading to the establishment of the state of Bangladesh.

The comparative realities and complexities of ethnic identity are undoubtedly far greater than outlined here, yet the force of ethnicity is clear. It is a strong referent to one's personal identity. When perceived as an idea of common origin, given ultimate loyalty, and translated into political behavior, ethnic ties then become the basis of a psychological nation of people. This national identity combines ethnic attributes into a myth of common origins, present life, and future destiny. Indeed, *ethno* is a Greek word element for "race" or "nation."

Ethnic Nationality

Nationality grows from a sense of common ethnic identity. The nation is at minimum an aggregation of persons who perceive themselves to be of the same ethnic family, who are highly conscious of their homogeneity, and who subjectively identify with a community united by common experiences and traditions. They constitute a kind of "we" group versus a "they" perception of other groups in the outside world. The outside observer may identify the presence of ethnic groups, e.g., members of a common race, culture, or people, but unless their own members selfconsciously so identify, then ethnicity has not been transformed into national awareness.

A nation, then, is at heart a group of people who share a real or imagined myth of their origins and destiny. Given the role of ethnicity

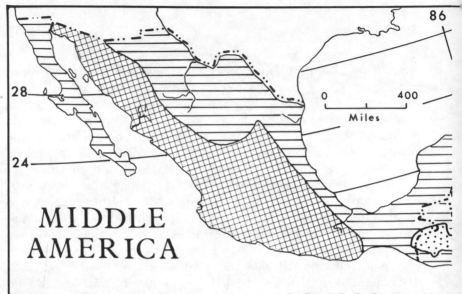

MAP 6

in national consciousness, it behooves one to study the nature of ethnic relationships, the degrees of ethnic self-perception, and the possibilities for emergent, common, ethnic consciousness among a developing state's population.

Ethnicity and Nationality in Latin America

Among the many elements inhibiting the growth of single nations in Latin America's states is that of separate cultural and racial groups and ethnic differences among the populations of the separate states. How diversified Latin America is from the point of view of racial distribution is denoted in Map 6 of Mexico and Central America, and by Map 7 of South America. Table 1, which follows, gives the racial breakdown of each state.

As Table 1 indicates, each Latin American state consists of distinct racial compositions. Brazil, Cuba, Haiti, and Panama contain large percentages of Negro groups. Argentina, Chile, Uruguay, and Costa Rica are predominantly "European." Bolivia, Ecuador, Peru, and Guatemala are strongly Indian states. Yet, as we shall see in more detail later, these discernible breakdowns do not tell the whole story. Negroes, Europeans, and Indians are composed of subgroups which

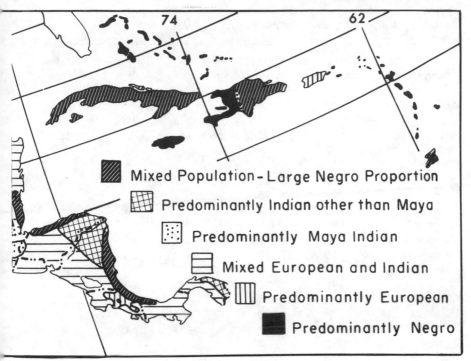

Mixed Population-Large Negro Proportion

Predominantly Indian other than Maya

Predominantly Maya Indian

Mixed European and Indian

Predominantly European

Predominantly Negro

separately identify along racial, cultural, and ethnic lines—e.g., as among mulatto versus Negro; Italian versus German or Spanish; Aymará versus Quechua Indian. Even more fascinating, but fragmentating as well, are the still more fragmented breakdowns in identity among these groups—e.g., one regional mulatto group versus another; one Indian community versus another; Catalans (from Catalonia in Spain) versus Basque (the Basque Provinces in Spain); Neapolitan versus Sicilian. Much research needs to be done on these ethnic differentiations, but the divisions caused by them and their implications for single nationality and politics are strong.

As long as these cultural and linguistic differences continue to be perceived by the people of Latin Amercan states, achievement of single national identity in any single state is difficult. In this sense one might conceive the task of nation-building as in fact the destruction of old ethnic identity and the creation of a new one for all the people of any given state. This task poses enormous issues of socialization (building new political attitudes and values) through systematic education, communication, language, and other forms of attitude and value formation. Some Latin American states—Mexico after its 1910 revolution, Cuba after Fidel Castro came to power in 1959, and Peru after Juan Velasco Alvarado assumed power in 1968—began to move in this direc-

TABLE 1 RACIAL COMPOSITION IN LATIN AMERICA

Country	Percent European	Percent Mestizo	Percent Mulatto	Percent Indian	Percent Negro
Argentina	90				
Bolivia	5	25		70	
Brazil	60	25 (mulatto, mestizo)			15
Chile	97			3.5	
Colombia	30	40		5	7
Ecuador	10	41		39	10
Paraguay		98		2	
Peru	12	42		46	
Uruguay	90	10			
Venezuela		Majority			
Mexico	10	60		30	
Costa Rica	90				10
El Salvador	10	70		20	
Guatemala	1	44		55	
Honduras		90			10
Nicaragua	1	77		4	
Panama	12		72	2	14
Cuba	73				26
Haiti			10		90
Dom. Rep.	28	60 (mestizo, mulatto)			11

Sources: *South American Handbook*. Chicago: Rand McNally, 1970. These percentages are estimates and do not always total 100.

tion. Other states—Chile, Costa Rica, and Paraguay—appear to have a relatively solid basis for national identity. But for much of Latin America, the systematic approach to national integration has not yet really begun, and states remain held together more by the older forces of corporatism, patron-client relations, authoritarian hierarchy, strong personal rulers, and militarism.

Other Conditioners of Missing Single Nations

Stress on ethnic identity should not obscure other forces that are inhibiting the growth of single nations in Latin America. Many of these are examined in subsequent chapters as the underpinnings to politics, but should be identified here as aspects of absent national community identification. Physical diversity and early settlement patterns, as well as underdeveloped transportation and communication facilities have been mentioned as accentuating the basic isolation of peoples along the Pacific and Atlantic shores from those deeper in the interior.

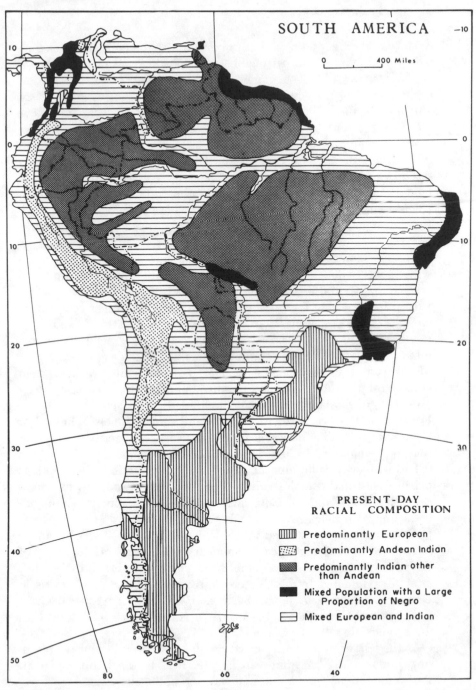

SOUTH AMERICA   −10

0   400 Miles

PRESENT-DAY
RACIAL COMPOSITION

Predominantly European

Predominantly Andean Indian

Predominantly Indian other
than Andean

Mixed Population with a Large
Proportion of Negro

Mixed European and Indian

MAP 7

Moreover, underdeveloped transportation and communication impede not only trade and personal contact, but the transmission of those symbols indicative of common nationality (flag, anthem, heroes, events, unifying themes vis-à-vis other national identifications). They also impede the communication of perceived similarities among people. In many outlying areas the inadequate availability of radios and television hampers communication of integration symbols. Added to this is another related deep source of division in the Andean countries—the widespread inability to read or speak Spanish, the "national" language and the tongue typically used in radio and television broadcasts. (This is changing to some extent in Peru, where broadcasting in native Indian languages began after the 1968 coup put a reform-minded military regime into power.)

This assessment of transportation and communication must be taken with great qualification, lest misleading assumptions be made. Increased transportation and communication traffic could have the reverse effect in some Latin American states and accentuate the differences of the population—from white to Indian and black and from extreme rich to extreme poor. As we have seen, the racial and ethnic mix makes Latin American states quite unlike those of nineteenth-century Western Europe, when the national spark was ignited within certain ethnic groups. There, common linguistic and cultural groups grew in awareness of similarity. The common ethnic tie that held for Germans, Frenchmen, Greeks, northern Italians, and others is not replicated in Central and South America, leaving the overall impact of transportation and communication development open to debate.

Latin America is an area of widespread immigration. The result is one of a vast and complex cultural melange, with European nationalities (Basques, Catalans, Castilians, Sicilians, Neapolitans, Germans) coexisting with black Africans and indigenous Indians. If the melting-pot thesis is now questioned in the United States,[7] it similarly can be questioned in Latin America. In summary, the framework for study of Latin American politics is different from that applicable to those kinds of states populated by highly conscious nations, such as Germans in Germany, Japanese in Japan, Serbs and Croats in Yugoslavia, Great Russians and Ukrainians in the USSR, or Han Chinese and Mongols in the People's Republic of China.

At the risk of oversimplifying, three distinct categories of people in stages of national transition can be identified in the Latin American states: prenational, immigrant national, and nationally conscious.

The prenational people are the more than 340 Indian tribes and 75 ethnolinguistic Indian groups identified in Central and South America—the Indians and blacks whose religious and linguistic ties date back to the Conquest and before, and the mixed-blooded mestizos and mulattoes, whose roots are partly European, partly Indian and African. Latin Americans identify along a range from pure white to pure black and Indian, and one's *casta* ("caste"—a term used since colonial days) is based upon a person's combined physical and cultural characteristics. During the colonial period, Spanish law recognized at least eighty racial combinations, and *casta* is still important today. The existence of prenational people suggests the tremendous complexity of self-identity and the extreme difficulties in evolution toward a single national consciousness as, say, Peruvian, Bolivian, or Ecuadorian.

The second category of people, immigrant national, includes European immigrants and their lineage who still are European in outlook. To be more succinct, they may typically identify with an ethnic European homeland—Germany; Sicily or Naples for Italians; the Basque Provinces, Galicia, Catalonia, or Andalucia for Spanish. Such older ties may be far stronger than such new ones as Argentines, or Venezuelans, as seen in the formation of Basque, Gallego, and other regional clubs upon arrival in the new country, the strong cultural affinity for all things European, and the continuing efforts of white Latin Americans to educate their children in a non-Spanish or Portuguese European language and culture. Undoubtedly an element of ethnic group status operates in the self-identities of these people, as with the Polish-Americans or Italo-Americans in the United States. This observation may help to account for the fact that the American elements in the United States do not seem to have counterparts in an Argentine or Colombian identity for many white *criollos* in the southern part of the hemisphere.[8]

The nationally conscious group can be categorized as having a strong ethnic national identity with all the people of their state. A number of government leaders, cultural elites, and intellectuals—past and present—fall into this category, and several states seem more likely seedbeds for this consciousness than others. Past and present government leaders and intellectuals who seem high in single national identity include José Martí and Fidel Castro (Cuba), Lázaro Cárdenas (Mexico), Eduardo Frei and Salvador Allende (Chile), José Figueres (Costa Rica), and Juan D. Perón (Argentina). Undoubtedly, others should be cited, but the point is clear.

As far as specific states are concerned, one expects the likelihood of more national consciousness today in Mexico and Cuba where revolutions spawned a strong Mexican and Cuban identity through education and mass communications; in Chile, where the land configuration (access along the coastline; few internal mountain barriers) and a history of successful wars and charismatic national heroes seems to have produced a degree of national consciousness; possibly Costa Rica, given its homogeneous population and small geographical size; and

Uruguay, with a homogeneous population concentrated principally in Montevideo.

THE PROBLEM OF NATIONALITY AND POLITICS IN LATIN AMERICAN STATES

Students of political development place exceptional emphasis on the priority of building a single national consciousness in Third World states. If these countries are to become "modern" or "developed" in the sense of possessing stable political institutions providing for the orderly and legitimate transfer of political power, as well as an integrated society reflecting popular interest through participation and representation in decision making and equality of opportunity, duties, and rights, impelling their people with a single national community consciousness seems paramount. Put another way, those identifying with a common national community (a common past, present, and future) should comprise most of the people within that state's boundaries.

Four major connecting links between a single national consciousness and a state's political system can be identified as far as Latin America is concerned. They are: high political stability in relation to the greater instability of other Latin American states, for those countries where some degree of single national consciousness exists; nation-building as a systematic program followed by certain governments, including Mexico, Cuba, Peru, and to some extent, Paraguay; legitimacy of state authority, leaders, programs, and institutions, which frequently seem weaker in countries where a single national consciousness is low; the existence of corporatism. A major aspect of Latin American politics, corporatism is in part a function of low single national identity in much of Latin America, just as it was in Spain—also an area where historically a "Spanish" national consciousness lags behind regional allegiances.

These four characteristics suggest that nation-building in Latin America is closely tied to, but certainly distinct from, state-building. The former is a psychological world of community identity, the latter embodies institutions and policies dealing with the performance, control, distribution, and use of political power. On a more somber note, the prospects for nation-building in Latin American states do not look particularly bright, especially in the light of the area's traditional culture. The best chances for success are with those states whose political elites determine to use the state's political process to build a sense of common national purpose, a process partly consonant with Hispanic corporatist politics more attuned to government-led policies from above instead of popularly led policies and reforms from below. But experiments of this kind will require long periods of time and an orchestration of the political process, and will impose strains within the social setting.

We can briefly examine the four aspects of nationality and politics in turn.

Nationality and Political Stability

A relationship between relative single national consciousness among a state's population and political stability is suggested in Table 2. Those Latin American states where one presumes some national consciousness to exist, incorporating all the people, are also those of relatively fewer

TABLE 2   NATIONAL IDENTITY AND POLITICAL STABILITY

	Coups: 1930–65
1. Countries likely to be high in national identity	
Chile (but experienced a coup in 1973)	3
Costa Rica	1
Mexico	1
Uruguay (but experienced military take-over in 1973)	0
2. Countries likely to be low in national identity	
Argentina	6
Bolivia	10
Brazil	6
Colombia	2
Dominican Republic	6
Ecuador	10
El Salvador	7
Guatemala	8
Haiti	7
Honduras	2
Nicaragua	3
Panama	5
Paraguay	7
Peru	5
Venezuela	5

Source: Warren Dean, "Latin American Golpes and Economic Fluctuations, 1823-1966," Social Science Quarterly 51 (June 1970): 72. Cuba is not included here insofar as the process of systematic nation-building by government leaders began only in the early 1960s. Between Cuban independence at the turn of the century and Castro's assumption of power in January, 1959, the country experienced seven extraconstitutional assumptions, and it was high in ethnic heterogeneity. The military coup that overthrew constitutionally elected President Salvador Allende of Chile in September, 1973, suggests the tentativeness of this proposition about national identity and political stability.

extraconstitutional assumptions of power. Again, these states are far from housing single nations. They are not nation-states, as a Germany or a Japan. But relative to other Latin American states, it can be argued that they probably have a greater percentage of their population sharing some common identity, for a number of historical reasons. It would appear, then, that the more nationally homogeneous a country is, the greater the chance of its people coming to share in percep- tions of the state's political authority as legitimate, or of leaders seen as in fact speaking for "a people," and of its developing institutional- ized, rational, and peaceful transitions of political power.

Nation-Building as a Systematic Government Program

The two countries that have pursued a program of single nation- building most systematically are Mexico and Cuba. Politics in both countries became a form of widening the number of people who might identify with a Mexican or Cuban population, and in qualitative terms deepening the emotional ties with fellow citizens.

The Mexican revolution of 1910 opened an era leading toward broadened political participation befitting a more "modern" para- digm of politics and magnified with a "Mexican" past, present, and fu- ture. While it is true that the revolution has passed through several stages and that "internal colonialism" still persists, that country is well advanced in single nationality when compared to sister Latin Ameri- can states. This advancement is a product of social, economic, politi- cal, and educational reforms that expanded the base of social and po- litical equality and participation in national life. The government sponsored mass-education policies (from the 1920s onward), land and labor reforms, extension of interest groups to incorporate white- collar workers, laborers, and *campesinos,* and a single party, the Insti- tutionalized Revolutionary Party (PRI, *Partido Revolucionario Institu- tional*).

Cuba followed a different ideological path than Mexico, but it is similar insofar as the accent is on stimulating in its populace a com- mon identity as Cubans. Fidel Castro opted for Marxism-Leninism as a guiding ideology, but with a distinctly Cuban beat. Similar to Mex- ico, he instituted mass-education policies, developed a single-party system linked to a host of interest groups that widened political par- ticipation in the state's institutions, and persistently referred to the revolution as a continuation of Cuban struggles that began in 1868 against Spain.

Castro also programmed into his speeches and policies what might be called a national social ethic, emphasizing the importance of work, unity, struggle, dignity, and commitment to Cuban development by all Cubans. Cuba went on a Marxist-Leninist footing after 1959, but the *leitmotif* of politics centered on Cuban identity, a Cuba run by Castro's followers rather than their being only Marxist-Leninists, and on Cuban nation-building in the authentic psychological meaning of the concept. That country's policies of course differed from Mexico's in terms of ideology, the nature of opposition groups, constitutional rule, elections, and style of political leadership. But as models of national integration, both countries pursued systematic attempts at national-identity formation, and in culture, literature, education, music, poetry, and architecture reflected nationalist orientations. Moreover, both encouraged not only national identity per se, but greater equality and participation in state politics.

Peru is a third country which more recently turned toward programmed nation-building through the state political system. Similarities exist when nation-building in Peru is compared to that of Mexico and Cuba. All three countries experienced earlier attempts at forming national identity before the major attempts discussed here got underway. Mexico had its positivist movement during the nineteenth century, which was a form of early national integration. Cuba experienced nationalist movements, principally by students and intellectuals, during the 1920s and 1930s. Peru, in turn, had its experiment with Aprismo beginning in the late 1920s, led by Víctor Raul Haya de la Torre, which attempted, in part, to integrate Peruvian Indians into national life.

In comparing the three countries, however, it must be said that Peru undoubtedly faces greater difficulty in nation-building than Mexico or Cuba, given the ethnic composition of its population. Mexico was predominantly mestizo at the turn of the century, a point recognized by one of its social critics, Andrés Molina Enríquez. Enríquez wrote in 1909, one year before the beginning of the revolution, that the repository of national identity lay potentially in the mestizo population, rather than in criollo whites or indigenous Indians. Cuba, in contrast, began its period of systematic nation-building with a white, mulatto, and black population.

Peru, divided by geography and underdeveloped in transportation and communication links, with an Indian population of about 46 percent, within which little widespread unity of identity is found, faces enormous obstacles.

Yet the military government that assumed power in October, 1968, is attempting to move in the nation-identity building direction. It pursued policies of land reform, with an emphasis on cooperatives, began an industrial community, with workers in an enterprise sharing equal control with those who provide investment capital, and began to broadcast these and other policies in native Indian languages. Unlike other military coups in Latin America, the Peruvian military government after 1968 was committed to radical but orderly social and economic change in the name of all the Peruvian people rather than for a narrow power elite, as in the past. It was designed to create long-run social democracy of full participation. In short, the government seemed dedicated to forging a new Peruvian identity of equality and participation for increasing numbers of the state's population.

Paraguay is another case. Pursuit of nation-building as a governmental process is less conspicuous or dramatic there than in Mexico, Cuba, or Peru. It is less comprehensive in terms of state governmental leaders moving toward greater participation and equality of opportunities in the country's political, economic, and social life. However, that country teaches the Guaraní Indian language in its schools, and Guaraní identity appears to have given that country's population a sense of nationhood stronger than that experienced by others elsewhere.

The Problem of Legitimizing State Authority
Where Nationality Is Weak

If weak national community identity exists within a state, it is difficult for people to perceive of state governmental institutions and leaders as legitimate. The government is not able to command their respect, loyalty, and obedience through voluntary acceptance and its rule as inherently right and proper. Why is national consciousness linked to legitimate state authority?

In the absence of a national community, people tend to give ultimate loyalty, commitment, and dedication to local or parochial rather than state institutions. Thus without this broad national identity, the state's political institutions are unable to draw upon an important integrating source of consensus and power. The consequence is fragmented consensus, weak political integration, and political instability.

That instability can be traced in part to weak nationality is not to say that national consciousness is a guarantee of harmony and stability. American, German, and Japanese politics illustrate this point. The point is also true of Chile and Uruguay, which even with relatively high levels of national consciousness succumbed to military interventions in 1973. But where national consciousness is present, government leaders are able to presume to speak for their people (or nation) and more likely to be perceived as doing just that by the population.

A state's authority is expressed through its institutions of government. These institutions—the constitution, executive, legislature, judiciary, and military—appear to command less legitimate authority than do the substate forces of individuals, interests, and factions. Any beginning student of Latin American politics is made aware quickly of the high rates of coups d'etat and military intervention, symbolic of the need for force and coercion as basic to stability, rather than wide consensus about nonviolent legitimate forms of authority under state auspices. Other well-known characteristics of Latin American politics—electoral tampering, party factionalism, corruption—illustrate the general difficulty of translating constitutional expressions of legitimate authority into practice. If a widespread, deeply felt, loyalty toward the state's institutional framework has been spawned through the psychological ties of nationality elsewhere in the world, Latin American countries have a ways to go.

Ibero-Latin Tradition and Nationality

One reason for the low levels of national identity in Latin America is the nature of Latin America's states, governments, and societies. They are essentially nondemocratic, elitist, corporate, hierarchical, and authoritarian. Due to the philosophical outlook inherited from Roman Law, Catholic thought, Vitoria, Soto, Suárez, Molina, and Mariana, Latin American governments emphasize little separation of powers, strong executive rule, and a patrimonial state viewed as the guardian of special, private, hierarchical, vested, and charted interests of society.[9]

The Ibero-Latin tradition is one of government's overseeing and protecting such elitist private interests as the military, the Church, the landed aristocracy, and the organic-corporate structures of the past. These governments are, however, capable of accommodating new interests and groups as they increase in influence, such as the educated *técnicos* (professionals), organized labor, and peasants. It is a tradition sanctifying the privileges of the past, while prepared to accommodate the new privileged elites as they are spawned, if they can demonstrate a power capability vis-à-vis the older elites.

The traditional Ibero-Latin tradition is thus distinctly undemocratic, anti-equalitarian, and nonindividualistic. Not a state for the public at large, it is rather for the private in power. It is unrepresentative of the majority, unequipped to translate minority demands into public policy, unrelated to a tradition of self-government, and unattached to an open, pluralistic, cooperative, and publicly oriented society.

Given this form of patrimonial state and government, it is not surprising that popular national identities do not flourish. Society is oriented toward the private interest rather than toward progressive, liberal, and public-spirited interests. It reflects patron-client ties, personal and family links as keys to official power, and identifying with a strong leader whose government regulates all associations and corporate bodies as well as access to all spoils and privileges,

A true national consciousness assumes a public aspect; corporate state and society is private and elitist. Nationality assumes sharing an identity with all the people. The corporate society stresses caste, hierarchy, and privilege. Nationalism is a nineteenth- and twentieth-century product. Corporate philosophy is rooted and sustained by modes of thought that far predate this era. In systems characterized by corporate privilege and vested power elites, human focus is drained away from what people share in common—a root of national consciousness—and toward what separates and divides: caste, elitism, authority.

The basic difficulty of grafting nationality onto corporate society has been magnified in the period following World War II. New claimants of power have arisen, posing new demands and expectations upon the state. New interests have been added to the old village community, *latifundia,* Church, *caudillos,* extended family, and landed oligarchy. These include educated *técnicos,* industrialists, entrepreneurs, professionals, mass-based political parties, organized labor and peasants, new progressive military interests, and modernized Church groups. The old state governmental systems do not always have the institutional capacity to resolve such conflicts and accommodate the pressures generated by increased participation by newly privileged interests. Bereft of a national community outlook, they are lacking in the qualities that might have formed a psychological foundation for comprehensive and sustained political integration based upon a common consensus about the state's past, present, and future policies. The nationless corporate states of Latin America are, in short, highly susceptible to polarized interests, fragmented consensus, fragmented self-identities, and political instability.

Given the nature of the corporate states in Latin America, they are not well prepared to undertake the tasks required of building a common national identity so long as the underlying privileged social structure remains unchanged. This, incidentally, suggests why social revolutions in Mexico and Cuba produced concentrated policies of building a national identity.

NOTES

1.   Walker Connor, "Nation-Building or Nation-Destroying," *World Politics* 24 (April 1972): 319-55.
2.   John Stuart Mill, *Consideration on Representative Government* (New York: Holt, Rinehart and Winston, 1972), p. 308.
3.   John Emerich Edward Dalberg Acton, 1st Baron Acton, *The History of Freedom and Other Essays,* ed. J. N. Figgis and R. V. Laurence (London, 1922), p. 297.
4.   J. P. Cole, *Latin America: An Economic and Social Geography* (London: Butterworth, 1965), p. 207.

5. Robert S. Platt, *Latin America: Countryside and United Regions* (New York and London: McGraw-Hill, 1942), pp. 13 and 18.
6. Sir Ernest Barker, *National Character and the Factors in Its Formation* (New York: Harper and Bros., 1927), p. 123.
7. See Mark R. Levy and Michael S. Kramer, *The Ethnic Factor: How America's Minorities Decide Elections* (New York: Simon and Schuster, 1972; Nathan Glazer and Daniel P. Moynihan, *Beyond the Melting Pot* (Cambridge: M.I.T. Press, 1970); and Michael Parenti, "Ethnic Politics and the Persistence of Ethnic Identification," *The American Political Science Review* 61 (September 1967): 717-26.
8. For a fascinating study of early child socialization experiences that contribute to low identity with the "nation," see Reid Reading, "Political Socialization in Colombia and the United States: An Exploratory Study," *The Midwest Journal of Political Science* 12 (August 1968): 352-81.
9. See Howard J. Wiarda's perceptive essay, "Toward a Framework for the Study of Political Change in the Iberic-Latin Tradition: The Corporative Model," *World Politics* 25 (January 1973): 206-35.

Suggested Reading

Alba, Victor. *Nationalists without Nations.* New York: Praeger, 1968.

Anderson, Charles W., Fred R. von der Medhden, and Crawford Young. *Issues of Political Development.* Englewood Cliffs, N.J.: Prentice-Hall, 1967, pp. 45-56.

Cole, J. P. *Latin America: An Economic and Social Geography.* London: Butterworth, 1965.

James, Preston E. *Introduction to Latin America; The Geographic Background of Economic and Political Problems.* New York: Odyssey Press, 1964.

Platt, Robert S. *Latin America; Countryside and United Regions.* New York and London: McGraw-Hill, 1942.

Silvert, Kalman H. *Expectant Peoples, Nationalism and Development.* New York: Random House, 1963.

Torres, James F. "Concentration of Political Power and Levels of Economic Development in Latin American Countries," *The Journal of Developing Areas* 7 (April 1973): 397-410.

Webb, Kempton E. *Geography of Latin America.* Englewood Cliffs, N.J.: Prentice-Hall, 1972.

Wiarda, Howard. "Toward a Framework for the Study of Political Change in the Iberic-Latin Tradition," *World Politics* 25 (January 1973): 206-35.

Zuvekas, Jr., Clarence. "Concentration of Political Power and Levels of Economic Development in Latin American Countries: A Comment," *The Journal of Developing Areas* 8 (July 1974): 507-12; also Grieb and Torres replies, pp. 513-24.

Six

Attitudes and Values

That value systems and personality traits condition political life in Latin America should come as no surprise, for these factors color politics within all countries. The power to influence and persuade, dominate or be dominated, and to play a role in the distribution, management, and control of political resources deeply involves personality. Who gets what, when, and how, in employment, income, patronage, education, housing, health care, and other valued elements in a society is affected by how attitudes and values condition interpersonal relations in the game of politics. These in turn are conditioned by a society's culutral values, child-rearing practices, familial patterns, racial configurations, and linguistic, religious, and social-class relations. The attitudes and values that we will be considering are both personal and aggregate, and they can often be lumped as types, as constellations of attitudes that seem to go together.

When attitudes and values—both personal and aggregate—operate in the political realm, they are frequently referred to as political culture. By this concept is meant the aggregate of outlooks and values that condition attitudes toward authority and political behavior. The range includes such attitudes as faith or little faith in elections, belief or lack of belief in the law, acceptance or not of violence as a legitimate form of political expression, the need or not to be emotional in politics, or easy domination of or desire to be dominated by others. A country's political culture also includes its political traditions, formal and informal rules of the political game, acceptance or not of the state's leaders and system (note that part of the country's population, such as Indians in the Andean countries, may not even know of the state's political system, thus constituting a special kind of political subculture), political stereotypes, and political moods. These attitudes and values are of course formed in the home, school, workplace, church—from childhood through adulthood—a process called political socialization.

TRADITION VERSUS MODERNITY

One set of values that seems useful in understanding the politics of Latin America is that provided by sociologists who study modern and traditional societies. Talcott Parsons, Marion J. Levy, and Seymour Martin Lipset, among others, describe the "modern" and "traditional" person in special terms denoting their values: achievement-ascription, universalism-particularism, equalitarian-elite, and rational-nonrational. To be "modern" is to base one's life on the values of achievement, universalism, equalitarianism, and rationality. By rationality is meant seeing the world in terms of achievement, universalism, and equalitarianism. The "traditional" is associated with the personal values of ascription, particularism, elitism, and nonrationality.

What do these terms imply? *Achievement* orientation means judging oneself and others on the basis of individual ability and skills, rather than on such inherited (or ascribed) qualities as family name, skin color, or racial identity. It also suggests a desire to "get ahead" in life through hard work and enterprise, rather than fatalistic acceptance of one's lot through an uncontrolled, predetermined set of circumstances. *Universalism* denotes the application of general standards for evaluating a person, such as examinations, instead of judging oneself and others on the basis of family and kinship connections (*particularism*). *Equalitarianism* suggests treatment of people equally (giving everyone equal opportunities) in most situations as against an elite dominance and non-elite submissiveness (or *elitism*) as the basis for interpersonal relations. Modernity, on the whole, implies a high degree of rationality, as the above values suggest, and an ability to adapt to a changing world. It is a set of values typically associated with a society that is urban, industrial, literate, economically interdependent, and participant.

Is Latin America Modern or Traditional?

Using the modern-traditional value scale, the obvious question is whether or not Latin American people are basically "modern" or "traditional." At which end of the attitude and value spectrum do the people within these states operate?

The answer is not simple. Some countries (Argentina, Brazil, Mexico, Costa Rica, Cuba, Uruguay) have experienced higher degrees of material change in literacy, urbanization, and per capita income growth than others (Bolivia, Guatemala, Haiti, Paraguay), which cannot but affect attitudes and values in a number of ways. Some countries (the Andean states) have a greater Indian Population than others, an important consideration because many Indian communities have their own lifestyles and do not wish to ape either white men or mestizo. Distinctions must be made between rural versus urban, literate versus illiterate, poor versus the rich, and so on. So any answers provided are conjectural and in need of qualification.

Secondly, experts disagree on this matter. Some suggest that the rising middle sectors (white-collar workers, service trades, government employees, bureaucrats, teachers, new industrialists, and progressive politicians among others) indicate a growth in the numbers of people who are essentially "modern."[1] According to this interpretation, the literate middle sectors are urban, trust blindly in industrialization as a key solution to national problems, are interested in advancing higher professional education, advocate agrarian reform, and are intensely nationalistic—often in highly anti-American forms. If accepted totally, underlying this popular middle-class or middle-sector thesis is the implicit assumption that these people embody achievement and a kind of individualism based upon merit, skills, and universalist criteria, rather than ascriptive and particularist norms. In other words, they are people of "modern" attitudes and values.

A counterargument also exists. Scholars such as Claudio Veliz and Lipset argue that in fact most people in Latin American societies are still basically traditional in personal relationships.[2] Their central thesis is that middle-sector population groups, like the upper classes they seek to emulate, still follow traditional values and personality patterns, and that their progressive and nationalist orientations are more myth than reality.

The problem is to put these arguments in perspective. A traditional psychocultural world does indeed predominate in Latin America. To identify its salient traits is not to suggest that individual exceptions, or even notable differences, between countries exist. Uruguay has a more equalitarian interpersonal setting than Guatemala. The Mexican and Cuban experiments in building a universalist-achievement-nationalist conscience in their peoples contrasts with continuing strong authoritarian traditions in Colombia and Bolivia. Many new professional elites are committed to changing attitudes and values; others are not. All are living within and conditioned by the past. No society is totally described below. But to depict collective attitude and value traits as basically traditional does help to explain much of political life south of the Rio Grande and the context within which whatever "modern"— however fewer—types are working.

Traditional Interpersonal Relations

Studies of Latin American societies indicate that self-perception and interpersonal relationships operate according to ascriptive, particularist, and elitist norms. For example, kinship and local communities, rather than impersonal state institutions, are stressed in personal identity. Kinship (particularism) is strong in selecting both government employees and personnel for private enterprise; use of such universalist criteria as standardized examinations is rare, even in such developed countries as Uruguay, Argentina, Brazil, and Mexico. Surveys of managerial elites and business executives alike show the continuation of ascription, particularism, and elitism.

Developing from these traits are a number of characteristics of public and private life. They include an unwillingness to cooperate with outsiders, an inability to trust and work with others not well known, difficulty in delegating responsibility, subservience to, rather than critical appraisals of, the ministers of bureaucracies, a tendency not to identify with society as a whole, and a general identity with individualist, familial, local, and subnational personal ties.

Traditional values permeate political culture in Latin America making the development of more equalitarian, open, democratic, and rational political institutions and procedures difficult. These traditional attitudes and values can be explored more in depth, especially their stress on personalism, interpersonal dominance and social hierarchy, and transcendentalist values. They add up to an authoritarian model personality, one of dominant-submissive attitudes, yet curiously not totalitarian. Democracy is greatly inhibited while, paradoxically, homage is paid to the individual. Military dictatorships traditionally dominate politics, yet organized mass parties, ideological purism, and systematic thought control, as in Nazi Germany, are alien to Latin American military rule.

PERSONALISMO

The distinctive traditional personality feature in Latin American societies might be coined by the word *personalismo* (personalism, individualism). The accent is on the individualized inner essence of a person, each having a unique value of "soul" or "spirit" typically described as the *dignidad de la persona* (dignity of the person). This refers to inner dignity, not to social or outward prestige, and implies the need to guard one's inner and unique subjective self and to preserve so far as possible one's own personal liberty.[3]

Personalism is closely associated with other traits inherited from Spanish culture. Establishing, expressing, and protecting inner personal identity is linked to distrust of those not bound by kinship or close friendship, for one is not predisposed to sacrifice the interests of one's own personality to larger group interests, particularly to any not known personally. This general aversion to strangers, collective action, group identity, or nonpersonal organizations is matched by an emphasis on pride, passion, and emotion in self-fulfillment, and a tendency to feel strongly, rarely to remain neutral, about key problems.

Emotion, passion, and pride express the personalist force. To exalt the individual is to concentrate on his emotional expression. One loves, hates, and feels intensely about life, for the neutral road is not that of Iberian attitudes and values. Individual honor and dignity are constantly on the line, expressed in daily life. "Pride is our national passion," writes José Ortega y Gasset, "our greatest sin."[4]

Pride is closely linked to the cultural forces of personal identity. Personal appearance, for example, is an element of pride, hence the stress on wearing a coat and tie if possible. These are signs of caste, of escape from the stigma of manual labor. A similar attachment to symbols of education, language competency, religion, occupation, and place of residence is natural in a psychocultural world of intense personal pride. But with pride and emotion on the line, equally understandable are the great levels of political violence, personalist factions, and interpersonal conflict arising from perceived threats to individual identity.

The outward symbols of individual importance and honor of course are stressed in daily life. Titles, decorations, citations, and even "manifestations," for example marches, strikes, or demonstrations for an individual, mirror *personalismo* at work. The environment exhalts the individual; deprecation of the personality is a major offense. Personalism means that *man* is the center of the universe; nations, states, government, and collective organizations are not.

Machismo

Personalism accentuates specific kinds of human relationships in politics. One traditional outgrowth is *machismo*, referring to emphasis on male sexual prowess, zest for action, daring, verbal agility, and supreme self-confidence. The upshot is the strong tendency in politics that politicians, as the Mexicans put it, *"tener pantalones,"* or literally, "wear the pants." The distinguishing political trait of *machismo* is intransigence, with each politician frequently convinced that one way and one way only exists to accomplish goals: his way.

Behind the *machismo*-personalist trait lie a number of explanatory propositions, many coming from studies on Mexico.[5] The Iberian tendency, socialized in the home and through other experiences, is to express oneself through emotion. That life is passion and tragic-fatalistic rather than rational-pragmatic is a theme found in novels, movies, and other cultural media. Hispano-Catholicism is fatalistic, especially in the closed societies of rural Latin America, but to some extent in the urban centers as well. A deeply ingrained inferiority complex affects mestizos and leads toward distrust, suspicion, and violent self-expression, stemming in part, it could be argued, from their existence "in-between" the Indian society left behind and the white society into which entry is incomplete. *Machismo* reflects emotional self-expression and protection of the inner self as higher in priority than self-criticism, self-improvement, and widespread social cooperation. Certainly *machismo* is socialized in the home, where the husband represents the family in public life, in trade, and in politics, and it is a constant theme in the arts.

Personalism and Politics

The effects of traditional personalism are wide ranging in Latin America. Strong-man rule and a political environment of men rather than such impersonal institutions as professional organizations, educational bulwarks, bureaucracies, and development planning show the imprint of personalism. Although it is changing under the pressure of new forces, it is still strong. Terms most frequently used to describe this phenomenon are the *caudillo* (regional strong boss), the *cacique* (local strong boss), or the *líder máximo* (maximum leader). Socialized in part through dominant-submissive relationships on the rural *latifundia* from the early settlement period onward, and by the historic Iberian hero worship of strong military leaders, Latin American political history is largely a history of rule by strong leaders, from Simón Bolívar and San Martín forward. Recent political history is replete with the roll call of dominant strong leaders—Fulgencio Batista, Porfirio Díaz, Manuel Odría, Rafael Trujillo, Juan Vicente Gómez, Marcos Pérez Jiménez, Jorge Ubico, Juan Perón, Getúlio Vargas, Rojas Pinilla, and so on.

Even today this phenomenon persists, as witnessed by Fidel Castro's personalist position in Cuba since January, 1959, General Augusto Ugarte Pinochet's overthrow of the constitutionally elected government of Salvador Allende Gossens in September, 1973, General Alfredo Stroessner's control of Paraguay and the Somoza family's dominance in Nicaragua. To be sure, the absolute dominance by single strong men has been modified by the emergence in some countries of juntas (several military men running the country), more complex civil services and public bureaucracies, private business and commercial groups, and modern parties, such as Mexico's *Partido Revolucionario Institucional* (Institutional Revolutionary Party). But even here personalism is at work within party, bureaucratic, and junta structure. Inherited cultural traits do not easily disappear.

Those politicians who win public office through elections frequently owe their success to their capacity to personify the inner values deemed important by the voters. These include charismatic qualities, verbal prowess, action, and self-confidence. Such perceptions of the candidate frequently outweigh the follower's pragmatic judgment about a candidate's party or his position on social, economic, or political issues.

Personal friendship and kinship ties are much the basis for getting things done. Patronage appointments and promotions, lack of effective delegation of power and responsibility, building networks of alliances through friendship, absence of criticism of superiors, accomplishing public business through private contacts rather than group conferences, and elite factionalism plague Latin American governments. Excessive formalism and legalism, perhaps defense mechanisms for self-worth and esteem, are key components of governmental life. To get ahead in public life often requires more "honesty, respect, and loyalty" to superiors than technical skills or competence, as perceived by both employees and employers. The new *técnicos* (technical experts in urban areas) show more modern tendencies than this, but the general system prevails.

The emphasis on favoritism in public life is strong, although in some countries in some departments (such as the public bureaucracies in Chile, Venezuela, and Mexico) achievement norms are sometimes mixed in with ascriptive criteria in recruitment and promotion. But the predominant force nonetheless is favoritism. The vocabulary of Latin American politics expresses this force, with numerous words to denote "pull" through family, friends, or influential contacts. Cases in point include *cuña* (Chile), *palanca* (Venezuela), *politiquería* (game of politics, Cuba), *clientelismo* (throughout Latin America), *jeito* (or *"dar un jeito,"* meaning improvisation, find a way, or oil the gears, Brazil), and in Mexico there are approximately fifteen words to describe the subtleties of graft! Indeed, a popular adage in Mexico, a country of relatively high institutional development and outwardly "modern" complexion, holds that "the thief who fails goes to jail; the thief who succeeds, to him all worldly goods." C. A. M. Hennessy uses the term *"empleocracia"* to denote the use of governmental bureaucracies for nepotism and finding jobs for friends and for using bureaucracies to relieve unemployment rather than administering the programs they were set up to carry out.[6] Helio Jaguaribe describes Brazil as a "cartorial state," a product "of clientele politics and, at the same time, the instrument that utilizes and perpetuates it . . . [in this system] public employment is not in actuality directed toward the rendering of any public service, but only toward the more or less indirect subsidization of clienteles in exchange for electoral support."[7]

The politician's relationship with other political leaders and willingness to compromise on key issues is based largely upon personal confidence and *personalismo*. It is extremely difficult in Latin American politics to divorce the procedures of politics—issues, platforms, bargaining, compromising—from perceptions of the opponent's personality, especially where the preservation of one's own personal liberty and independence is at stake.

Personalism thus helps to explain the enormous political instability in Latin America. Factional conflict, weak political parties typically torn into personalist opposing camps, and in general the difficulty in establishing organized political life as we know it in Western Europe or the United States radiates from *personalismo*. *Homo burocratis* is not easily found in Latin America, and social cooperation on a large scale is extremely difficult.

DOMINANCE AND HIERARCHY

Dominance and hierarchy, which characterize Latin American societies, indicate a social system arranged in hierarchical interpersonal social, economic, and political terms. Within it, some people and groups—the elites—tend to dominate those lower down on the social scale. This has occurred since the first *conquistador* set foot in the new world; it occurred on the large landed estates and still does, as it does in the home; and although modified today by the larger numbers of people, *intereses*, and groups playing elite roles, dominance and hierarchy continue to shape the political world.

Colonial government imposed rule from above, and rather than encouraging self-government from below, independence substituted a new set of elites—large landowners, military officers, the Church—for the deposed colonial rulers, leaving the social and political structure of elite-mass hierarchy basically intact. The Hispanic-Catholic tradition, moreover, encouraged an essentially hierarchical society. Its own system of internal governance was hierarchical, combined with emphasis on otherworldliness, fatalism, and general acceptance of one's fate in this life—especially if one were a peasant. These socializing experiences are cues to understanding Latin American political cultures.

While it may appear to contradict the emphasis on *personalismo*, the hierarchy-dominance syndrome means that self-perceptions and interpersonal relations in fact operate within a special human context not inconsistent with individualism. As John P. Gillin puts it, the individual tends to see things "on a scale ranging from 'lower' to 'higher,'" within which individualism can be expressed within social rank. In Gillin's words, the "distinctive worth of each individual has nothing to do with his social position or his recognized distinction; advancement within the hierarchy may come, although not necessarily so, as a result of fulfilling one's unique potentialities."[8] As we know, it is possible to rise to a higher social position through change of language, occupation, dress, education, and other symbols of prestige. The emergence of middle-sector people into new positions of status and power during the past half-century, particularly since World War II, illustrates this.

A number of aspects of governmental life express the strength of dominance and hierarchy. Most executive branches, as we will see more in detail later, control basic policies and major appointments; legislatures tend to be weak, although exceptions to the rule exist, as in Chile's unique political history of strong legislative power. But the general rule holds even in so-called "developed" or "modern" systems, like that of Mexico, where state governors control patronage and appointments below them, but owe their own jobs to the federal executive.

In public as well as private bureaucratic life, patronage both reflects and conditions the basic pattern, as do other behavioral traits. Fear of responsibility, centralized but not well-organized authority, and constant referral to higher officials suggests, in addition to protection of individual dignity and self-esteem, a system of subordination, deference, and loyalty. One should not appear to frustrate a superior's needs, should not question the superior's wishes, for promotion and job security largely hang on loyalty and the communication of deference within the pecking order. While this attitude permeates all levels of bureaucratic life—supervisory, professional, technical, clerical, service, and security personnel—it appears in some surveys to be especially strong for the lowest-level personnel, as one might expect.

More than the Iberian trait of being a gentleman, respectful and respect-worthy, are involved here. First, ethnic hierarchy can infuse bureaucratic hierarchy, where those of lower ethnic identity are subservient to those of higher ethnic identity. Guatemalan Indians, for example, who have recently "passed" as ladinos and entered the service and security sectors of bureaucratic life are highly conscious of the cultural gap between them and upper-class ladinos above them. This could also be said of people recently in from rural areas who face urbanites of higher status within the bureaucratic structure. Paradoxically, then, cultural divisions of hierarchy and dominance-submissiveness help stratify government life, partly nullifying the integrative effects of governmental participation.

Second, some governmental systems, as in Guatemala, may not have strong institutional safeguards against whimsical or capricious treatment by superiors. In the absence of tenure, merit protection, a uniform wage scale, examinations for advancement, a public employee's union or other protective group, and other universalist criteria for protection and advancement, building a network of loyalty through friendship and being subservient and respectful of authority is simply a means of survival.

Third, traditional attitudes and values in Latin America do not stress strong achievement and civic culture. By civic culture is meant a number of related traits that include identity with and allegiance to leaders and organizations which transcend the parochial and primordial; an interest in public affairs validated by keeping informed and expressed through participation in civic (community-wide) action; and being oriented toward political and governmental processes that recognize and accept the necessity for a rational structure of rules and regulations.[9] The psychocultural world does not always reinforce such modern notions as the ability of those below to challenge those above, the willingness to be self-critical, the equality of all, or the idea that authority should be delegated on the belief that self-government is the natural order. Instead, prevalent attitudes reinforce a tendency to dominate those below while being subservient and loyal to those above—on whom one personally depends for economic security and protection of one's own inner personality. In addition, dominance at some level is a natural component of individualistic pride, self-esteem, emotion as fulfillment of self, inner dignity, and privilege—all aspects of traditional attitudes and values.

Patron-Client Relations

Social-class identity and the ability to influence and be influenced by others bring certain expectations about power, influence, and author-·ity. Those in lower social strata expect, look for, and cultivate protection from those above.

Patron-client relations, sometimes called *clientelismo*, were linked to landholding early in Latin America's history, an important socializing experience. To be sure, the landholders dominated then (as now) those *campesinos* associated with the *latifundia*. The *repartimiento* (assignment of a number of natives to work for the individual Spaniard), *encomienda* (a specific grant of land together with the right to the labor of the Indians who lived on it), and the *mita* (a system of forced labor, also used by the Incas) of colonial days and similar contemporary forms of internal colonialism could not but produce dominance and hierarchy. As a corollary system, patron-client relationships developed in the rural areas. In return for work, obedience, and loyalty, the patron provided housing, tools, individual plots of land, and protection for his workers or tenants.

This "protector" notion is no longer restricted to rural society. It operates even in urban settings, where small *patrones* have their own *patrones*, and where *clientelismo* is prominent in public service, political life, and certainly in obtaining jobs for young people graduating from universities and seeking employment. Even presidents of some countries are looked upon as great *patrones* vis-à-vis their constituents. It is evident from all this that hierarchy has a built-in tendency to divide people into dominating and dominated roles, albeit not in a complete sense, for *clientelismo* involves a certain amount of interdependence between the two roles.

Clientelismo and *Compadrazgo*

Anthropological studies attest to the continuing importance of *clientelismo* in the form of the fictive kinship relationship called *compadrazgo*. This is the godparent system arising from the Catholic custom of requiring spiritual sponsorship at baptism. Although it serves different functions throughout Latin America, it exists as a form of power- and influence-seeking through influential people by those with less accessibility to goods and services, where those of higher status frequently become *compadres* to those of lower status. As one anthropologist summarizes *compadrazgo* in Spanish America:

The compadrazgo plays a highly important role in promoting social stability, both within classes and ethnic groups, and between them.

Compadres are morally bound to stand by each other in time of all need and danger.[10]

Studies show that *compadrazgo* continues to function in rural and urban areas, and during periods of rapid social and economic change.

Clientelismo *and* Caciquismo

Caciquismo, as discussed above, is found in both rural and urban areas of Latin America. It mirrors the patterns of dominance and hierarchy in modal personality. The *cacique* has been defined as "a strong and autocratic leader in local and/or regional politics whose characteristically informal, personalistic, and often arbitrary rule is buttressed by a core of relatives, 'fighters,' and dependents, and is marked by the diagnostic threat and practice of violence."[11] *Caciquismo* always implies "strong individual power over a territorial group held together by some socio-economic or cultural system," and a degree of "detachment or freedom from the normative, formal, and duly instituted system of government." Recognized by community and state leaders as the most powerful person in the local political area, he becomes an important source of influence unaccountable to external governmental authorities.

Two key points are related to the *cacique*. First, while most dominant historically in rural Latin America, he continues to operate in urban areas today. Secondly, the *cacique's* "following" is often bound to him not only through patronage rewards but by ties of *compadrazgo,* helping form a cohesive "political family." It should be noted not only that *caciquismo* helps explain the enormously strong impact of nonformal, nonlegal, nonconstitutional political processes in Latin America's fragmented societies, but also helps illuminate a source of fragmentation itself.

THE TRANSCENDENTAL SPIRIT

Why does so much of governmental life in Latin America seem more talk than action, plans than implementation, and maintenance of the status quo than substantive institutional change? Why so much debate and verbal gymnastics? Why the elaborate constitutions without equivalent constitutionalism, or their translation into practice? While these characteristic phenomenon can be explained partly by individualism, *personalismo,* dominance and hierarchy, another major force merits attention: the transcendentalist spirit.

Transcendentalism may be defined as "transcending ordinary or common experience, thought, or belief; idealistic, lofty, or extravagant;

extraordinary, supernatural, or abstract." These transcendentalist values permeate Latin American thought, and are embodied as "the something beyond" (*lo algo mas alla*).[12] This self-perception results in a modal personality ranging between two extremes: (1) focus on and protection of one's own inner dignity, *personalism*, and (2) belief in and concentration on universal values; the search for universal truths; appreciation of the aesthetic, arts, and philosophy, *transcendentalism*. Transcendentalism emphasizes words, ideals, lofty expression, and concepts with universal meaning; less emphasized is pragmatic utilitarian action to implement elaborate plans and ideals.

The transcendentalist aspect of modal personality ultimately bears upon politics. It stimulates, for example, the sense that a project or plan is completed once the Idea of it has been grasped, completely identified, and given elegant expression in a constitution, party platform, or legal code. When combined with personalism, the transcendentalist force helps account for the verbal pyrotechnics of Latin American political legislation without implementation and the proliferation of constitutions and party platforms. Each leader, after all, seeks to leave his personal version of the "ultimate" or "something beyond" imprinted for posterity.

The Word, verbal as well as written, carries heavy weight in the transcendentalist world. The importance of elaborate creative verbal communication is hard to underestimate, especially in Latin American educational systems, an important socializing medium, from primary to university levels. Its obvious culmination is the importance of oratory to assembled masses—from professor to class, president to student, or labor leader to worker in downtown central plazas, factories, or open fields. José María Valasco Ibarra, Ecuador's many-times president, is said to have boasted, "Give me a balcony and the country is mine!" and he proved it precisely five times. More familiar are the lengthy speeches of Fidel Castro to assembled masses since he came to power in 1959.

Verbal communication occupies a peculiar role in the transcendentalist tradition. More than expressing the lofty, creative, and ideal, it in some ways seems to *legitimize* the Ideal, the ultimate, the "something beyond." Thus, not only is verbal prowess a key to attaining power, verbal communication is used to legitimize decisions, to sanctify a leader's position. Thus, orating to large masses is not only important, but also critical to the running of public bureaucracies, in transmitting orders and decisions from heads of departments to those in lower echelons. The simple written set of rules and regulations, or decisions made, will not do. Closely related to this phenomenon is the prestigious role played by the lecture in university life, where lecture notes are more important than outside reading. Again, we have the transmission of ideas by the spoken word. It would be difficult to pin-point the origins of this variant of transcendentalism, but undoubtedly the Hispano-Catholic tradition (authoritarianism, higher destiny, ulti-mate truth spoken by priest or pope) is a pervasive factor.

Transcendentalism also helps explain other features of Latin Ameri-can social and political life. Politicians, civil servants, and diplomats are frequently gifted speakers and writers, and more than willing to show off their poetic, literary, and philosophic talents. Not illogically, José Martí (1853-95), the great Cuban patriot and revolutionary, was also a Doctor of Law, an art critic for the *New York Sun*, and wrote seventeen volumes on life in the United States, several volumes of poems, and many political essays. Salvador Allende, Chile's recent president, was a medical doctor and enjoyed the finer artistic things of life, for which some of his left-wing allies criticized him. Still another aspect of transcendentalism is the role that fate and luck play in Latin American societies, where gambling and the lottery are well-known phenomena.

Transcendentalism seems connected to the low development of a na-tional consciousness in Latin American countries, where intellectual concern has centered on more universal issues. For example, fascina-tion with the notion of "Latin America" versus "North America" tradi-tionally left the idea of "Brazilian," or "Venezuelan," or "Uruguayan" identity less explored. Two countries where this general rule does not seem to apply are Cuba and Mexico, but remember that only these two countries experienced full-fledged social revolutions with a consequent search for a national identity. For the most part, the universalist con-cern is sharper, as evidenced in the debate over Latin American versus North American culture, an argument involving also the question of race. Some Latin American scholars attacked what they saw as racial inferiority south of the Rio Grande, while others extolled the Latin Americans. The classic statement of Latin American superiority is that of the Uruguayan thinker, José Enrique Rodó (1871-1917), author of *Ariel*, which praised the intuitive and spiritual qualities of Latin Amer-icans, and condemned the empirical and material outlooks of North America.

THE INDIAN VERSUS NON-INDIAN WORLD

To a large extent we have been discussing the world of the white man and those mixed groups that aspire to emulate the Iberian values of upper-class status. But implied in our discussion is that the Indian world is distinct from the white man's or mixed group's domain. In-deed, it would be accurate to state that the way political cultural patterns operate for self-perceiving Indians is in contrast with those of non-Indian norms of behavior.

Studies on Guatemala, for example, suggest that the attitudes and values discussed so far fit for ladinos but not for Indians. Friendship, to use one illustration, has a practical utility in the realm of economic and political influence for ladinos. This use of friends to obtain patronage or political influence is called *cuello*, and it leads to a desire to have friends among urban ladinos—ones, it is hoped, of superior status and political power.

By contrast the Indian notion of friendship is different, for friendship is maintained not for political influence or economic gain, but for emotional satisfaction. It is called the *camarada* pattern. The ladinos look down upon Indian *camarada* as foolish, possible only for "uncivilized" individuals. This of course means that friendship between ladinos and Indians is highly unlikely, for they literally live in distinctly different psychological worlds.

The case of Mexico illustrates the different worlds of mestizo and Indian. The Mexican governmental system is of course authoritarian and hierarchical, befitting our traditional political-culture outline, with authority coming from the top, and where *caudillismo* and *caciquismo* together with personal influence and patronage still prevail at regional and local levels of government. But for the Yaqui Indians, authority is more diffuse and the need for consensus among leaders as well as led is strong. All levels of authority discuss issues in the Yaqui Indian tradition, and then feedback is sought from the people. The structure of hierarchy, dominance, and submissiveness does not exist.

Traditional Attitudes and Values on Balance

One should not conclude from this overview that the traditional attitudes prevailing in Latin America severely or impossibly constrain development. Development, it is suggested, will occur within, be conditioned by, and reflect traditional political culture and patterns of socialization.

A combination of new styles, linked with traditional political culture, is already becoming clear. Cuba illustrates traditional personalism (Castro's role as *líder máximo*) and dominance-hierarchy (as is shown by the central influence of the men of the 26th of July Movement in political decision making), combined with emphasis on new attitudes of achievement, equality, hard work, nationalism, participation, and personal self-criticism as a basis for self-improvement. Cuba's educational system inculcates attitudes of study combined with manual labor in an equalitarian framework. Children and young adults study in the classroom, then go to the fields and factories.

Other examples illustrate the point. Brazil is a combination of old and new values, emphasizing dominance-hierarchy (as in the military role in government), but also promotes private economic achievement. Peru is experimenting with agrarian reform and worker participation in factory management that may affect attitudes in the future. Mexican primary-school textbooks stress participatory citizenship values, the need to work for Mexico, and the importance of political unification. These are only a few examples of the interaction of old modal personality and new institutional-attitudinal forces for change.

Then there is the matter of education and where a person lives. Those isolated in rural areas may quite likely be cynical toward political objects, particularly if government is perceived as divorced from the lives of the common person, usually corrupt, favoring the wealthy, and unequal in its treatment of the public at large. The adult will pass these attitudes along to the child. The urban dweller in contrast is more likely to be socialized to the potential benefits of positive political action, if surrounded by newspapers, radios, television sets, parades, political activists, mass rallies, and other political activities. The amount of organized political activity and the opportunities for political participation of some kind surrounding the growing individual is part of the socializing experience, hence urban dwellers have more potential for developing attitudes of civic awareness than rural dwellers who may live on a *latifundia* (and be *campesinos* on it) or in a village, Indian community, or tribe. Yet being urban by no means guarantees the growth of a civic culture, as defined at the outset of this chapter, nor is the rural dweller necessarily immune from being socialized to the belief in political action per se, as the rise of rural guerrilla movements, peasants leagues, and *campesino* land occupations illustrates.

Formal education is another avenue of socialization. The more educated a person, the more aware that person is of the state's political system and, hence, the more available as a political participant. While education does not determine the kind of participation, it does raise knowledge, awareness, and opinions about the state's political system; often one's activities with it increase as a result of higher education. Increased education also tends to cause higher expectations of equal treatment in the political system—an important aspect of modern civic culture. So local habitation and level of education are important socializing experiences, contributing to the building of attitudes and values. Income levels, place of employment, occupation, and religion are undoubtedly also important.

A final observation must be made about government itself as a socializing mechanism—either in forging modern cultural syndromes or sustaining older ones. If effective political participation is low, corruption high, laxity in law enforcement notorious, human rights consistently violated, and elections seldom, one would expect much of the population to continue to be attached to traditional attitudes about government. These attitudes may include alienation, suspicion, untrusting feelings, and general cynicism. Some of the countries discussed in chapters three and four would reinforce these tendencies. If, on the other hand, political leaders begin to move the political institutions toward more enlightened development, as is also occurring in many Latin American countries, then we can reasonably expect a fruitful setting for an evolution toward more civic-mindedness, albeit in a distinct Latin American style.

NOTES

1. See John J. Johnson, *Political Change in Latin America: The Emergence of the Middle Sectors* (Stanford, Calif.: Stanford University Press, 1966), pp. 5ff.; and Jacques Lambert, *Latin America: Social Structures and Political Institutions,* trans. Helen Katel (Berkeley: University of California Press, 1971), ch. 12.

2. Claudio Veliz (ed.), *The Politics of Conformity in Latin America* (New York: Oxford University Press, 1970); Claudio Veliz (ed.), *Obstacles to Change in Latin America* (New York: Oxford University Press, 1969); Seymour Martin Lipset and Aldo Solari (eds.), *Elites in Latin America* (New York: Oxford University Press, 1967); and see Rodolfo Stavenhagen, "Seven Fallacies about Latin America," in *Latin America, Reform or Revolution,* ed. James Petras and Maurice Zeitlin (New York: Fawcett, 1968), pp. 23-26.

3. Personalism is frequently cited as a major personality feature of Latin America. See John P. Gillin, "Some Signposts for Policy," in Richard N. Adams, et al., *Social Change in Latin America Today* (New York: Vintage Books, 1960), pp. 29-33; John P. Gillin, "Ethos Components in Modern Latin American Culture," *American Anthropologist* 57 (1955): 488-500; William Lytle Schurtz, *This New World* (New York: Dutton, 1964), pp. 92-99; Salvadore de Madariaga, *Spain: A Modern History* (New York: Praeger, 1958), pp. 17-18, 20-23, reprinted in Hugh Hamill, Jr., *Dictatorship in Spanish America* (New York: Knopf, 1965), pp. 30-34; and Francois Chevalier, "The Roots of Personalism," in Hamill, *op. cit.,* pp. 36-51.

4. José Ortega y Gasset, *Invertebrate Spain* (New York: Norton, 1937), p. 146.

5. Octavio Paz, *The Labyrinth of Solitude; Life and Thought in Mexico* (New York: Grove Press, 1961); Samuel Ramos, *Profile of Man and Culture in Mexico,* trans. Peter G. Earle (New York: McGraw-Hill, 1963); and Patrick Romanell, *Making of the Mexican Mind* (Lincoln: University of Nebraska Press, 1952).

6. Clarence E. Thurber, "Islands of Development; A Political and Social Approach to Development Administration in Latin America," in *Development Administration in Latin America*, ed. Clarence E. Thurber and Lawrence S. Graham (Durham, N.C.: Duke University Press, 1973), p. 33. See Thurber's perceptive collection of essays for other aspects of bureaucratic behavior in Latin America, some of which are discussed here.

7. Quoted by Charles J. Parrish, "Bureaucracy, Democracy, and Development: Some Considerations Based on the Chilean Case," in Thurber and Graham, *op. cit.*, p. 245.

8. John P. Gillin, "Some Signposts for Policy," in Richard N. Adams, et al., *Social Change in Latin America Today* (New York: Vintage Books, 1960), p. 35.

9. Alex Inkeles, "Participant Citizenship in Six Developing Countries," *The American Political Science Review* 68 (December 1969): 1122-23; and Gabriel Almond and Sidney Verba, *The Civic Culture* (Princeton, N.J.: Princeton University Press, 1963).

10. George M. Foster, "Cofradia and Compadrazgo in Spain and Spanish America," *Southwestern Journal of Anthropology* 9 (Spring 1953): 3ff.

11. Wayne A. Cornelius, "A Structural Analysis of Urban Caciquismo in Mexico," *Urban Anthropology* 1 (Fall 1972): 237.

12. Gillin, *op. cit.*, p. 41.

Suggested Readings

Fillol, Tomas Roberto. *Social Factors in Economic Development; The Argentine Case.* Cambridge: M.I.T. Press, 1961.

Horowitz, Michael (ed.). *Peoples and Cultures of the Caribbean: An Anthropological Reader.* New York: Natural History Press, 1971.

Lipset, Seymour Martin. "Values, Education, and Entrepreneurship," in *Elites in Latin America*, ed. Seymour Martin Lipset and Aldo Solari. New York: Oxford University Press, 1967, ch. 1.

Liss, Sheldon B. and Peggy K. Liss (eds.) *Man, State, and Society in Latin American History.* New York: Praeger, 1972.

Moreno, Francisco José and Barbara Mitrand (eds.), *Conflict and Violence in Latin American Politics.* New York: Thomas Y. Crowell, 1971, pts. 1 and 2.

Silvert, Kalman H. *The Conflict Society; Reaction and Revolution in Latin America*, rev. ed. New York: American Universities Field Staff, Inc., 1966.

Smith, T. Lynn. *Studies of Latin American Societies.* New York: Doubleday, 1970.

Thurber, Clarence E. and Lawrence S. Graham (eds.), *Development Administration in Latin America.* Durham, N.C.: Duke University Press, 1973.

Wolf, Eric R., and Edward C. Hansen. *The Human Condition in Latin America.* New York: Oxford University Press, 1972.

Seven

Ethnicity and Class

Much of our earlier discussion touched on questions of personal identity and politics in Latin America. It was shown how geography divides the Latin American population into clusters of people who tend to identify more with *latifundias,* communities, villages, and regions than with modern legal states. The literate middle sectors and upper-class elites of capital cities were shown to see themselves as separate from people in outlying rural provinces. A related phenomenon is the general absence of large numbers of people from capital city to landed estate, from the literate to the illiterate, from the white creole to the Indian who shares a common national identity.

Personal identity affects government and politics in Latin America. When people perceive themselves as inferior or superior to others, as occupying a lower or higher scale of social status, as possessing less or more of the elements of prestige, they are conditioned to be less or more influential vis-à-vis others. Identity, then, is another kind of political resource. It is in a sense as powerful as money, employment, food, and weapons, which exert an influence on patterns of who controls whom, and who gets what, when, and how. When we inquire into the system and distribution of political control and political resources, we come headlong into the complex, often illusive, question of "Who am I?"

This fascinating issue is particularly accentuated in Latin American societies, where people are highly conscious of social, class, caste, cultural, and racial distinctions. One's level on the social hierarchy conditions a person's attitudes and values in his relationships with others. While we have already explored the nature of the authoritarian attitudes and values that predominate in Latin America's political culture, we are concerned here with how people perceive themselves, on what bases, why, and with what general consequences.

ETHNIC IDENTITY AND POLITICS

Ethnic identity is increasingly recognized as a major force in politics. Its persistence is no illusion, and recent research has shown its effects on the political life of developed and developing states throughout the world. By such political criteria, as exercising power and influence over others, making decisions and resolving conflicts, exercising control, use, and distribution of such political resources as money, status, and patronage, or positing legitimate authority, ethnicity repeatedly appears as a key variable. Yet analyzing ethnic identity in Latin American politics is made difficult by the region's unique ethnic setting and by conflicting interpretations.

The Assimilationist Argument

It can be argued that Latin American societies are the true "melting pots" of ethnically different people. Taken to its logical conclusion, the argument would state that ethnic identity plays no (or at best, a minimal) role in Latin American politics because the people are a highly racially mixed people, unconcerned about ethnic differences.

What is the evidence? First, physical characteristics such as skin color do not lead to de jure segregation of blacks and Indians within Latin American countries, as occurred in the United States. Secondly, Latin Americans are considered to be less racially prejudiced than North Americans as a result of the Hispano-Catholic religion, the Iberian experience with slavery, and the influence of African people and culture on the Iberian peninsula before colonization in the New World. Third, depending upon the specific social setting, physical characteristics frequently relate to such cultural and economic indicators as language, family name, dress, place of residence, and religion in the final determination of one's social class.

Fourth, as we already know, Latin American societies are comprised of mixed groups—white, mestizo, Indian, mulatto, and Negro. Argentina, Chile, Costa Rica, and Uruguay are highly populated with white Europeans. Bolivia, Ecuador, Peru, and Guatemala are highly Indian. Others, such as Cuba, Brazil, and Haiti, are African in racial composition. Indians are generally found in the interior areas of Latin America, whites, mestizos and blacks on the coast. Finally, Latin American societies are not multi-ethnonational states, where separate self-identifying ethnic nations coexist, as Tamil and Sinhalese in Ceylon or Czechs and Slovaks in Czechoslovakia.

These circumstances distinguish the more fluid and flexible Latin America from other parts of the world, where ethnic groups are more visibly self-contained, hermetically sealed off from each other, and frequently hostile. It could appear that personal identity on the basis of being white European, a mixed group mulatto or mestizo, or a black or Indian, would on the whole play a relatively minor role in politics.

Nonassimilation: A Counterargument

In contrast to the conclusions that might be drawn from the above argument, studies show that nonassimilation is also a distinct and powerful force in Latin America. Interethnic and cultural-racial differentiation affects daily life, and the whiter a person is the better his chances in life, the more status he enjoys, and the more likely he will be to harbor feelings of superiority over Indian and black people. Color is a factor in social relations, stereotyping by phenotype occurs, and ethnocentrism—the judging of one's own group as better than others—exists. The Altiplano Indians of Bolivia, for example, show pride in being what they are, just as the white ladino of Guatemala is proud of his ethnicity and superiority over Guatemalan Indian groups.

White skin and European, principally Iberian, heritage is of the highest status in most Latin American countries. Certainly people with white or lighter skin are highly conscious of their phenotype, and difference from blacks, mestizos, mulattoes, or Indians. But it should be kept in mind that cultural-racial consciousness is also high among Indians, Negroes, and mulattoes. These interethnic differentiations are partly due to de facto discrimination in employment, clubs, and culture, and to a host of phrases and clichés denoting Indians and blacks as inferior people.

One's cultural-racial status is important. For example, in São Paulo, Brazil, it has been estimated that about thirty-one different cultural-racial categories are used by residents answering the question "Who am I?"[1] During the colonial period in Mexico, about sixteen different categories of *castas* were accepted elements of identity.

Color continues to be a factor in social relations, particularly when it comes to sex, marriage, and offspring. Indeed, some popular Latin

American magazines carry marriage want ads, in which the person looking for a spouse will designate his or her color of skin, for example, trigueño (swarthy), moreno (brown), and that desired in the spouse.

Ethnic identity is not a simple matter of all whites seeing themselves as one group, all blacks as another, all Indians as still another. Regional, linguistic, cultural, and religious differentiations tend to break these larger segments into many smaller groups. Differences prevail among the white Spanish, depending upon their family name, or region of Spain from which they came. Spaniards are different from Italians or Germans, but then "Spain" may in fact mean the Basque region, Catalonia, or Galicia, while "Italy" may in fact refer to Sicily or Naples.

Differences among Indians also exist. Not only do they see themselves as different from whites, but they also differentiate between highland and lowland Indians in Bolivia or village identities in Guatemala or Peru. Linguistic differentiation between Quechua, Aymará and Guaraní throughout the Andean countries also fragments the Indian community. Indian groupings are far more than the casual observer of Latin America might suspect. At least 73 languages are spoken and more than 335 separate tribes have been identified. The tenacity of Indian traditions is amazing, and if one visits La Paz, Bolivia, one encounters Indians living much as they did four hundred years ago, albeit adapting somewhat to the entrepreneurial opportunities of urban life. Some Indians do, of course, know the city mayor with whom arrangements are made for sidewalk space to sell chewing gum, trinkets, and the like.

Just as differences between whites and Indians complicate the ethnic portrait of Latin America, the situation among black groups is equally intricate. Darker blacks tend to be on the lower end of the social totem pole than lighter blacks, a situation validated by studies on Brazil, Panama, and certainly in prerevolutionary Cuba. It should be relatively clear from all this that ethnic and cultural-racial relations, with their corresponding cultures are not of homogeneous consistency. People do not identify themselves with a single group. The picture is further complicated by regional differences in the way people identify each other, ranging from ancestry to sociocultural criteria (Mexico and Guatemala), to physical appearances (Brazil and the Caribbean).

The central point is that people are distinguished by a number of familial, linguistic, regional, cultural-racial, and ethnic differences that produce polyethnic rather than monoethnic status. Once an individual is relegated into an ethnic category, moreover, he is frequently not considered as "one of *us*," but as "one of *them*." This occurs even in Brazil, the country frequently cited as high in assimilation, in Mexico, where the 1910 revolution presumably began a process of common ethnic identification with the Indian past, and in Guatemala, Peru, Bolivia, Guyana, and the Caribbean.

Ethnicity and Politics

Varieties of ethnic groups and levels of ethnic identity exist throughout the world. These contain distinct qualities of ethnic identification and different values, attitudes, and expectations. Logically, their effects on political systems vary, but should not be underestimated in political analysis. Ethnicity is linked to politics in various ways, as verified by a number of specific political arrangements inside different states and by a wide range of policies applied to ethnic groups by state leaders.

Power and influence are conditioned by different types of ethnic situations. Patronage, nepotism, and clientelist politics continue along ethnic lines throughout the world and form basic power relationships. Machines, cliques, factions, and "followings" are cases in point. Operating well into the development process of new states, they typically supersede relationships between citizens and representative or between party member and party leaders as occurs in modern Western European or United States politics. Accentuated here is the importance of private *substate* politics behind governments, rather than the modern *state* realm of formal constitutional authority, legality, and public accountability.

How does Latin American ethnicity compare with the general world situations? It is becoming increasingly apparent that, viewed from a number of different perspectives, ethnic and cultural-racial identity conditions politics in Latin America, too. As a general observation, unequal distribution and control of political resources, especially such influential resources as status, prestige, money, jobs, are in part a function of ethnic perceptions and typing. Whites are clearly in the dominant position over blacks and Indians, just as mulattoes and mestizos are typically less powerful than whites, but more than blacks and Indians. The whiter people, or those evincing white Iberian values, typically control the labor market, distribution of goods and services, and most of the arable land. They also hold positions of authority and bureaucratic offices not only in capital cities and large urban settings, but also in rural areas.

Given these ethnic divisions, the allocation of a country's valued goods and services typically finds blacks and Indians at the short end. They generally receive less of the state's money, education, housing, well-paying employment, and social services. Employment opportunities are less for blacks and Indians partly due to their inferior status, lower literacy, skills, and cultural characteristics (including speech, clothing, place of residence). They are stereotyped as "dirty," "lazy," "stupid," "inferior" (and so on), characterization not conducive to a more equitable sharing in society's valued goods. According to some sociological evidence, for example, blacks in Brazil suffer from discrimination due to ethnic identity. Discrimination officially ended in 1951 and laws exist to prohibit mention of color in police reports, employment applications, and Federal census questionnaires. Unofficially, discrimination continues. Segregation is still a current practice in the Brazilian business world, color is a basic factor in employment practices, and the Brazilian armed forces has no blacks in its hierarchy.

In what are already culturally authoritarian societies, those most consistently dominated are not surprisingly of inferior ethnic status as defined by white society, and at times by Indians and blacks themselves—although pride in being Indian or black appears to be increasing. This trend of white domination has been summarized lately in the term "internal colonialism," used by several Latin Americans in describing their societies.

The patterns of white domination over Indian and black groups dates back to the colonial period, which led to black slavery and a subjugated Indian people. Indian cultures were quite different from Iberian, being more highly stratified, relatively stable, and having unified systems of control. Compared to the highly individual Spaniard, who emphasized self-dignity, pride, and nongroup orientations, the Indian demonstrated far less individual consciousness and was more attached to land and to the community. As it turned out, the Indian orientation to authority and the Spanish drive for individual wealth in some ways conditioned these different cultural groups to a master-slave relationship even before the Spanish arrived. A cultural identity associated with subjugation (the Indians) or slavery (blacks) cannot but affect self-perceptions and politics today.

Interethnic Violence

The numbers of people killed in interethnic violence in the Third World are staggering. One assumes high casualty rates in declared wars between great powers, but not from isolated cases of ethnic civil wars. Yet the magnitude of ethnic conflict is there, showing how easy it is to kill one of "them" as opposed to one of "us"—the potential negative result of ethnic identity. More than half a million people died in a northern Arabic Moslem versus southern pagan black conflict in the Sudan during a sixteen-year civil war, before a political arrangement was reached in Februray, 1972. An estimated eighty thousand educated Hutu's were killed by the ruling Tutsi tribe in Burundi during 1972, and earlier, in 1963, it is said that twenty thousand Tutsi were killed. In the weeks following the abortive coup of October, 1965, in

Indonesia, an estimated three million people were killed, many of them Chinese at the hands of militant Moslems. An estimated two million people died in the Biafran war that ended in January, 1970. A large number of those were Ibos participating in the Biafran breakaway movement. Similarly, the Bengali-Bangladesh movement produced massacres of thousands and enormous bloodshed in East Pakistan.

How does the Latin American record of violence due to interethnic identity and antagonistic politics compare with the general Third World scene?

Interethnic violence in Latin America has not been studied extensively. This undoubtedly is due to the general absence of the ethnic group civil wars and ethnic national self-determination movements found in Africa, South Asia, and Southeast Asia. Cases of clear interethnic war, to be sure, exist in historical Latin America, including white Spanish against Indian Aztec, Mayan, and Inca tribes during the Conquest, the Yucatán caste war of 1848, the Black Rebellion in Cuba in 1912, or recent white-Indian conflict in Brazil. These exceptions to the general rule that Indians and blacks do not form self-identifying self-determination or resistance movements suggest that ethnicity or cultural-racial identity has not played the kind of role in political instability and violence experienced elsewhere.

But one wonders. Speculating with numbers and facts about ethnic composition in Latin American states yields interesting propositions on the impact of ethnicity on violence and instability. Latin America's predominantly Indian societies, for example, rank as the most violent if numbers of coups are used as the indices.[2] This is indicated in Table 3. Martin Needler argues that this correlation may arise from the Indian's "lack of social mobilization and integration into national society (which fails) to inhibit the occurrence of coups."[3]

A second proposition can be advanced. Those societies of highly mixed racial components have experienced periods of extreme violence, suggesting that the absence of large ethnically homogeneous and ethnically self-identifying groups may in part condition interethnic violence and bloodshed. This postulate is based upon the assumption that it is easier to kill one of "them" than one of "us" and that multiethnic situations are conducive to this distinction. Colombia was torn by violence between 1948 and 1953, resulting in approximately three hundred thousand killed in the famous period of *la violencia*. Cuba experienced a very high rate of killings, assassinations, and bloodshed in the late 1950s. And an estimated three to four thousand died in the streets of Santo Domingo during its 1965 civil war. These are very ethnically and cultural-racially mixed countries.

Similarly, three countries of ethnically mixed settings produced dramatic social revolutions with substantial violence. These were Mexico

TABLE 3 INCIDENCE OF COUPS IN STRONGLY INDIAN COUNTRIES, 1823-1965 and 1930-65

	Percent of Indians in Population	1823-1965	1930-65
Bolivia	70	26	10
Guatemala	55	21	8
Peru	46	27	5
Ecuador	39	27	10
Mexico	30	21	1
El Salvador	20	21	7
Latin American average		17.5	5

Sources: Martin C. Needler, "The Causality of the Latin American Coup d'Etat: Some Numbers, Some Speculations," paper prepared for the American Political Science Association meeting, Washington, D.C., September 1972, p. 16. Needler's numbers of coups are drawn from Warren Dean, "Latin American *Golpes* and Economic Fluctuations, 1823-1966," *Social Science Quarterly* 51 (June 1970): 72.

(1910), Bolivia (1952), and Cuba (1959). Interethnic conflict accompanied these revolutions, particularly in Mexico, where Indians fought to regain land earlier taken from them by white landowners; many of them battled with Emiliano Zapata and Pancho Villa, both of Indian parentage. This is not to suggest the Mexican revolution was a pure interethnic war, for Indians fought against Indians where their commanders disagreed, but the interethnic element is there.

Indians in Bolivia had awakened to a new consciousness after the Chaco War (1932-35), which exposed them to "Bolivian" national concepts and to a stake in the successful conclusion of the war. Returning from the war, many of them organized into syndicates for the purpose of renting land for cash payments. Later, political victory by the leftist-leaning *Movimiento Nacional Revolucionario* (MNR, National Revolutionary Movement) in 1952 spurred some Indians to begin sporadic land expropriation which in turn prompted the MNR to pass an agrarian reform law.

In Mexico, Bolivia, and Cuba, revolutionary policies were followed that aimed at incorporating Indians (Mexico and Bolivia) and blacks (Cuba) into the life of the state, and attempted to give them identity as Mexicans, Bolivians, or Cubans. Thus, the interethnic aspect of revolution, civil war, and incipient violence in Latin America should not be omitted from analysis. Table 4 illustrates that ethnically mixed societies have experienced periods of extreme violence, compared to the more institutionalized violence and greater stability of more homo-

TABLE 4 VIOLENCE IN ETHNICALLY MIXED SOCIETIES COMPARED TO MORE HOMOGENEOUS SOCIETIES

Country	European	Mestizo	Mulatto	Indian	Negro	High Violence*
Argentina	+90					
Bolivia	5	25		70		*
Chile	96.5			3.5		
Colombia	30	40		5	7	*
Costa Rica	90				10	
Cuba	73				26 (Negro and mulatto)	*
Dominican Rep.	28	60 (mestizo and mulatto)			11	*
Mexico	10	60		30		*
Uruguay	90	10				

* Denotes high violence.

geneous countries such as Argentina, Chile, Costa Rica, and Uruguay. However, the Chilean military coup of September, 1973, followed by military violence and repression certainly qualifies this proposition.

Meanwhile, ethnic divisions are clear in other states, accompanied by distinct ethnopolitical effects. Guyana's politics experience ethnic pressures of East Indians versus Negroes, including bombings, assaults, and houseburnings. Black Power movements in Trinidad and Tobago show the force of ethnic identity in the Caribbean, but one complicated by divisions among blacks and East Indians, the latter being both Hindu and Moslem. In summarizing this evidence, one suspects the presence of a key ethnic factor in Latin American violence to match that of world ethnopolitics, a point requiring more extensive research.

Ethnicity and Modernization in Latin America

Contrary to the predicated assimilation of diverse ethnic groups as modernization and mobilization proceeds, a thesis expounded in much political development literature, separate and distinct ethnic self-perceptions do not appear to be decreasing under these conditions in Latin America. Increased education, urbanization, transportation, communications, per capita income, and general social mobility—far from having the effect of showing ethnically different people what they have in common—brings to perception interethnic differences and intra-ethnic similarities. This trend parallels that found in South Asia, Southeast Asia, Africa, and the United States.

A number of examples illustrate how assimilation is not automatically strengthened through modernization. A growing body of literature suggests that as individuals move from a rural to an urban setting, they retain their sense of regional and ethnic focus rather than losing it in the "melting-pot" experience of the city. One researcher finds migrants to Lima, Peru, forming regional associations which officially represent their members' specific places of origin.[4] Migrants reconstitute their family, circle of friends, and community in the city based upon common place of origin. These community organizations of the city lobby in government offices and congress on behalf of the hometowns or "homelands" and their people, which indicates the political significance of one's continuing identity with his *tierra* (land) and its people rather than with a broader, mythical, in this case "Peruvian," nation of people.[5]

We know also that black unity based upon black pride is increasing under the influence of education and continued ethnic prejudice in employment.[6] So is pride in black people's achievements in the face of persistent discrimination by whiter people, and increased contact with blacks facing common obstacles to social mobility. Where the black man perceives greater sharing of identity with other Negroes, counterposed against similar prejudices and typing, the winds of common ethnic consciousness begin to blow. These changes are most visible in the British West Indies, but are also potential trends in Brazil, Colombia, and Ecuador.

One of the truly fascinating issues during the latter part of the twentieth century will be the question of Indian nationalism. Notwithstanding the possibility of passing from Indian into mestizo society, which affects a number of Indians who adopt mestizo linguistic, religious, and cultural patterns, another process appears to be at work. Rather than increased passing, the future may hold increased identity of being *Indian*. The potential of increased awareness of Indian origin may already be underway in parts of Latin America, illustrated by the Quechua nationalism now emerging around Cuzco in the south of Peru.

The modernization of cities should not be overestimated in its effects on ethnic identity. Traditional perceptions continue to operate in urban settings. Beyond the regional clubs, a visit to La Paz, Bolivia, attests to the striking continuance of Indian customs inside the city, even though forces of change have existed for more than four hundred years.[7] Beyond the cities, in hundreds of mountain valleys, many Indians continue to maintain a distinctive Indian culture and way of life. Since modernization and mobilization are never uniform throughout an entire country, clusters of traditional life must be measured against the more visible urban settings.

These examples suggest a different rate and direction of development than the postulated single ethnonational consciousness of developmentalist theories. First, tradition is strong; people do not easily acquire new ethnic self-identities. Those who do are replaced by many born into their ethnic status who do not leave. Secondly, multi-ethnonational groups may be spawned inside Latin America's states, instead of a single ethnonational consciousness. Thus, being Guyanese will be a different self-perception for Negroes than for East Indians; being Peruvian different for whites in Lima than Quechua-speaking Indians near Cuzco. Politics will be affected by these trends, and in the future may even have to make adjustments for multinational groups inside the states.

SOCIAL CLASS AND STATUS

Social class and status runs along a line from pure white to pure black and Indian. If one is whiter than others, one's horizons are typically wider in many parts of Latin America. But it is also true that sociocultural factors are a major component of social class and status. How one perceives oneself, what sort of relationships he or she might expect with others in society and politics, the range of economic and political opportunities available, and a host of political aspects are in part tied to questions of one's class and status position as defined by sociocultural norms. In identifying these norms, it should be stressed again that regional differences in classification exist throughout Latin America, including ancestry, physical type, or sociocultural traits.

A checklist of key cultural traits in class and status position would include language, education, occupation or profession, clothing worn, location and type of residence, manners and social graces, and religion.

Language

Language shapes personal identity. As an extension of the self, it conditions our learning and interpretation of nature, our impressions of reality, and our organization of the outside world. Moreover, since one identifies with one's fellow speakers, language can divide or unite a country's population, and the colonial language tends to become dominant, thus perpetuating social divisions in all parts of the world. Language also performs social functions in terms of designating class and status position. What are the specific effects in Latin America?

Language, given its identity-shaping role, affects nation-building in Latin America. In trying to build one national identity, for example, in any multilinguistic state, consider the obstacles. How does a political leader create a Guatemalan, Peruvian, or Bolivian identity when faced by multilinguistic, and hence multi-identifying, interpreting, and reasoning Indian groups? How does one even communicate with non-Spanish speaking people in the territory? To use native languages, as Quechua in the case of Peru, to instill a sense of identity with Peru and its reforms may simply encourage reaffirmation of the native psychocultural world rather than identity with a new world implied by Peruvian government programs and decrees.

Nation-building problems are only one area of the linguistic-identity-politics network of communication. As in other colonial settings, the language of power, influence, and access to expanded opportunities is typically that of the colonizers—German, French, and English in Africa; Spanish or Portuguese in Latin America. Speakers of the Indian dialects of Aymara, Quechua, or Guaraní wield far less power in Latin America within the elite political, economic, and social life of the state. Guaraní is a possible exception in Paraguay, where it is commonly used as a common tie to the Indian past.

Language is one key to maintenance of class advantages, class distinctions, and class privileges. Spanish and Portuguese are the upper- and middle-class languages in Latin America; to speak an Indian language is to be "typed" in the lower levels of society with fewer and more restricted opportunities. Indian subcultures include tribal Indians and modern Indians, the latter being possibly bilingual. Above these are peasant types who typically speak the national language, but whose vocabulary is far more limited than the upper-middle and upper-class urban and rural dwellers, whose control and mastery of the national language is superior.

If good Spanish and Portuguese, for example, are the languages used by the influential and powerful in politics, economics, and society, then its possession and mastery are a key to many aspects of an individual's life. It promotes social and economic mobility; it helps access to power, wealth, or at least a well-paying job; and it is a necessity in most countries for participation in modern political processes, there being a literacy requirement for voting in some Latin American states. Mastery of the country's main language may be critical in guaranteeing defense against encroachments by others, since legal processes are conducted, and administrative documents written, in it.

The problem of social mobility through language alone is not easily conquered. New habits and ways of thought must be learned, and the old must be forgotten in the jump from Indian to mestizo status. This is difficult, given the imprint of the native language and culture, in addition to possibly incurring ostracism from the old linguistic group with no absolute guarantee of acceptance by the new. Not all Indians are prepared to take this gamble, even if they have the urge to do so, and not all will be able to emulate Benito Juárez, the full-blooded Zapotec Indian who became president of Mexico in the nineteenth century.

Education

Like language, education is a basic factor of personal identity and status in Latin America. Lower-middle and lower-class parents typically envision education as a central, if not the central, path to upward mobility for their children. This path, unfortunately, is fraught with a high drop-out rate often due to its cost and the parent's low economic positions. Upper-middle and upper-class sons and daughters place strong emphasis on academic degrees. As symbols of educational attainment, degrees help to identify one's position in society and consequently are heavily in use, appearing on calling cards, stationery, name plates, front doors, in salutations, and in the rhetoric of government and politics. Such symbols include "Dr.," "Ing." (engineer), "Lic." (lawyer), "Arq." (architect), and "Prof." (teacher).

Although increasing numbers of young people in some Latin American countries are selecting careers for their utility in building more economically advanced societies, the traditional selection of fields of study for reasons of prestige and social mobility remains enormously strong. The university degree is typically seen as the route to professional middle-class status if one comes from the lower middle class of artisans, shopkeepers, and white-collar workers. Higher education for these and others is a major route of social mobility, and if one is already from the established upper-middle or upper class, the university degree helps to preserve one's status. The prestigious function performed by education has led to what William S. Stokes calls the "cult of the doctor," a force so strong that lower-class individuals will frequently address upper-class people as "doctor" whether they have the degree or not.

Prestigious fields in Latin America tend to be law, medicine, engineering, and the humanities. Aesthetic pursuits are deemed of high value, hence the high ranking of more aesthetic subjects—part of the Latin American emphasis on transcendental values. Degrees in these fields frequently become the necessary symbols for admission into positions of influence, power, and wealth in the government or business bureaucracy. Less prestigious, but certainly needed, professions are agronomy, mining engineering, public administration, and nursing and technicians of various types are always in demand. Practical scientific studies and research, in short, are generally underdeveloped, in part owing to the continuing attraction of traditionally prestigious careers, and the weight of the transcendental heritage.

Given the role of education, the illiterate sector of the population is far down on the scale of status identity, and hence with substantially less power and influence to shape their destinies. Those of the lowest strata are, as they have been since the Conquest, the indigenous illiterate Indians. Higher up are the more literate, with mixed Indian, black, and European ancestry, who try to follow a predominantly European way of life that includes at least some primary education to push them into the "literate" identity. These include mestizos, ladinos, mulattoes, and other designated middle-sector groups—the fastest growing classes of Latin America's populations.

Education, like language, is a route for upward mobility. In Guatemala and other countries, for example, such lower levels of bureaucracy as the service and security personnel are composed of rural laboring and *campesino* families. Since the definition of Indian refers as much (perhaps more in some areas) to cultural as to biological criteria, the Indian who can speak Spanish, attain some education, drop the Indian costume, and attain even a low-level bureaucratic position can be said to have passed into mestizo or ladino (mestizo in Guatemala) society. Another example of education leading to upward mobility is the newer category of bureaucratic personnel in Latin American life called the *técnico* (technically trained). These are typically sons and daughters of lower-class families trained in special skills, whose commitments to public service appear stronger than many other types of bureaucrats.

Occupation and Profession

In terms of occupation or profession, upper-class identity is associated with intellectual activities, lower status with manual labor. The Iberian cultural concept that work is not noble, early associated with the use of Indians to do the Spaniard's manual labor on landed estates and in the mines, shows some erosion over the past several hundred years, but its tenacity is monumental. That work is debasing and leisure or creative intellectual activity is enobling remains strong and is evidenced in typical contempt for terms such as manual labor, physical labor, mechanical labor, or working with the hands.

One avenue of social entry from lower manual-labor identity into higher status is through change in occupation. A typical pattern occurs through urbanization, where those formerly associated with agricultural *campesino* or peasant activities attempt to find new, non-manual employment. The next level up from manual labor includes such jobs as small merchant (perhaps in an urban slum area or shantytown), retail or wholesale merchant, proprietor of an artisan workshop, service trade employment, or petty officialdom, which might include standing guard at a government functionary's office or ushering visitors to the official's inner sanctum. It is not strange to see a number of these types floating around government bureaucracies in Latin American cities, particularly capital cities. Frequently, however, economic necessity forces many of these people to return to some form of manual labor for the ruling elites or for more successful middle groups.

The higher-status professions are naturally associated with non-manual labor. Their practitioners include lawyers, doctors, engineers (more theoretical than practical), poets, priests, and the upper brackets of governmental bureaucracy. White-collar jobs are more prestigious than blue-collar, and education is the route to a nonmanual labor position in both public and private sectors.

Clothing, Residence, Manners, and Religion

Type of clothing worn, location and type of residence, manners and social graces, and religion also affect one's identity and interpersonal contacts. They condition the flow and direction of power and influence within Latin America's societies.

One dresses formally if seeking to preserve or attain middle- or upper-class identity. This includes wearing a suit, tie, and highly polished shoes—hence the plethora of shoe-shine boys and men with incredibly decorated shoe-shine boxes and booths. The Indian must divest himself of Indian clothing to gain higher status, which some do. But to qualify this process, it should be noted that in Bolivia, while an Indian man may have turned to Western clothing, his spouse, walking by his side, may remain in traditional Indian clothing. Upper classes, it should be added, sometimes flout the rules of dress.

Prestigious residences exist in the urban areas. In manners and social graces, formality and ceremony is the essence; mastery of such social graces as the art of polite and expressive conversation in Spanish or Portuguese at weddings, church services, or political gatherings is critical to higher-status identity. Upper-status religion is Roman Catholic, lower class the pure or mixed Indian-Roman Catholic worship where the indigenous and Iberian interact.

SOCIOECONOMIC CLASS

The cultural factors of identity indicate the attention paid to social class or status in Latin America. One's self-identity is conditioned by awareness of and response to one's social-sector position within society. Interpersonal relations, social distance between individuals and groups, the division of people into haves and have-nots, and into those with and without power, are class-based or class-related. Beyond these general observations, however, the precise role of class identity in Latin American politics is difficult to nail down.

The problem is not so much identifying which people are in the upper, lower, or middle classes—although some debate exists even here—but rather assessing the impact of class status on personal identity and politics. It is possible to identify basic changes in the class structure of Latin American countries since independence, along with related change in the structure of political action. It is also possible to indicate roughly what types of people fall into upper, lower, and middle classes, and to suggest the effect of this structure on sources of power and influence. Beyond this, we enter the realm of attitudes, values, and beliefs that may or may not be conditioned by class position—an issue about which little consensus exists.

Class structures and relations have changed in Latin America, albeit at different rates in different countries, since the early nineteenth century when these states first gained political independence. During the colonial period and much of the nineteenth century, Latin America was dominated by a typically rigid two-class system. It was composed of the aristocratic landholding groups, plus the influential Hispano-Catholic Church and military organizations, on the one hand, and a lower class of landless or small landowning peasants and domestic servants, on the other.

Politics in those days reflected this social system. Political structures were not highly diversified, decentralized, nor open to large scale political participation. Elites and people of influence were those of agrarian wealth and religious influence, or were located in the higher echelons of the military, a source of coercive influence and personal status. The bases of political power were highly stratified and limited; the numbers of influential groups were few.

Latin America's class structure today is more complicated, as is its system of politics, largely owing to the affect of economic development upon class structure. As industrialization occurs, as it has in Mexico, Cuba, parts of Central America, Venezuela, Colombia, Chile, Argentina, and Brazil, it opens new opportunities in employment. The effects of industrialization and economic development on the class structure is typically shown in the trends of economically active activities found in a population over time, as the economy moves away from a purely agrarian base. New divisions occur within the upper and lower sectors, and an emerging middle sector is spawned between them. Much debate surrounds the identity, composition, and political effects of this new middle class. Some students argue that it is the source of innovation, modernization, and positive political change, while others see it as an extension of the upper classes, composed of people imitating upper-class values, and essentially a force of stagnation and underdevelopment.

Contemporary divisions of society in many Latin American countries are composed of an old and new upper class; a lower class divided into at least three types of people; and between them a broad middle-sector group embracing a large number of people with different white-collar occupations. The old upper classes are the remnants of the great landowners, those whose present or past heritage and identity go back to the large *latifundias*. The newer upper classes are composed of essentially self-made men and their families, who have accumulated fortunes through business, industry, commerce, or government, and who, like the older upper classes, have claims to power, status, and prestige.[8]

Three types of people characterize the lower classes. There are peasants and agricultural workers, industrial workers in factories and extractive industries (some of whom are fairly well off compared to the other two groups), and slum dwellers, who surround most capital cities in Latin America. These people typically earn their living by manual labor and are not completely literate. Much has been written about them, given their rapid expansion in recent years due to population explosion, high rates of unemployment, stagnating economies, and their limited base of political power to exert influence.

The middle classes are the rest of the people not within these two polar groupings. They range from school teachers, village storekeepers, and regular army officers to intellectuals, clerks, bureaucratic leaders in labor unions, agrarian leagues, and mass political organizations, technicians, professional people and skilled laborers, university professors, and professional politicians. The precise nature and function of this middle class is subject to much debate in Latin American studies. But this class is sharply on the increase in Mexico, Costa Rica, Argentina, Brazil, Venezuela, Colombia, Uruguay, and Chile since World War II. Nicaragua and Paraguay, on the other hand, retain much of the nineteenth-century two-class structure. Cuba lost much of its middle classes through emigration after Castro's assumption of power.

The size of the middle class varies enormously from country to country. It is estimated to have grown in Mexico between 1895 and 1960 from 7.8 percent to 33.5 percent of the total population. The lower class is estimated to have declined from 90.7 to 40.0 percent during that period. The middle class is estimated at about 50 percent or more of the population in Argentina, Chile, and Uruguay, and in Brazil at about 30 percent. A major cue to upper-class status are the landholding and wealth distribution patterns discussed in the country profiles of Chapters 3 and 4. In countries like Nicaragua, Paraguay, and Haiti a very small percentage of the population enjoys upper-class status with a concomitantly huge proportion in lower-class categories.

The Middle-Class Debate

Some observers insist that the middle classes represent the hope of Latin America. The middle classes, in their view, are urban, strong advocates of industrialization as a key solution to national problems, interested in advancing higher and professional education, support agrarian reform, and are intensely nationalistic, often in highly anti-American forms. This positive interpretation holds that the middle sectors favor labor unions and social legislation, public over private foreign investment in domestic sectors, governmental intervention, and believe strongly in democracy with liberal and socialist overtones. They see themselves in this view as innovators of change and reform. They are confident and progressive.

The rise of the middle classes in this positive assessment is associated with the development of political parties that began to take the initiative in social, economic, and political reforms. These parties include the Democratic Action Party of Venezuela (AD), the National Liberation Party of Costa Rica, the *Alianza Popular Revolucionaria Americana* (APRA) of Peru, the Institutionalized Revolutionary Party of Mexico (PRI), Christian Democratic parties throughout Latin America, notably in Chile, and even the Marxist-Leninist parties, including the traditional Communist parties of Argentina, Chile, Brazil, and Cuba. The thesis is that Latin American development and political change toward greater equalitarianism and sharing in national economic, social, and political life rests upon middle-sector identity.

The rise of the middle sectors and their positive contribution toward equalizing the control over and distribution of valued resources, toward checking and balancing political power through the creation of new power bases, and instituting some form of separation of power and influence is associated with another major thesis. That thesis is the impact of incipient industrialization, which is supposed to break down traditional class structures and diffuse power through the increased functional specialization of labor. Industry, commerce, and technology, for example, move people from the rural to urban areas, break down the traditional occupational structure of heavy agrarian employment, and create new demands for such skills as electricians, technicians, plumbers, governmental employees, bankers, teachers, clerks, all of which potentially can form into unions or mass-based organizations. Industrialization thus creates new bases of power. It should be remembered that the positive assessment of middle-class emergence suggests not only that these new power bases have developed, which is true, but that the leaders and followers in them are oriented toward a greater spread of opportunities, wealth, and influence for all people within society.

The middle-class argument is this: Not only has structural change occurred within Latin America's class relations and identity, but the new middle sectors have distinctly different attitudes than the old upper classes. The new middle classes are presumed to be progressive and modern. Their identities and attitudes are deemed to be geared to a kind of individualism based upon merit, skills, and achievement, not upon ascription, particularism, and fatalism. Equal opportunity for political participation will therefore make the system more equitable. Pragmatism and public responsibility in planning, conflict resolution, and decision making replace fatalism and attention to strictly parochial interests. The middle-sector people presumably identify with a common nation, politically organized within a state under which all men are ostensibly equal. An expanding middle class brings with it universalist, not particularist, values, empathy with a broad range of others rather than a closed group, and tremendous initiative for social and political reforms. These reforms will lead toward more pluralistic, equalitarian, and democratic systems, and a redistribution of valued resources from the elite haves to the less influential have-nots.

A different assessment of middle-class identity can also be made. This thesis argues that it is possible to distinguish a growing middle-income sector, but that its impact as a force of change has been far exaggerated. The basic negative evaluations of middle-class identity are many. The better known ones are that the concept of a middle class contains many ambiguities, including the lack of any personal class identity by those presumed to be its members; that its members are nothing less than an extension of the old and new upper classes in terms of goals (money, status, power, and influence), economic position, and dominance over others, and occupy not a middle position, but rather in many countries a ruling one as politicians, entrepreneurs, financiers, and industrialists; and finally that the attitudes, values, and behavior of the middle sectors are existentially *traditional*, i.e., status seeking, concerned with prestige, personalistic, family oriented, and authoritarian.

It must be said that the negative evaluation is extremely persuasive. As numerous works on the rising middle sectors attest, their activities, attitudes, and values tend to be in large measure conformist, traditional, and little prepared psychologically to carry out the reforms needed for advanced economic development.

The rise of the middle classes is not, unfortunately, paralleled by the demise of traditional influences at work in Latin American politics. Patronage, weakness in organizational capability, elite factionalism, personal interests, manipulation of job rewards, licenses, and contracts by government officials continue under middle-class influence. Fear of making decisions, inability to delegate authority, desire to be of service to superiors, and the search for personal alliances to guarantee job security and elite status remain part of the middle-class scene. Many people of the so-called "modern," middle-sector in Latin America re-enact the strong traditional thrust of maintaining the status quo, show an unwillingness to share economic rewards and political power with the popular sector, and continue to identify with authoritarian traditions.

This is not to say that progressive change in government life and public bureaucracy is completely impeded due to traditional middle-sector identity. To be totally negative or totally positive in assessing the middle sectors is to miss the complicated variety of experiences and histories of the different Latin American countries. We noted, for example, the important evolution of a new type of middle-sector person—the *técnico*—an indication of the growing professionalization of the public bureaucracy, planning, and decision making. Increased professional training and education may also help to spawn a growing national consciousness, a missing dimension of identity in Latin America. The recent histories of some countries, especially Chile, Cuba, Mexico, Peru, and Venezuela, moreover, show great commitment to development through creation of development institutions, development ideologies, and the training of human resources to solve problems.

These changes involve issues of personal identity, in this case elite identity with the problems of change rather than acceptance of the status quo. Naturally, personal identity is not going to change totally overnight. Equally important, it is sharply conditioned by traditional cultural values and attitudes. It is the slowness of identity changes, the different experiences of different countries, plus the intricate blending of new and old that makes assessment so difficult and that raises so much scholarly debate over the subject.

NOTES

1. Marvin Harris, "Referential Ambiguity in the Calculus of Brazilian Identity," *Southwestern Journal of Anthropology* 26 (Spring 1970): 3-5.
2. Martin C. Needler, "The Causality of the Latin American Coup d'Etat: Some Numbers, Some Speculations." Paper prepared for the American Political Science Association Meeting, Washington, D.C., September 1972.
3. *Ibid.*, p. 17.
4. Paul L. Doughty, "Behind the Back of the City: 'Provincial Life in

Lima, Peru,'" in *Peasants in Cities: Readings and Anthropology of Urbanization,* ed. William Mangin (Boston: Houghton Mifflin, 1970), p. 33; see also William Mangin, "The Role of Regional Associations in the Adaptation of Rural Migrants to Cities in Peru," *op. cit.,* where the multiplicity of clubs in urban settings is discussed.

5. Doughty, *op. cit.,* p. 32.

6. On this specific issue, see Jean-Claude Garcia-Zamour, "Social Mobility of Negroes in Brazil," *Journal of International Studies and World Affairs* 12 (April 1970): 242-54; Thomas A. Johnson, "Black Power Flourishing in the Caribbean," *New York Times,* April 24, 1970; and John Biesanz, "Cultural and Economic Factors in Panamanian Race Relations," *American Sociology Review* 14 (December 1949): 775.

7. On Indian resistance to change, see Frank Tannenbaum, "Agrarismo, Indianismo, and Nacionalismo," *Hispanic American Historical Review* 23 (August 1943): 394-423. Any of us who have researched in La Paz cannot but agree with Tannenbaum.

8. John P. Gillin, "Some Signposts for Policy," in Richard N. Adams, et al., *Social Change in Latin America Today* (New York: Harper and Brothers, 1960), pp. 22-23.

Suggested Readings

Bastide, Roger and Pierre van den Berghe. "Stereotypes, Norms and Interracial Behavior in São Paulo, Brazil," *American Sociological Review* 22 (December 1957): 689-94.

Bretton, Henry. "Language, Politics, and Political Science," in *Language and Politics,* ed. William M. O'Barr. The Hague: Mouton, 1975.

Fernandez, Florestan. "The Weight of the Past," *Daedalus* 96 (Spring 1967): 560-79.

Garcia-Zamour, Jean-Claude. "Social Mobility of Negroes in Brazil," *Journal of Inter-American Studies and World Affairs* 12 (April 1970): 242-55.

Harris, Marvin. *Patterns of Race in the Americas.* New York: Walker, 1964.

Hoetink, H. *The Two Variants in Caribbean Race Relations.* New York: Oxford University Press, 1967.

Morner, Magnus. *Race Mixture in the History of Latin America.* Boston: Little, Brown, 1967.

Pitt-Rivers, Julian. "Race, Color, and Class in Central America and the Andes," *Daedalus* 94 (Spring 1967): 542-59.

Tannenbaum, Frank. "Agrarismo, Indianismo, and Nacionalismo," *Hispanic American Historical Review* 23 (August 1943): 394-423.

Van den Berghe, Pierre. "Racialism and Assimilation in Africa and the Americas," *Southwestern Journal of Anthropology* 19 (Winter 1963): 424-33.

Wagley, Charles. "On the Concept of Social Race in the Americas," pp. 531-45 in *Contemporary Cultures and Societies of Latin America,* ed. Dwight B. Heath and Richard N. Adams. New York: Random House, 1965.

Political
Patterns

Eight

Constitutions and Presidents

Each Latin American country has a written constitution that divides the government into executive, legislative, and judicial branches, all theoretically equal and coordinate in power. Although most of these constitutions resemble that of the United States, having a system of checks and balances and separation of powers, in fact the executive branch predominates in Latin America, following the Hispanic tradition of the strong leader, with the legislative and judiciary taking a secondary position. The legislatures, which typically cater to the president's whims, are of two forms. One form is the unicameral, one house, system, as in Costa Rica, El Salvador, and Guatemala. The other form is bicameral, with an upper and lower house, as in Mexico and Venezuela.

The overall organization of government also takes one of two forms. One is federal, with decentralized power theoretically being of prime importance through states and provinces exercising a good deal of self-government, as in Argentina, Mexico, Brazil, and Venezuela. Another is unitary, where the central authority in the country's capital exercises full and complete power over the whole land, as in Costa Rica, El Salvador, Paraguay, and Honduras. The federal countries of Argentina, Mexico, Brazil, and Venezuela in fact tend to operate as centralized forms of government—again illustrating the centralized nature of power in Latin American government, and the importance of capital cities.

The constitutions seem to guarantee *limited* government, where power is proscribed and procedures are prescribed. They declare that the people are sovereign, and they include extensive detail about citizen rights, such as freedom of speech and press, freedom of religion, the rights of persons accused of crimes, social and economic guarantees, and the right of political asylum. Recent constitutions, moreover, have paid extensive attention to social and economic functions such as social welfare, land reform, and the protection of labor, thereby at least indicating increased awareness of problems of development and attention to their goals.[1] The Mexican constitution of 1917, which in many ways set the tone for other post-World War II constitutions in Latin America, as, for example, Venezuela's 1961 version, subordinates private ownership of property to general social welfare, guarantees free public education, and protects labor. All this is spelled out in elaborate detail, such as the guarantee of eight hours as the maximum working day, seven hours for night work, six hours for children over twelve and under sixteen, and one day's rest for every six days work. Minimum wages also are guaranteed in the Mexican constitution, and it prohibits payment in script or merchandise rather than legal currency. When it comes to issues relevant to economic development, then, Latin America's constitutions can be highly specific.

Constitutions, however, are misleading when it comes to the political dynamics operating within governmental structures. Political struggles, rather than involving the checking and balancing of legislatures and executives, more typically take other forms. These include political infighting within a dominating military (Brazil and Bolivia), palace intrigue within a dictatorship (Haiti), and clashes of various interest and pressure groups contending for power and dramatic change, such as guerrillas, trade unions, students, or peasants—assassinating, kidnapping, striking, marching, and demonstrating in support of their objectives—against the established power contenders protecting their own place in economic and political life. In countries where society is less industrialized and economically developed and where reformist leaders and movements have not emerged (Nicaragua and Paraguay, for example), groups pressing for change are virtually nonexistent, and the country is dominated largely by the older military and landed interests.[2] Thus, constitutions may outline systems of democratic equalitarian politics with strong development overtones, when in fact the real issues are what political leaders, reformist movements, and established power contenders are doing, how they mobilize their forces, and whether or not the matrix of pressure groups and their power capabilities are changing.

The actual politics of a country differ from stated constitutional forms in other respects. Chief executives often invoke special powers, such as the decree and state of siege, not to reshape government policy toward development, but to nullify many constitutionally guaranteed civil rights. This occurred in Colombia, Chile, and Argentina in the early to mid-1970s, as presidents sought to curb civil strife generated by politically antagonistic interest and pressure groups. Constitutions normally make provision for civil unrest and give presidents special powers, such as the state of siege, to deal with it—which frequently off-sets other guaranteed civil rights. Local *caudillos* and *caciques,* more-over, maintain order in many outlying regions of Latin American coun-tries and their power outweighs government guarantees of social and economic improvement for all citizens, as well as the general priority of human rights over individual property rights. Personalism and au-thoritarianism also seep into everyday political life, from capital city to rural province, reflecting the region's political culture, rather than the constitutional norms of equalitarianism and republicanism.

Latin America's constitutions must be viewed in part as descriptions of governmental structures—for the governments are in fact divided into three branches—and in part as a set of goals and objectives—in-cluding development—rather than as procedural ground rules and op-erative norms for the political system. Excessive in detail, lengthy, and elaborate in stating the functions of government in the lives of the citi-zenry, they show Hispanic transcendentalism—stress on words, ideals, and elegance of expression. Many of the ideals of equalitarianism, rep-resentation, checks and balances, and separation of power of course are imported. They are drawn from the Spanish constitution of 1812, from France after its revolution, and from the United States constitu-tion—all of which became part of Latin America's goals and objectives after independence from Spain had been won. Later constitutions be-gan to incorporate social and economic objectives, showing a strong preoccupation with development problems, starting in the 1930s and continuing during the years following World War II. It should be re-membered in viewing Latin America's constitutions that the under-lying culture tends to stress the importance of stating objectives rather than taking steps toward attaining them, and this declaration of intent shows itself in the constitutions. Yet in many countries the goals of constitutions began to be matched by deeds; Mexico first after its 1910 revolution, then Bolivia in 1952, and later other countries such as Chile (before 1973), Peru, Venezuela, Brazil, and some countries in Central America.

Many constitutions are promulgated in Latin America—more than two hundred by 1965, averaging ten to a country—making these states different from most Western democracies. How does one account for such a large turnover? In addition to the cultural and historic under-pinnings above, new constitutions legitimize new governments and set forth their ideals and objectives. They thus tend to reflect liberal or conservative trends within a country and establish the philosophic base of the new government.

To get into the substance of Latin America's political dynamics, we must examine the nature of executive predominance and the clash of personalities, interest groups, and political parties more in detail. This chapter concentrates on executive predominance while the following looks at interest groups.

EXECUTIVE PREDOMINANCE

Latin American chief executives hold supreme power for a number of reasons, one of which is the impact of tradition.[3] Admittedly infatuated with equalitarian and republican ideals on attaining independence, the new countries were none the less inheritors of hundreds of years of centralized executive power. This heritage extended back to the Iberian monarchs who exercised absolute centralized control through the viceroy, a kind of regional king. The de facto political culture, then, is one of a tradition lacking strong representative institutions, but per-meated with authoritarian attitudes and values, and a cult of central-ized power. The strong leader is found throughout Latin America's nineteenth- and twentieth-century politics, and modern executives are not immune to this heritage. As part of this Hispanic tradition, modern chief executives control a number of political resources.

Command Over Political Resources

Political resources are those valued elements used to exercise power in society. They include, among others, legal rights, money, jobs, patron-age, personality, ethnic and racial status, and prestige. Their control and distribution vary from one country to the next, but are never equally controlled or divided. Yet one thing is clear. The chief execu-tive's command over them is vast, and he (or she) is in the driver's seat when it comes to the politics of governing.*

The president controls the formal legal resources allocated to him by

---

* On the death of Juan D. Perón, July 1, 1974, at age 78, his wife Isabel Perón, 43, assumed presidential power to become the first female chief of state in the Americas.

the constitution, as well as informal ones not included in that document. His formal legal powers are immense, far greater than those at the disposal of the president of the United States, and his informal power is broad.

Commander in Chief

A Latin American president is the commander in chief of the armed forces, charged with the responsibility for maintaining internal order and defending the state against external aggression. This power is potentially enormous, given the extraordinary role played by the military in preserving internal order, compared to its less expansive activities in external defense. The power of the military to back up presidential authority, and hence presidential power, in internal affairs cannot be underestimated. Salvador Allende, for example, brought the military into his cabinet in late 1972 and also in 1973 as a means of enforcing his domestic policies, one of which at the time was a newly passed gun-control law to quell civil violence.

Yet the military eventually overthrew Allende, as military organizations have overthrown many a civilian and military president, suggesting that being commander in chief can be a mixed blessing. What happens to the military during a president's administration can lead to blame or praise of the president. Should military budgets fall or military perquisites (salaries, land and commercial rewards, retirement benefits) decline, military leaders can easily become restless, as they did under President Juan Bosch in the Dominican Republic during the mid-1960s. As an established contender for power with recognized capabilities, they are a force to be reckoned with by both civilian and military presidents, whether they be reformist or conservative in their views. Even military presidents face disaffection within their own establishments, frequently divided between reformist or conservative officers who yearn for power themselves. President Hugo Bánzer, a conservative president, faced these problems in Bolivia, as did President Velasco Alvarado, a reformist, in Peru, during the early 1970s.

A number of methods have been adopted by civilian and military chief executives to keep their military establishments happy or somehow neutralize their potential as a threat to overturn the presidency during a period of reformist or conservative change. These methods include keeping the military budget and perquisites high, rotating officers around command posts to avoid their building a base of power, building one's own faction and power base within the military, or establishing a nonmilitary base of power through another interest group, as Perón in Argentina, Vargas in Brazil, and Lázaro Cárdenas in Mexico did through the laboring classes. Colonel Arturo Armand Molina, President of El Salvador, coming to power in February, 1972, strengthened his hand over the military by sending potential rivals abroad as ambassadors.

Appointment and Removal Power

The president has virtually unlimited power to appoint administrative officials and government employees. The president and his men exert almost complete control over the tenure of high-ranking government employees, as well as their salaries, promotions, pensions, and leaves of absence. In the federal states, moreover, the president has the power to select his own state appointees. This appointment and removal power is different from the president's power in the United States. It goes deeper into the bureaucracy, is traditionally sanctioned by the senate without opposition,* and is not restricted by a highly organized civil service under which promotions occur by merit or universal examinations. The civil service operates through political paths and patronage when it comes to appointments and promotions.

One can imagine how important this power over appointment and removal is, because it affects patronage at all levels of government. Its use as a means to influence other people's compliance, opinion, and support is understandable. President Luís Echeverría of Mexico, for example, personally intervened in the eastern state of Veracruz in April, 1973, to determine who should be the PRI (Institutional Revolutionary Party, the government party) candidate in the upcoming gubernatorial election (which meant who would be the new governor, since the PRI candidate always wins). The new president of Venezuela, Carlos Andrés Pérez, followed tradition by appointing men of his own party (Democratic Action) to his key ministries, and the crucial Ministry of Mines and Hydrocarbons went to a technician without political weight. This indicated that the new president intended to manage the oil policy himself, and it shows that executives can enhance their power to spur or retard the development process. How, when, and where they use the appointment power, as well as their decree power, depends upon their own power base and the nature of other power contenders within the political system. All groups, whether reformist or conservative, are affected by executive decisions that alter or maintain the distribution of the state's goods and services.

---

* Latin American senates, as in Mexico, must by the constitution approve the appointment of high officials, such as ambassadors, ministers, and high-court judges, but the president's desires are typically served.

Decree Power

The decree power is another legal, political resource possessed by Latin American presidents, and it is enormous. Laws are formulated in rather general terms, as they are in democratic states, to allow the president discretion for implementing them through administrative regulations. This general principle has been greatly extended by Latin American presidents, who issue decrees to cover practically any matter of legislation they wish, thus translating the decree authority into extensive power applied in almost unlimited form, unlike in other Western democracies. The ranges of circumstances in which it can be used are shown by Mexico where most of the important legislation between 1920-38—years of extraordinary development—was accomplished by decree-law drafted by the president under authority of powers delegated by Congress. President Carlos Castillo Armas governed by decree in Guatamala in 1954-56, issuing nearly six hundred decrees. Given the president's control over the congress in most of the Latin American countries, and in many cases the virtual gift of law-making power to the president, whose wishes are then ratified by the legislature, the chief executive's decree power is truly enormous.

Presidential use of decree power is extensive. President Juan Perón issued decree-law 1774 in 1973 to ban the import of any kind of material that could contribute to formation of ideologies that were "against the republican and representative form of government." This decree empowered customs officials to decide what literature, tapes, or films should be stopped at the border. The decree power in this case allowed the president to control public opinion.

The Chilean military junta that overthrew Salvador Allende in September, 1973, used decree powers to increase the work week, dissolve the national congress, and curtail political opposition by outlawing all political parties that had supported the former president. The latter decree affected the Communist, Socialist, and Popular Socialist Party, part of the Radical Party, the Christian Left, and the Independent Popular Action.

President Velasco Alvarado of Peru used the decree power to accomplish a number of reforms, including the nationalization of insurance companies during the summer of 1973. The decree power has also been used to close down opposition (and to control all) radio or television stations, curtail various political activities, provide amnesty for political prisoners, deport undesirable political activists, and expand the economic role of the state by such actions as nationalizing domestic and foreign businesses. Another use of decrees is to acquire juridical power, as has been done in Brazil since 1968. The executive virtually placed itself above the law then by Institutional Act 5, leading to many complaints of physical abuse and incommunicado detentions without legal help. The point is that all Latin American legislatures delegate power to the executive to issue decrees to implement the laws, and in many cases to draft laws or whole codes of law—all of which leads to the extensive use of the decree power.

State of Siege

Power to declare a state of siege is an additional legal, political resource showing traditional Hispanic sensitivity to political instability. It allows the president, with the consent of the legislature if it is in session, to suspend individual freedoms and constitutional guarantees. Its origins lie in the French institution of *etat de siege,* used to contain threats to the public order. The *estado-de-sitio* power, as one might expect, lends itself to abuse since it can be invoked not only if the state is threatened by external invasion, but also for serious internal disturbances that threaten the president.

Extensive adoption of the state of siege throughout Latin America, used almost any time internal disorder threatens, has perverted it into a broad executive power dominating the legislative and judiciary branches of government and frequently curtailing human and civil rights. The state of siege, in effect, gives the military the right to intervene on questions relating to public order, such as strikes, student demonstrations, and peasant protests. It can be perverted easily into brutal repression, summary executions, use of terror tactics in interrogation, detainment of thousands of people in jails, military installations, and sports arenas without charges, and suppression of all forms of opposition—all of these occurred in Chile after the fall of Salvador Allende. It can also justify the killing of unarmed demonstrators, as occurred in Cochabamba, Bolivia, in January, 1974, and other atrocities.

When the storm clouds of opposition darken over a ruling regime, the state of siege is routinely invoked. It limits, among other things, vehicle and pedestrian traffic—one method of curtailing organizational meetings and mass demonstrations. State-of-siege power thus legitimizes the use of physical force to squelch opposition. Student protests in support of arrested teachers in Cuzco, Peru, in November, 1973, for example, led to a state of siege in Cuzco during which the government was placed under the command of General José Villalobos, the local garrison commander. Nicaragua went under martial law after December, 1974, when guerrillas seized twelve prominent Nicaraguans at a Christmas party and exchanged them for fourteen political prisoners, who were flown to Cuba. After that all constitutional guarantees were suspended by President Somoza, who also imposed censorship of press and broadcasting. States of siege may be of short or long duration. The

Colombian government announced in December, 1973, that it was lifting a twenty-five year state of siege! The state was applied again by President Alfonso López Michelsen in July, 1975, as part of an anti-bandit drive.

Finance and the Economy

The power of the executive branch in Latin America has grown enormously during the years since World War II due to another important reason: the increased role of government in the economy. The evolving accent on economic development, particularly during the 1960s, brought about the expansion of government agencies to deal with developmental problems. These generally come under the control of the executive branch. Nationalization of domestic and foreign business, for example, lengthen a president's shadow over his state's economic system, as do an increase in the size and scope of social welfare, educational, and health and housing agencies.

The president's political resources in the financial and economic domain are large. Delegated wide discretion and authority to use public tax money allocated to the central government, the chief executive's office grants export licenses, government bank loans, and the rights to construct public projects (such as roads and irrigation outlets). Patronage naturally follows. Secondly, the new development agencies created to oversee economic growth are under executive jurisdiction, which means more money, patronage, and influence. With increasing emphasis on agrarian reform, social welfare, public education, health, and housing, expanded executive power in the future is likely.

Legislative Powers

The executive has a number of legislative powers which augment his list of political resources. In addition to legislation by decree, he is usually authorized by the constitution to initiate specific kinds of legislation. These deal with the budget, new positions in the executive office, the armed forces, and regulating government employees. President Juan Bordaberry of Uruguay, for example, announced a 33 percent wage increase, higher fuel prices, and a general increase in the price of consumer goods and services in January, 1974. Latin American chief executives also can veto legislation, as can the United States' president.

The range of formal legal powers is wide, and it gives the Latin American president tremendous control over political resources. These in turn allow him great latitude in the art of influencing and legitimizing his rule. They form an array of legal means by which to gain compliance and support.

POLITICAL STRUCTURE AND PROCESSES: INFORMAL POWERS

The nature of Latin American political structures and processes augment presidential power. The president is elected by a popular vote, making him one of the leading politicians in the country and a dominant political figure. Given the role of *personalismo* in Latin America, this role is particularly strong. Latin American presidents are frequently seen as the big patron or largest *caudillo* within the country by the masses at large. Equally important are the subordinate roles played by Latin American legislatures and judiciaries.

Legislatures

The legislatures, as already noted, tend to be weak, notwithstanding the check-and-balance role assigned to them by most Latin American constitutions.[4] A number of circumstances help account for weakened legislatures. Parties tend to proliferate around personalities and narrow political interests. Voters switch party identification rather freely from one election to the next, and parties often fall apart after elections. Strong participation in political parties drops rapidly outside such core areas as the capital city or second largest city. Factionalism within legislatures is strong because of the emphasis that is put on personalities as opposed to programs.

These characteristics of the legislature make political bargaining and tight congressional organization extremely difficult. Given the weak political-party base—in terms of participation, programs, institutions, and organizations—effective brokerage and interest-group politics does not come easy. The proliferation of parties, moreover, adds to the problem of conducting and organizing matters which come before the legislature. The formal legislative powers granted to the congress—levying and collecting taxes, control over appropriations for the armed services, regulating domestic and foreign commerce, industry, and agriculture, among others—are weakened by the realities of the political process. Political resources available to legislatures are fewer than those at the president's disposal, and even these resources are unequally controlled and divided.

This is not to say that all legislatures are totally without power or that they never challenge the executive branch. The Chilean congress, before the onset of the military dictatorship after September, 1973, was well known for its role in playing an independent part in expressing opinions different from the president and in creating a major obstacle in the president's path when he wanted specific legislation passed. Congress also played a strong role in Uruguay before its dissolution by President Juan Bordaberry—pressured by the military—in June, 1973. Costa Rica shows similar trends of strong congressional roles. The legislative branches in Latin America, moreover, have effective power over a number of areas, such as levying taxes to support the government (but not in any way likely to hurt the upper classes if large landowners are the principal congressmen, as is true in a number of countries), appropriation power to support the military, control over riverine, land, and maritime trade with foreign countries, and passing laws governing the conduct of elections. In some cases the legislative branch may even select the president of the country if election results are inconclusive, as it did in the case of Salvadore Allende in Chile in 1970.

Strong legislatures, as in the case of Chile before Allende's fall in 1973, do not necessarily guarantee efficient governance of the country nor effective solutions to its economic and social problems. The democratic multiparty system in Chile's legislature made it extremely difficult for any president to deal effectively with that country's major social and economic issues.[5] Its divergent bases of power impeded presidential authority, undermined a sustained consensus on reform, and set up the conditions for waning presidential popularity—and this was as true for Salvadore Allende (1970-73) as it was for Eduardo Frei (1964-70). The Conservative and Liberal representatives of the right, for example, represented large landowners, industrialists, businessmen, professionals, in short the upper classes, which held sufficient power to block legislation affecting any drastic alteration of their power base. Those seeking change included the Communist and Socialist representatives, and spokesmen for workers, intellectuals, and peasants. But this did not exhaust the political spectrum in the Chilean legislature.

The Chilean Christian Democrats—left of center representatives—constituted Catholic members of the middle sectors, intellectuals, professionals, and technicians who also sought major changes. More to the center were the radicals, comprised of some people desiring sweeping changes and others more in agreement with Conservatives and Liberals. In this divided legislature, which much resembled those of the French Third and Fourth republics, the traditional pattern of presidential initiatives toward economic reform resulted in bargaining and exchanges of favors resulting in greatly modified legislation. Indeed, the amount of compromise between left, center, and right over the years gave rise to what some observers call an "equilibrium" or "stalemated" congress. The term refers to a congress in which all groups bargain and compromise in such a way that no group threatens to destroy the interests of any other. This situation had been altered somewhat during the term of Eduardo Frei, as his agrarian and copper (partial nationalization of the copper industry) reforms indicated. But the need for a president to compromise with a divided, obstructionist legislature remained strong when Allende came to power in 1970, producing discontent among those who wished him to move more quickly as well as those who saw him as a too-fast-moving revolutionary. Ultimately this led to conditions virtually outside his control and his demise at the hands of the military.

The Judiciary

The judicial branches in Latin American governments are not in a strong position to check the executive.[6] The judicial system emphasizes Roman law, which puts stress upon the interpretation of an extensive code of laws within each Latin American country. This system, leading back to the colonial period, contrasts to the Anglo-Saxon tradition of common law as it is practiced in the United States. Our legal system rests strongly on the doctrine of stare decisis—decisions based upon precedent—and recognizes custom and usage as key components of the law. The judiciary in Latin America has little leeway to "make law" itself.

Other factors also help explain the weak role that the courts play in Latin American politics. A highly complex court system, coupled with the emphasis on personal influence in Latin American politics, leads most individuals to avoid civil litigation and rely instead upon personal contacts. The prestige of the supreme court is not particularly high in most countries, given the heavy interference in judicial affairs by the executive. The executive initiates legislation relating to the courts, grants pardons and reprieves to the condemned, and can respect or ignore the ruling of the courts in his capacity as chief executor of the laws of the country. The president's decree and state-of-siege powers, moreover, can make a mockery out of the judicial system.

The independence and strength of the judicial branch, as formally outlined in Latin American constitutions, is thus more fictive than true. The constitutions emphasize the importance of the law as interpreted by the judicial branch, but the political processes undermine this desired norm. An independent power base for the courts, a necessary prerequisite for effectiveness, is simply nonexistent. Its chief power base would of course be the adherence to and loyalty felt for the law itself. But given the nature of Roman law and the overpowering influence of personal forces in Latin America, this effective power base is lacking.

The judiciary branch, of course, does perform a number of functions in Latin American countries; it is not as if jurists were totally powerless or merely window dressing for presidential dictatorships everywhere. The supreme courts, which head the judicial system in each of the Latin American countries, are staffed by professional lawyers who ostensibly must meet exacting professional qualifications. This court has wide appellate jurisdiction over constitutional and legal questions, including original jurisdiction in proceedings against a president and other officials representing the central government, and in disputes between foreign countries and the home country, as well as issues dealing with international law. Contempt of court is a serious offense in several countries, such as Colombia, and the supreme court has a large measure of control over the lower courts of the land. The lower courts also operate rather extensively throughout the Latin American countries, settling judicial controversies in cities, towns, and villages with different degrees of justice. It must also be stressed that as literacy and the general political development of a country advances, the prestige and professionalism of the courts tends to be heightened, in part reflecting the increased influence of professional qualifications in the selection of judges rather than their being appointed for out-and-out political reasons.

Other Political Processes

Imposición is a recurrent phenomenon in Latin America. It occurs when political leaders pick a candidate and then rig the election to guarantee his victory.[7] Justification for this activity is that experienced leadership can better pick a candidate than the inexperienced and uneducated masses. It is one way to perpetuate the power of a president or to transfer power to one of the president's closest friends.

Continuismo, another political phenomenon of Latin America, is a peaceful constitutional method of maintaining a chief executive in power. Most constitutions limit the president's tenure in office. *Continuismo* entails amending the constitution or drafting a new document in which the major change will be a new legal interpretation allowing the chief executive to remain in power. If the constitution is not amended, the chief executive will obtain a favorable court interpretation of the constitution allowing him to stay in power. Presidents who have used this include Getulio Vargas (Brazil), Juan Domingo Perón (Argentina), and General Rojas Pinilla (Colombia).

Candidato Único is a third means to perpetuate an elected executive's supremacy. It occurs occasionally when a strong-man leader becomes so powerful that no other political figure dares oppose him. This tactic occurs much less frequently than *imposición*, and is typically used when a major party is fairly unified while the others are disunited.

Latin America's chief executives derive power from the nature of corporate interest groups as they are structured and interact. Since the Ibero-Latin tradition is one of corporate interest groups arranged in a social hierarchy and regulated in a harmonized state headed by an all powerful executive, the chief executive plays an immensely important role both in regulating older corporate groups and incorporating newer interests within the state fabric. The older groups include landowners, businessmen, the older Church structure, older extended family relations, and traditional parties (Conservatives and Liberals). Newer bases have emerged in the twentieth century, producing newer corporate interests such as the educated *técnicos,* professional groups, organized labor, peasant groups, more mass-based political parties, and in professionalized and progressive military officers as well as new Church orientations.

The president is the chief *patrón* who dispenses available favors to these groups. He also heads the state's government, through which the corporate interests are linked, receiving hierarchic recognition and more concrete benefits. The task of maintaining an equilibrium among these groups is designated to the chief executive by virtue of the corporate state value system. As an accepted historical part of the Latin American political ethos, it gives the president a kind of political power not found elsewhere in the Third World nor in the developed countries. But the president rules in an arena of competing pressure groups, which accounts for much of the political instability within Latin America. These competing interest groups, whose pressures the chief executive must deal with, are the subject of the next chapter.

NOTES

1. See Alexander T. Edelmann, *Latin American Government and Politics* (Homewood, Ill.: Dorsey Press, 1969), ch. 13; William S. Stokes, *Latin American Politics* (New York: Thomas Y. Crowell, 1964), ch. 19; *The Constitutions of Latin America,* ed. Gerald E. Fitzgerald (Chicago: Regnery, 1968); *The Constitutions of the Americas,* ed. Russell H. Fitzgibbon (Chicago: University of Chicago Press, 1948).

2. On the various interest and pressure groups in Latin America, see Robert F. Adie and Guy E. Poitras, *Latin America: the Politics of Immobility* (Englewood Cliffs, N.J.: Prentice-Hall, 1974); and Edward J. Williams and Freeman J. Wright, *Latin American Politics; A Developmental Approach* (Palo Alto, Calif.: Mayfield, 1975), pt. III.

3. Stokes, *op. cit.,* ch. 16; Edelmann, *op. cit.,* ch. 11; Hugh M. Hamill, Jr., *Dictatorship in Spanish America* (New York: Knopf, 1965); *Latin American Politics,* ed. Robert D. Tomasek (Garden City, N.Y.: Doubleday, 1966).

4. Edelmann, *op. cit.* ch. 15; Stokes, *op. cit.* ch. 17; and Robert E. Scott,

"Legislatures," in *Government and Politics in Latin America,* ed. Harold E. Davis (New York: Ronald Press, 1958).

5. Federico G. Gil, *The Political System of Chile* (Boston: Houghton Mifflin, 1966), ch. 6; Arpad von Lazar and Luis Quiros Varela, "Chilean Christian Democracy: Lessons in the Politics of Reform Management," *Inter-American Economic Affairs* 21 (Spring 1968).

6. Edelmann, *op. cit.,* ch. 16; Stokes, *op. cit.,* p. 19.

7. William S. Stokes, "Violence as a Power Factor in Latin American Politics," *Western Political Quarterly* 5 (September 1952).

Suggested Readings

Edelmann, Alexander T. *Latin American Government and Politics,* 2d ed. Homewood, Ill.: Dorsey Press, 1969.

Fagen, Richard R. and Wayne A. Cornelius. *Political Power in Latin America: Seven Confrontations.* Englewood Cliffs, N.J.: Prentice-Hall, 1970.

Hamill, Jr., Hugh M. (ed.). *Dictatorship in Latin America.* New York: Knopf, 1965.

Keehen, Norman H. "Building Authority: A Return to Fundamentals," *World Politics* 26 (April 1974): 331-52.

Mander, John. *The Unrevolutionary Society.* New York: Harper and Row, 1969.

Martz, John D. (ed.). *The Dynamics of Change in Latin American Politics,* 2d ed. Englewood Cliffs, N.J.: Prentice-Hall, 1971.

Needler, Martin C. *Latin American Politics in Perspective.* New York: Van Nostrand, 1963.

Sigmund, Paul E. (ed.). *Models of Political Change in Latin America.* New York: Praeger, 1970.

Von Lazar, Arpad. *Latin American Politics: A Primer.* Boston: Allyn and Bacon, 1971.

Williams, Edward J. and Freeman J. Wright. *Latin American Politics: A Developmental Approach.* Palo Alto, Calif.: Mayfield, 1975.

Nine

Pressure Groups

Latin American politics is in part the product of conflict among pressure groups—corporate interests in the Ibero-Latin tradition—competing for recognition and entrance into, or a continued place within, the corporate structure of politics. Latin American political instability, as discussed in Chapter 2, arises largely as the result of discord between new groups seeking entry into the political system and older, established pressure groups already there. Each group seeks to make demands on the political system, and in the general absence of institutionalized problem-solving mechanisms, these demands often lead to one form of violence or another. The general strike by workers, land occupations and protests by peasants, urban violence by students, a military coup d'etat, manifestos from the Church, and other forms of demonstations are instances of displaying power and making demands on the government. Political development in Latin America can be viewed as the process by which new groups are admitted into the political system and through which its members come to share in the state's goods and resources.

Three key points bear stressing when we consider the role of pressure groups in Latin America. First, given the cultural underpinnings of personalism, *machismo*, emotionalism, *dignidad*, and other attitudes and values, pressure groups are far less organized than in other Western democracies.[1] They simply do not articulate interests in a regular and consistent manner, as one might expect of an interest group or pressure group in the North American or European tradition. Like Latin America's political parties, they are faction ridden, frequently form around the personality of a charismatic leader, tend to split like kindling wood, and cover a wide range of individuals who organize to influence government and politics only in ways beneficial to themselves.

Disorganization is rampant in Latin America. The peasants often have little idea of what is happening away from their *latifundias* or isolated enclaves; the military squabble among themselves; priests dispute bishops; students split into factions; labor unions follow different ideological paths (from Communist, to Christian Democratic, to more conservative); civil servants are poorly organized; and businessmen and landed interests are often at loggerheads. So in considering Latin American groups, one cannot compare them to counterparts in more developed countries, where tight organization, permanence, cohesiveness, regularity of expression, group consensus, and durability over time are the major features. Yet in the Latin American setting, as confusing as it might seem, these ill-organized groups are nevertheless very active in influencing and controlling government. They are part of the Latin American corporate-structure system.

Second, Latin America's pressure groups do not agree upon the legitimate means of expressing their demands to the government. Given the lack of consensus on how to influence or even run the government—for government's day-to-day operations are in part the effects of interest-group pressures on it—the upshot is frequently a violent demonstration of power involving assassination, student riots, urban bloodshed, rural deaths and demonstrations, or kidnappings. These are means to incite government response and gain a share in the benefits of the political system during the more quiet periods when violent news is otherwise scarce. Lack of consensus on legitimate means of political expression in turn impedes the forging of institutions through which to resolve the conflict among various interests. All this leads back to the beginning: violent expression. These features of the "legitimacy vacuum" in Latin America have their roots in society and economy, as discussed in Chapters five and six.

Third, one rule of the game does seem agreed upon. Groups will be admitted into the hierarchical corporate structure of the political system after they have demonstrated a capability for power and so long as they do not threaten the position of other established groups in the system.[2] This happens in many Latin American countries, making swift-moving political development and economic reform exceedingly difficult. Chile under Presidents Eduardo Frei and Salvador Allende is a good example of this basic rule in action. But even as Allende sought to accommodate increasing numbers of groups into the political system—at a time when the state's resources and institutional problem-solving mechanism were limited—the final curtain fell as the military took the center of the political stage. Argentina appeared to be facing similar problems, but accommodating its new groups far more slowly, in the 1960s and 1970s. To coin a phrase, too many groups can spoil the broth, and political decay, not development, results.

Three Latin American countries illustrate that keeping all established groups within the political system, while admitting new ones, does not always occur. In the cases of Mexico after 1910, Bolivia after 1952, and Cuba after 1959, the basic rule was not followed. These were full-blooded social revolutions that radically altered the old structure of interests. Mexico's revolution led to the eventual demise of the military, landed oligarchy, and Church as dominating power groups, and the rise of labor, peasants, and white-collar workers, all incorporated into the PRI structure under forceful presidential leadership. Bolivia's revolution under the MNR and Víctor Paz Estenssoro, broke the back of the landed interests and of foreign and domestic giants in the tin industry, and helped to begin the formation of strong peasant organizations. Cuba, the most far-reaching and radical of the three, squashed the old landed aristocracy, the powerful United States interests in sugar, petroleum refining, and public utilities, the Church, and the old military, replacing these—under Castro's forceful rule—with the interests of laborers in the city and countryside. Cuba's revolution also eventually wiped out the old middle sector *intereses*—professionals and *técnicos* (technicians)—replacing them with new revolutionary professionals and *técnicos*. So the basic principles of allowing established interests to remain alongside new ones are not always followed—a situation that continued in the late 1960s, as Peru's military moved toward building the interests of peasants (land reform), urban works (worker-management organizations), and Indians (linguistic and educational reforms), while reducing the established power of urban businessmen and commercial interests, foreign business, and landed power.

With these observations in mind, we can turn to a brief overview of the major groups vying for power in Latin America's different countries with their different rates of development.

CONSERVATIVE LANDED INTERESTS

The conservative landed interests are a major force in Latin America favoring the established order and opposed to any state action that might be detrimental to their elite and privileged status. They began to form a dominating group at the outset of Latin America's independence period through control of a major natural resource, land, and its use as a political weapon. The vast inequality of landholding, with a few families owning much and many families owning little, perpetuated landholders' control through the nineteenth and into the twentieth century. The rise of new groups and political leaders through urbanization and industrialization, and the consequent pressures for agrarian reform, began to erode their power in several countries during the twentieth century, particularly after World War II. But they continue to be strong in countries like El Salvador where 7 percent of the rural population own 81.3 percent of the land, dominated by huge coffee, sugar, and cotton farms.

Land constitutes a political resource in several different ways. First, it is a major source of prestige and status, recognized by the population at large, which gives the owner a distinct advantage in terms of influencing decisions within the government. Where dignity and hierarchy are so closely woven into interpersonal relationships, owning land keeps one at the top of the social structure and, consequently, the political power structure as well. Secondly, land is a source of occupation for masses of people in settings where manual labor predominates over mechanized farming, where agricultural employment is a major source of income, and where supply of agricultural laborers is plentiful. The need to work operates here, particularly since working for a large landowner often brings with it a small piece of land for the campesino's own use, something he may not be able to acquire through other peaceful means. Thirdly, the large landed estates of rural Latin America today, as in the past, form dominate-submissive relationships between the wealthy, typically white owners and the poor, mixed-blooded campesinos. This social stratification perpetuates power relationships between large landholders and masses of the rural landless. Finally, the large landed estate in Latin America, the latifundia, with its patron-peon relationships, is in fact accepted as a way of life for the typical peasant.[3]

Members of the landed elite are found as legislators in congress, usually as members of Conservative or Liberal parties within the various countries, sometimes as presidents (Stroessner in Paraguay, Somoza of Nicaragua), in pressure-group organizations, and of late in some extreme right-wing, violence-oriented groups. They are part of the corporate-interest group structure that virtually controls government in parts of Central America, but have been substantially reduced in power in Bolivia, Cuba, and Mexico, and must share power with newer middle- and lower-class groups in Argentina, Brazil, Chile, Costa Rica, and Venezuela.

Landed groups tend to be better organized than peasant organizations for pressure politics. The powerful *Sociedad Rural* of Argentina, formed in 1866 and with over nine thousand members of elite Argentina, has played a powerful role in politics, as have Chile's National Society of Agriculture, the Consortium of Agricultural Societies of the South, and the Agricultural Associations of the North. The strong Honduran Cattle Farmers Federation is another landed group resisting agrarian reform in that country by claiming that the government's National Agrarian Institute is controlled by Communists and blaming a number of Roman Catholic priests for unrest among rural peasants. Needless to say, the large landowners are a far more powerful interest group than the largely illiterate peasants. And they tend to remain strong in most of Latin America despite agrarian reform. Even in Mexico, with its revolution of 1910 and years of commitment to land redistribution, less than 1 percent of all farms possessed 50 percent of all agriculture land as late as 1961—fifty years after the revolution! Cuba after 1959 is the one major exception to continuing inequality in land distribution.

THE MILITARY: REFORMERS
AND CONSERVATIVES

The military organizations of Latin America, discussed in Chapter 11, are divided between those officers advocating change and those more in favor of the status quo. The military has provided leaders in development in a number of countries, most notably Peru and Brazil, but also in Cuba after 1959, when Castro forged his own military organization and socialized it to new revolutionary imperatives. The experiences in Peru and Brazil, moreover, will undoubtedly have an effect on the thinking of officers in other countries, as in fact it already has in Colombia, Honduras, and Venezuela. But in other Latin American lands, as Guatemala, Nicaragua, Paraguay, and Ecuador, it is far less an agent of change than of maintaining the existing order.

The puzzle of the military constituting or not an organized agent of development is not simple. The fact is that military officers often dispute among themselves over questions of if, where, when, and how to alter the state's matrix of power contenders and its distribution of goods and services. This division of goals is shown again and again in Latin American military politics, as in Guatemala in the mid-1950s, Peru after the 1968 coup, in Bolivia from the late 1960s onward, and to a certain extent in Brazil after 1964. Understanding Latin American politics, then, requires a close look at divisions within the military establishment, including not only those among Army, Navy, and Air Force, but also those within each branch. Chile's military, for example, went through severe internal strains during 1972 and 1973, as Marxist President Allende pressed for radical reforms within Chile's traditional constitutional order and as civil unrest mounted.

That the military can play the trump card in politics, and must therefore be reckoned with in any conflict, is sharply underscored by its dominating presence in Latin America's political systems by 1973. It either directly controlled, or was the major force behind, governmental systems in eight South American countries (all but Colombia and Venezuela), five Central American lands (all but Costa Rica, Nicaragua's armed force being the National Guard), and the Dominican Republic. Out of the twenty Latin American countries, the military dominated in fourteen! We go much more deeply into the role of the military in Chapter 11.

THE CHURCH

The role of the Hispano-Catholic Church as an autonomous interest group promoting change in Latin America's political, social, and economic development is fascinating but complex. The Roman Catholic clergy, for example, share no common view of the Church's functions in development. The Church's official policies, as might be suspected, often diverge from the attitudes and practices of some of its priests. The separation of Church and state, secondly, is an uneven and as yet incomplete process, not only on a comparative country-to-country basis, but also within countries. Third, the Roman Catholic philosophy has become a base for new political parties and labor movements in some countries, while in others it is committed to a defense of the status quo. Finally, Hispano-Catholicism, as a religion, is not necessarily a firm value system for democracy and economic development (given its fatalistic and authoritarian aspects), but has become precisely that in parts of Latin America. Even more paradoxical, some Catholic priests have become either guerrilla fighters or Marxists!

The Church is involved in political action promoting development along different avenues. First, some of the clergy show themselves to be motivated agents in promoting change. The famous young excommunicated priest of Colombia, Camilo Torres, who gave his life in 1966 (age 37) in a guerrilla movement is a case in point. Indeed, a wide range of political activism on the part of Latin America's clergy emerged in the 1960s and 1970s, covering a spectrum, as some analysts see it, from moderate and progressive, to radical (not to mention conservative and reactionary). Leftist and moderate clergy are found, in addition to the countries already discussed, in Brazil, Chile before Allende's overthrow in September, 1973, Colombia, Venezuela, and Mexico. It should be noted that the progressive clergy have a regional forum for expressing their demands: the Latin American Bishops Council (CELAM), through which progressive bishops advocate social and economic development.

Roman Catholic theology forms another base for progressive development in Latin America. It can legitimize change through political organizations and political action. As a major part of the traditional value system of the region, religion can help expand the government's role in fulfilling public needs.

This theological value system, as a base for political action, served precisely that function in two important ways during the 1960s and after. The first is the rise to power of the Christian Democratic Party as a party of major governmental strength in its role as the president's party. This occurred in Chile and Venezuela in 1964 and 1968. The second is the growth of Roman Catholic-oriented labor movements.

Chile's Christian Democratic party came to power under the leadership of Eduardo Frei (1964-70). It served as a key political mechanism for motivating political leadership to the partial nationalization of Chilean copper, and to new housing, agricultural reform, and educational projects. It was also instrumental in recruiting young Chileans into the political process. The party, however, suffered severe internal splits during the Frei years, which in part set up the conditions for its defeat in the 1970 presidential elections. The Christian Democratic Party of Venezuela (COPEI) came to power in 1968, putting into the presidency its founder, Rafael Caldera. This party and the Church in Venezuela are generally agreed on the principle of initiating changes to promote the socioeconomic development of Venezuela. These two parties clearly contribute to widening the participation of people in government in Venezuela and Chile.

The Roman Catholic-oriented labor movement in Latin America is the Latin American Confederation of Christian Trade Unionists (Confederación Latino-Americana de Sindicalistas Cristianos, CLASC). This organization was associated with significant change in the labor picture during the 1960s, since CLASC is ideologically committed to a complete change in Latin American social structure, with specific emphasis on income redistribution through a comprehensive social-welfare system. An affiliate of CLASC is the Rural Labor Federation of Latin America (Federación Campesina de Americana Latina, FCAL), organized in December, 1961. It has a large following among peasants and agricultural workers. CLASC and FCAL, then, represent movements of both political and economic development, thus linking them to a commitment to expanding citizenship.

The Church has also been active in condemning a number of governments for their repression of human rights, making it a new protector of civil liberties since World War II. Church groups were active in Brazil and Paraguay in 1974, for example, and their leaders publicly suffered for their efforts. Three archbishops and ten bishops of the northeastern region of Brazil accused the Brazilian government of repression in May, 1973. This heralded a renewed conflict between Church and state in that country, aggravated by a number of arrests and trials of members of the religious community, including one French priest who was sentenced to ten years' imprisonment for subversion, after he had helped peasants in the Araguaia region to resist eviction by land developers. Thirty-two priests—including five Dominican Friars—went on trial in early June, 1973, on charges of having "promoted disaffection against the authorities" in 1968. These priests were subsequently acquitted. The pope appealed to the Brazilian government in August, 1973, to "respect the rights of men" and to "guarantee economic justice in the country," while in November, 1973, the National Conference of Brazilian Bishops published a document accusing the government of persecuting the Church and torturing its political adversaries.

Paraguay is another area of Church-state conflict. A serious confrontation developed between President Stroessner and the Church from 1969 onward. The Church strongly opposed the President's measures to extend his powers. The Paraguayan Bishops' Conference publicly opposed President Stroessner in August, 1969, and several priests were subsequently arrested. This conflict continued through the early 1970s.

The role of the Church in Latin American development, however, is by no means totally progressive. The progressive, moderate, and radical left-wing clergy are matched by conservative and reactionary counterparts. This dimension of the clergy acts in a number of ways to impede or restrict the forces of enlightened development. Examples include supporting right-wing military contenders (Rojas Pinilla in Colombia, Trujillo in the Dominican Republic, Batista in Cuba, Pérez Jiménez in Venezuela); leading violent attacks against liberals (Colombia, Mexico); resisting state efforts to control education (Mexico); emphasizing spiritual concerns rather than participation in politics. When these efforts are combined with many (some would say "most") of the clergy who remain politically apathetic and inactive, the role of the Church in building citizenship and promoting broad developmental change is unclear.

Secondly, the uniformity of separation of Church and state is uneven in Latin America. The Hispano-Catholic religion is the approved religion of the state in Argentina, Colombia, Costa Rica, Ecuador, Paraguay, Peru, and Venezuela. But in Bolivia, Brazil, Chile, the Dominican

Republic, El Salvador, Guatemala, Haiti, Honduras, Nicaragua, Pan-ama, and Uruguay, the Church and its religion are more independent of the state. Mexico, on the other hand, has a fascinating historical record of sharp state repression of Church activities (over its control of land, marriage, and education; see its 1917 constitution), but is still a country where the Church is intact and quite strong. Many of its government leaders still send their children to Church schools, and recruitment to the priesthood remains relatively high.

The Church and its Hispano-Catholic religion, to conclude, remains in a stage of complex transition, showing considerable concern among the clergy as to what its future role is to be. Its future role, in turn, is affected by a shortage of priests (rising population is a factor), difficulty in recruiting personnel, dependence on foreign-born priests, fragmented views on its clergy, and the limitations of financial resources. The future role of the Church and its clergy in promoting or containing citizenship and development is by no means clear.

ORGANIZED LABOR

The setting for the rise of labor groups in Latin America is one of increased urbanization and a slow shift of population from agriculture to industry. Professional occupations, administrative positions, clerical work, sales and services, blue-collar work, and other related activities associated with industrialization, have grown steadily during the twentieth century, and particularly since World War II. By the early 1970s, Latin America had experienced a continuously high rate of urbanization, with twenty-two of the largest cities more than tripling their population between 1930 and 1960. Some demographers were predicting that by the year 2000, Latin America's urban population would be two hundred and fifty million, or 60 to 70 percent of the total population. Countries of high urban and industrial growth are Argentina, Brazil, Cuba, Chile, Colombia, Mexico, Uruguay, Venezuela, and to a lesser extent, Peru. The urban sector ranges from 46.3 percent in Brazil to 80.8 percent in Uruguay.

As part of the urban and industrial processes of change, labor unions in the early twentieth century were products of ideological movements, specifically anarchosyndicalism, socialism, populism, or Communism. Anarchosyndicalists, for example, were strong in Mexico, Chile, Argentina, and Brazil. They stressed direct action, bombing, arson, and terror, first to weaken, then abolish, the state. The Socialists and Communists urged the destruction of capitalism and the substitution of state ownership of the means of production. The populist movements were inspired by the concepts of Peru's Víctor Raúl Haya de la Torre, em-

phasizing more of a revolutionary nationalism. The common underlying themes of these different ideological movements were basic distrust of capitalist forms of government and the general desire for a
classless society. These broad, total solutions to the laboring man's
problems gave way over time, and the unions began to stress more immediate economic gains for their memberships.

Has organized labor been effective in achieving economic gains?
The answer on balance must be in the negative. Labor unions, to be
sure, conduct strikes and engage in collective bargaining to gain substantial wage increases. Chile and Argentina are good examples. Chilean copper miners, the elite labor group there, manage to gain large
pay raises each year to keep up with—and contribute to—inflation and
this was true during Allende's term in office, notwithstanding his appeal to the copper miners to forego large wage increases to help in his
austerity program. The stronger unions in Argentina won better than
100 percent wage increases in collective bargaining with management
in 1975—much against President Isabel Perón's wishes, for she too was
trying to use wage-increase ceilings to help curb inflation. Labor
strikes also articulate discontent with other aspects of government
austerity programs, making it difficult for the president to govern, as
in the general workers' strike in Argentina in June, 1975, and in Chile
in early 1973, as workers illegally seized factories and engaged in urban violence. These events made the task of governing exceedingly
difficult for Allende, helping to set up conditions leading to the eventual military intervention, and they undermined Isabel Perón's base of
support in Argentina in 1975. Despite these situations, the record of
labor as an organized, tightly knit, autonomous group within the political system is not all that positive.

Labor tends not to be an autonomous group, nor is it organized into
tightly knit, unified organizations. This situation is brought about by
a number of forces. Financial weakness, the need to be recognized by
the government (including government recognition of the strike to
make it legal), the low level of politicization of the urban worker, and
multitudinous restrictions affecting their internal organization create a
central overriding concern: the general dependence of labor unions on
government for continued union activities. Unions, then, are more
concerned with keeping themselves politically strong—the basis of
their security to operate—which leads them to establish alliances with
those people, parties, or government officials who influence government decisions. The net result is a kind of patron-client relationship,
with unions cast in the role of client. They tend, in the end, to be dominated by personalities and political parties that are strongly linked to
government—the ultimate source of decisions concerning wages and
working conditions.

Many examples show the dominance of Latin America's organized labor by strong personalities and political parties. Cuba's Confederation of Cuban Workers is locked into the Cuban Communist Party under Castro's personal rule. Organized labor in Mexico owes its twentieth-century fruits to the PRI structure. The Democratic Action party in Venezuela promoted unionism and labor organization during the postwar period, while the Christian Democratic party (COPEI) is also active in the labor movement. This results in some posts of the Confederation of Venezuelan Workers being held by each party. Chilean labor is historically split between Socialist, Communist, and Christian Democratic party activities. Argentina's labor movement is divided into Perónist, Communist, and independent unions. Peru is currently experimenting with labor involvement in managerial decisions, but the force behind the movement is the military.

The different party and personality alignments of Latin America's labor unions illustrate the absence of centralized organization, which helps perpetuate their low degree of autonomy. Division within the labor movement and its dependence on other forces is equally apparent at the regional level. Some unions are in the Inter-American Regional Organization of Workers (ORIT), created under the efforts of the American Federation of Labor. Others are associated with the Latin American Confederation of Christian Trade Unions (CLASC), which is heavily financed by the International Solidarity Institute, in turn financed by West Germany. These two organizations, both competing for union following in Latin America, must look outside Latin America for financial support, showing another aspect of low autonomy of organized labor and the dependence on extraneous groups for political power.

It must be stressed in studying Latin America's labor unions that all workers are by no means organized, and those that are do not evince high aspirations to overthrow the existing order. The number of workers not unionized in Latin America remains high due to continued disorganization of farm workers and the low level of organization in such areas of employment as textiles and service industries. Meanwhile, a number of obstacles inhibit organization, such as the need to file formal petitions with employers and labor inspectors before organizing, the illegality of strike funds once organized, and the stipulation that no potential union leader may be salaried by the organization. The last hurdle means that the leader must work full time elsewhere, or be independently wealthy, before turning his attention to organizational activities. Moreover, the typical union member tends to be conservative, wanting simply a larger share of the economic pie, rather than a wild-eyed revolutionary bent on violent overthrow or reform of the system.

PEASANTS

Peasants in Latin America enjoy even much less of an autonomous status than the groups discussed above. Their environment, as many a study shows, is one of extreme powerlessness against the many threats in their life. Violence, exploitation, and injustice from those more powerful than the peasant combine with disease, death, ignorance, low social status, and accident to produce an outlook of fatalism and pessimism. Although a number of social outlets offset this perception of the outside world, such as extended family relations and patron-client systems, the peasant is typically conditioned to be dominated by his environment and by those in power within it, such as the large landowners. The peasant's life of paternalist dominance by others, usually the landholder, leads him to be controlled by others who may seek his participation in elections, party support, or peasant syndicates to advance their own political interests.

This is not to say that peasants are totally passive or have little interest in changing the landholding system to their benefit. Nor is it true that many are no better off today than during the nineteenth century in terms of landholding. Available studies indicate that the peasant working on the *latifundia*, the landless seasonal worker, and the squatter in fact would like to have land of their own that they can count upon retaining. This desire predisposes the peasants to become supporters of those who advocate agrarian reform and prepares them to be clients of syndicate or political party patrons. Given this predisposition, they formed a mass support for the Democratic Action (AD) and Social Christian (COPEI) parties after 1945, for the PRI party structure in Mexico from the mid-1930s to the present, and for the MNR in Bolivia from 1952 through 1964. Agrarian reform became a form of patronage in these cases—consolidating and ratifying changes stimulated by peasant land invasions and widening the distribution of other goods and services throughout peasant areas. In all cases, the peasants formerly had lost land to the upper and middle classes; this, combined with long economic suffering, prepared them to follow other organized groups.

A number of events in the 1960s and 1970s further illustrate peasant willingness to engage in militant action to gain access to the land and express discontent when so inspired by effective leadership promising some new form of land distribution. Peasants invaded land in southern Chile under the leadership of the radical Movement of the Revolutionary Left (MIR), and migrant workers (*inquilinos*) and other rural peasants allowed themselves to be bused into Santiago for demonstrations, painting walls, and discussing political tactics in support of President Allende between 1970 and 1973. The National Union of *Campesinos* in Honduras engaged in land seizures, leading to the arrest of a hundred peasant-league leaders in June, 1975, and an estimated twenty-five thousand peasants and workers barricaded the main roads leading to Cochabamba, Bolivia, in protest against President Banzer's austere economic policies in January, 1974. These events attest to the peasant as a potential political actor, but one typically requiring outside leadership to organize and often able to be manipulated by others.

The point is that peasants, much in contrast to the view that the rural areas form the base of future revolutions in Latin America and elsewhere, do not show enthusiastic support for violent revolution within the existing social and political system. Their yearning for land does not appear to go much beyond that, and once attained, their revolutionary horizons quickly narrow, as experiences in Mexico, Bolivia, Peru, Chile, and Venezuela show. Peasants in Mexico, for example, engaged in land seizures after 1910, but later joined in with government party organization. A similar experience occurred in Bolivia in 1952, when *campesinos* occupied land, then became linked to the government through MNR peasant syndicates.

This in part stems from the basically authoritarian political culture of which they are a part and in which they typically are the client rather than the patron. When *campesino* syndicates emerge in areas where *latifundias* were expropriated, for example, the syndicate leadership in many cases takes over the role of the former patron in organizing work to be done, as in Bolivia after 1952. They become the clients of government parties, as in Venezuela, typically resisting the efforts of the Communists, left-wing splinter groups, and guerrillas because they do not wish to bite the hand that feeds them—their patron, the government itself. Che Guevara's notable failure to rouse the peasants who already owned their own land in Bolivia during 1967 is another case of peasant apathy in rising to the revolutionary call. Other studies show that many peasants actually support the current *latifundia* system, and that their support for change stops once they have gained land.[4]

That peasants do not form autonomous, independent, well-organized groups does not mean that the *campesino* is forever doomed to live a landless existence of extreme poverty with no future. It does mean that any development affecting peasants typically occurs through the actions of strong leaders above—by a government patron in the form of party or strong leader—rather than from below, as in the classic Western democratic "interest-group" model. President Lázaro Cárdenas (1934-40) and the PRI structure benefited thousands of *campesinos* in Mexico, in exchange for their political support, although that job is far from finished and in fact began to slow considerably after the Cár-denas years. Democratic Action (AD) and COPEI have encouraged agrarian reform in Venezuela to forge a peasant base there—which of course does benefit the peasant. Presidents Frei (1964-70) and Al-lende (1970-73) and their Christian Democratic and Unidad Popular movements did much for rural peasants before Allende's overthrow, in return for peasant political support. So the picture is not totally dim, but certainly different from what one would expect in terms of organ-ized interest group behavior in developed Western democracies.

Cuba is a case of rather large benefits coming the way of peasants, once the old regime was toppled and a new leader and party system emerged. In terms of its totality of change for the average peasant, it stands at sharp relief against the continuing abysmal conditions for millions of landless peasants and squatters throughout Latin America. Measures to achieve greater equality of opportunity were wide-ranging after Castro's rise to power in Cuba. They included new low-income housing programs and rent reduction, with a large percent of new con-struction occurring in the countryside. Land reforms opened new land and redistributed confiscated land to renters, sharecroppers, and land-less peasants. Other nationalized land became state farms, which pro vided year-around employment opportunities for Cuba's low-income rural workers. Land reforms and new construction projects (homes, hydroelectric plants, irrigation projects) increased the employment op-portunities for all Cubans, including those in rural areas. All Cubans—urban and rural—began to receive equitable salaries and minimum pensions, and were expected to work side-by-side on an equal basis in the new agricultural programs, factories, and sugar-related industries.

Other institutional innovations, as Cuba moved toward income re-distribution, increased equality, economic security, and equalization of opportunity, can be cited. Such public services as electricity, sewage disposal, and road maintenance were expanded and reduced in cost throughout the land. Free services in medicine, education, public tele-phones, burials, and weddings were expanded and reduced in cost to the Cuban public, greatly benefiting blacks and mulattoes. These community-development changes resulted from the fidelista's deliber-ate policy of regional equalization. This policy emphasized the integra-tion of the country through the development of smaller communities and rural areas rather than the capital city, as in most of the rest of Latin America. Havana's growth after 1959, significantly, is estimated at approximately 1 percent, compared to the booming urbanization and slums of other Latin American capital cities as rural migrants poured into the cities.

Throughout Latin America the landless and squatter peasants want land. Their desire generates discontent with the status quo and the basis for political support of more organized groups able to tap the peasant political resource. While the peasant may wind up as a client in the traditional patron-client relationship, he stands to increase his opportunity for owning land. Yet this is far from the end of his troubles. The remaining problems are many. How much land does he get? Is it a small inefficient *minifundia?* How arable is it? How productive can he be on it? Can he sell his produce and earn a living from it? Can he borrow money to buy tools? Does he know the techniques of efficient farming and are commercial outlets available? These and a host of other related issues stymie effective agrarian reform in Latin America.

UNIVERSITY STUDENTS

University students constitute another interest group, frequently cited in studies as having a major effect on social and economic reforms in Latin America. To the extent this view is true depends upon the specific condition in each country and the way one interprets "having an effect upon." It is certainly true that many student activists later became prominent leaders, thus effecting change from above. Fidel Castro of Cuba, Rómulo Betancourt and Raúl Leoni of Venezuela, Víctor Raúl Haya de la Torre of Peru, and Salvador Allende of Chile are cases in point. Political activism—in the form of strikes, boycotts, demonstrations, marches, and urban violence—also alerts the domestic and foreign public to repressive political conditions and unequal social and economic relations in the Latin American lands, which in turn contributes to the matrix of pressures operating upon government leaders. But as to the underlying reasons for university student political activism and its long-term effects on fundamental conditions in Latin America, there is considerable debate and conflicting evidence.

Why do students engage in heated political conflict? Are they all oriented to social and economic change? Are they all politically radical? As to why they engage in political activism, the answers found by researchers range from political activism being an extension of the University Reform Movement begun at Córdoba University in Argentina in 1918 (advocating, among other things, that the university must be autonomous from the government, and also that the university must be involved with great national problems) to student idealism, to political activism as the stepping stone to a political career.[5] Hence, no conclusive answers are found. All students are not oriented to radical social and economic change, and many are more concerned with serious professional preparation for entry into a career of upper-middle or upper-class status. Most of them, however, do appear to favor the principle of university autonomy and resistance to military take-over of government. The culturally ingrained attitudes of university students tend, of course, to weaken their potential to form strong, autonomous, and cohesive interest groups.

University students in Latin America, contrary to the image often portrayed by newspaper reports, are far from single organized groups articulating identical demands. Students spread themselves across the political spectrum, from anti-Communist, conservative in the traditional Liberal and Conservative Party views, Christian Democratic, Soviet or Chinese Communist, guerrilla warfare, to just apolitical. Factionalism is very much a part of Latin American student politics. Students were militantly divided in Chile in 1970-73, with Christian Democrats and Conservatives opposing left-wing groups supporting Allende—a clear example of a fragmented student population within one country under a period of extreme political stress. Another type of division is found in the various university fields of study within a single university. For example, of students interviewed at the Central University of Venezuela (UCV) in 1973, only those enrolled in civil engineering showed concern with social issues.[6] It should be remembered, too, that in addition to students not all being politically active, many who do engage in riots, marches, urban violence, and the like, later become solid members of the establishment, particularly since most university students are members of the middle, upper-middle, and upper classes.

It also seems clear from the available evidence that outside political organizations compete for student support of their movements and programs. Christian Democrats, Socialists, and Communists, for example, were strong in wooing Chilean student followings from the early 1960s onward—a period during which Chilean university life became increasingly polarized. It also seems clear that Christian Democratic strength declined during the late 1960s within the student movement, owing partly to competition from other parties and to a decline in Christian Democratic political socialization of the students. Similarly, the Popular Action and Christian Democratic parties worked hard in Peru to create a student base before military intervention in 1968, and the PRI organization in Mexico has an enormous operation directed at students—although not with complete success, as the 1968 student riots in Mexico City illustrate.

The record of student activism in bringing about significant social, economic, and political change is mixed. Student activism in Cuba has a long record and is undoubtedly one of the major political forces that leaders had to reckon with, particularly at the large University of Havana between 1920 and the eventual fall of Batista, which students also helped bring about. Students also appear to have played a role in the struggle against Juan Vicente Gómez in the late 1920s and the demise of Marcos Pérez Jiménez. Christian Democratic university students also worked hard for some of Eduardo Frei's reform programs in Chile between 1964 and 1970. It is also true that a number of students have taken to the hills as guerrillas, but not with a great amount of success. Students in Panama support the efforts of President Torrijos to gain increased Panama Canal rights. Many students will continue to call attention to the need for more equitable distribution of goods and services within their countries, thus indirectly contributing to the development process.

Many student strikes and demonstrations, on the other hand, result in negative government reactions. These include the strafing of the university with airplanes, as in La Paz, Bolivia, in the late 1960s, imprisonment of student leaders, as in a number of countries, the closing of the university, as in Montevideo, Uruguay, in 1973, or killing students, as in Mexico City in 1968 and Puno, Peru, in 1973. These negative reactions, far from stimulating social and economic change, may in effect stiffen government resistance to it.

Student activism, then, continues, as do the efforts of other political organizations to capture student support. If the students are not a direct major force in stimulating the social and economic changes some of them talk so much about, they are nevertheless a potential source of power for other leaders and groups who can lead in the development process. This is clear in student support of Christian Democratic activities during the early years of Eduardo Frei in Chile, and support for Torrijos in Panama. University student support of Fidel Castro's revolution in Cuba also shows their potential strength. Cuban students contribute part of their time to cutting sugar cane, working in factories, and engaging in a wide range of field work.

The understanding of political activism among Latin America's students, then, requires scrutinizing them within the region's political culture and each country's political dynamics. Violent confrontation in the form of strikes, demonstrations, and guerrilla warfare on the part of students clearly reflects another dimension of the culture of emotion as fulfillment of self, idealism, *machismo*, and personalism.

BUSINESSMEN

The social, economic, and political attitudes of Latin American businessmen differ considerably from those in the United States and condition pressure-group activities within the political system. By businessmen is meant the upper- and middle-income brackets, rather than the street vendors and lottery-ticket salesmen, who might also be so termed.

One major difference is that the economic philosophy of United States businessmen traditionally emphasizes a positive role by the state in the economy, nurturing a number of development and other activities for business growth.[7] Latin American businessmen, while capitalist in outlook, expect a large degree of governmental protection when taking entrepreneurial risks—a kind of spill-over of paternalist attitudes within Latin American political culture, extending back to colonial times. Secondly, businesses are typically family owned and operated, and are viewed as a principal, if not the major, means of entering into or staying within the upper-middle or upper-class brackets of society. This closeness of social status and business activity, gives businessmen added incentive to curry favor and to pressure the government for policies favorable to business.

Since government policies play a vital role in the success of Latin American businesses and businessmen, the latter must possess political skills and be adept at forming close contacts with the government officials. The typical businessmen will petition government on a wide range of issues, including tax exemptions, government aid to private business, export subsidies, cheap and adequate credit, and reduction of export duties for machinery and raw materials. The business community also favors government intervention in such areas as irrigation, communications, power facilities, land reclamation, education, and health and related social projects. In terms of agrarian reform and other social-welfare development programs, the business community is usually, but not always, more conservative. Business groups in Mexico, Uruguay, and Venezuela, however, tend to be more progressive on welfare matters. In the case of Cuba, of course, the state has assumed the prior domain of private business.

Business groups in Latin America, as might be expected, tend to be well organized and closely linked to government and other upper-middle and upper-class social groups. This gives them an effective formal and informal voice in helping to shape government policies and programs. They are organized into central business confederations, whose members sit on bureaucratic organizations dealing with monetary policy, credit, banking, and development programs. Businessmen, as in Chile, also arrange to be represented on committees drafting legislation—key legislation, including the 1962 tax reform that affected all Chileans.[8] The business sector also prepares new statutes or administrative rules affecting business, testifies before legislative committees, and has access to government representatives through their own upper-middle and upper-class social ties.

Business organizations abound in Latin America. Mexico, for example, has two large centralized organizations, the CONCAMIN, embracing more than fifty chambers, each including all the industries in key areas of manufacturing, and the CONCANACO, comprising more than two hundred and fifty local chambers of commerce. One of Colombia's strongest groups is the ANDI, the National Association of Industrialists, and FENALCO, the National Merchants Federation. These groups sharply influence legislative initiatives and executive decrees affecting the economy. They also oppose some tax laws that provide charges on corporate profits. They are joined in this opposition by the Association of Agriculturalists and Cattlemen, a landed-interest group. Chile's central business organization, the Sociedad de Fomento Fabril, is equally strong, as are the Industrial Union, the Argentine Chamber of Commerce, and the General Economic Federation in Argentina.

It seems clear from prevailing government-business relations in Latin America that government, rather than private industry as in early American industrial growth, will play an increasing role in the development of Latin America. Economic development tends to be seen as a public responsibility, as is the economic climate for private business, and the contemporary models of development are strongly state directed, as in Brazil, Cuba, Peru, Mexico, Venezuela.

BUREAUCRATS

Latin American scholars began to pay increased attention to the role and significance of bureaucrats in Latin America after World War II. This is due in large part to the growth of government agencies overseeing a number of development programs, which is consistent with the belief of Latin Americans that government is the decisive element in promoting and creating socioeconomic change. As development agencies grew, so did the number of those people in positions of responsibility within their bureaucracies. Ultimately came the question of how bureaucrats affect political decisions, and what is their overall contribution to the process of development?

Bureaucrats occupying responsible positions in public-sector agencies deal with a wide range of activities, including welfare, health, education, agrarian reform, state banking, transportation and communication agencies, the oil industry, natural-resource control, and a host of other civil-service concerns. They may likely be military officers in military-dominated governments or civilians in other settings, and their positions are gained by appointment rather than election. Many bureaucrats exert strong political pressures within the governmental system when other parties and interest groups are too weak to do so. In other cases, however, bureaucrats are politically weak, particularly where chief personnel officers are appointed by the president and are directly responsible to him, as in Paraguay. But bureaucrats as a whole are very important when it comes to carrying out government policies, because decisions, presumably, have to be implemented. Here the bureaucrat's attitudes, values, perceptions, and abilities come into play—either executing the mandate of his office or creating major obstacles to it.

Of all the potential interest groups operating within Latin America's political systems, the bureaucrats have been sharply criticized by students of development for their essentially negative role. The key point is that by the nature of bureaucratic appointments and lifestyles within bureaucratic organizations, overall productivity in relation to development priorities tends to end up on the debit side. Since bureaucrats are the very lifeblood of the day-to-day operations of the state—itself viewed as the central mechanism for development—one would hope for great contributions from them; but alas, this is often not the case.

Among the many notable problems of Latin American bureaucracy several merit attention. Appointments to public office tend to be made more on the basis of patronage than merit. This results in a network of intricate alliances involving high bureaucratic careers within the state, a situation that tends to make many bureaucrats fearful of doing anything that might terminate their employment, even at the sacrifice of sound administration and management within their office. The state's public sector thus becomes an employment agency for loyal followers of those in power, rather than an efficient complex leading development.

Other aspects of bureaucratic life within the civil service should be mentioned. Deferring to superiors, overcentralization, endless red tape, departmental jealousies, and corruption are well-known features of the public-sector agencies. Overstaffing, since civil-service laws usually prevent firing, is an equally common practice. The problems also include unwillingness to delegate responsibility, excessive legalism (codifying every administrative contingency), and passing decisions on to the highest executive. This leads to upper-level civil servants faced with reams of paper, petitions, memos, and requests for decisions, and middle levels of bureaucracy with little responsibility. Factionalism within bureaucracies exists, as does the desire of higher bureaucrats to build personal empires within their organizations.

The result of this bureaucratic morass was an enormous expansion of the state's public-sector bureaucracies following World War II. The politics and internal life of the bureaucracy inhibited bureaucrats from becoming leaders in change and reform. Even Fidel Castro ran into these problems after he had presumably swept away the old order and built a new one after 1959. Mexican bureaucracy, many years after the 1910 revolution, also suffers from many of the same problems.

The state becomes a product and promoter of clientelist politics in this setting. Long-range goals may be set by development agencies such as Chile's Institute of Agrarian Development (INDAP) or the Agrarian Reform Corporation (CORA), but the realities of bureaucratic recruitment, staffing, and internal politics can hold back any momentum for change, as occurred in the later years of Eduardo Frei's administration (1964-70). All chief executives have difficulty in dealing with political patronage, size, and other problems within their bureaucracies, especially when they want to move ahead swiftly with major reforms. The growth of governmental bureaucracy means that the president cannot run the government alone, as in the old days of one-man dictatorship. Even military regimes show this effect as they now govern by juntas, not by one man.

Another type of problem is the symbolic attention paid to progress rather than to actual working projects. Lots of plans and intents are drafted without ever taking physical shape, as in the much-legislated, but totally unimplemented, land reforms of some Latin American countries. The lack of continuity of planning and execution of public-works programs, for example, is to be seen in empty hospitals, skeletons of buildings without interiors, schools built near noisy highways, and lack of provisions for maintenance of buildings even when they are completed. Meanwhile, hiring of incompetents, duplication of effort, overlapping agencies, and poorly administered programs continue, and the bureaucratic structure continually expands.

The bureaucrats, as with other interest groups, are concerned with what one might expect—prestige, salary, status symbols, security, welfare, and other perquisites. The individual bureaucrat, typically from the middle class, has a variety of political options that can be used to attain these goals—depending upon the specific country and level of position occupied. Mexican civil servants are linked automatically into the dominant PRI structure through their powerful Government Employees Union. Venezuelan bureaucrats can use the services of the Venezuelan Labor Confederation. They can also rely upon *palanca* (political pull) in Venezuela, or some form of patron-client relationship in most countries. The Paraguayan and Guatemalan bureaucrat, by contrast, has no public-employees union to protect him. But, as in other countries, higher officials can decide whether or not to apply the law in a variety of situations, can hold up plans and funds, and can delay public projects. These are ways of exerting influence within the political system, to the detriment of sustained development even though the symbolic commitment to change may exist.

The overall picture is, however, not hopeless, despite these negative influences. Some agencies are paying close attention to thinking out the problems in their sector, leading to more feasible and better coordinated planning and programs, as with Venezuela's central planning agency, CORDIPLAN. A number of public-sector agencies throughout Latin America are turning more to merit considerations as the basis for hiring and promotion; again, Venezuela is a case in point, as is Cuba since 1959. A number of countries are experimenting with innovations in education to try to stimulate training in needed areas such as engineering, agronomy, science, and increasing the number of paramedical personnel. Cuba began to move swiftly in this direction in the 1960s, stimulated greatly by the exodus of middle-class, trained manpower as Castro moved toward Communism.

Finally, in parts of Latin America there is emerging a new type of professional public servant, who has specialized knowledge and training, called the *técnico*. While many of the Latin American bureaucracies still have great difficulty in assimilating this skilled technician, the trend is toward more professionally trained economists, engineers, scientists, and agronomists. The problem, of course, is still how to manage their talents effectively.

CONCLUSION

Many pressure groups operate within the Latin American political systems. The newer ones are products of increased urbanization, industrialization, commercial relations, and new leaders building new bases of power as compared to the old days. Their variety depends upon the specific country, and the range of traditional and new interest group activity is wide from Mexico to Tierra del Fuego. They cannot be considered interest groups in the Western democratic sense, for they are less autonomous, organized, and independent than in the United States or Western Europe.

The rapid growth of these interest associations affects the power of Latin American presidents. Even though chief executives dominate the formal government structures, the task of managing conflict between groups in an era of new demands for change is very tough. This is doubly true since so few political systems in Latin America have evolved nonpersonal problem-solving institutions to handle conflicts. So the older-style systems of patronage, patron-client relations, personalism, and demonstrations of power by a wide variety of means on the part of many different groups come into play. The upshot can be great instability and civil disorder when management breaks down, as occurred in Chile under Salvador Allende between 1970 and 1973. In an effort to abort the civil disorder connected with managerial conflict of interest, many regimes resort to repressive measures. The rise of military-run societies is frequently a natural outcome.

The nature of interest-group activity in Latin America suggests that development will occur with a distinct Latin American beat and not according to models imported from the United States or elsewhere. Brazil follows its own distinct path—repressive on the political side, but innovative on the economic. Peru uses strong military dominance to enforce economic changes more on a socialist model. Cuba, even though in close coordination with the Soviet Union, shows the imprint of Latin American culture: A personalist leader dominates interest-group performance, and the new interest groups—peasant unions, labor organization, the military—were created by none other than the socialist *caudillo* himself. Future interest-group activity within a development syndrome may follow still other models, but with a Latin American rhythm.

NOTES

1. See Robert F. Adie and Guy E. Poitras, *Latin America: The Politics of Immobility* (Englewood Cliffs, N.J.: Prentice-Hall, 1974); and Edward J. Williams and Freeman J. Wright, *Latin American Politics: A Developmental Approach* (Palo Alto, Calif.: Mayfield, 1975), pts. 2 and 3.
2. Charles W. Anderson, *Politics and Economic Change in Latin America* (Princeton, N.J.: Van Nostrand, 1967), ch. 11; and Howard J. Wiarda, "Toward a Framework for the Study of Political Change in the Iberic-Latin Tradition: The Corporative Model," *World Politics* 25 (January 1973): 206-35.
3. George Foster, "Peasant Society and the Image of the Limited Good," in *Peasant Society: A Reader,* ed. Potter, Diaz, and Foster (Boston: Little, Brown, 1967); and John Duncan Powell, "Peasant Society and Clientelist Politics," *American Political Science Review* 64 (June 1970): 411-25, on which part of the following discussion is drawn.
4. See Adie and Poitras, *op. cit.*, ch. 2.
5. *Student Politics in Latin America,* ed. David Spencer (United States National Student Association, 1965); and Walter Washington, "The Students," in *Latin American Politics: Twenty-four Studies of the Contemporary Scene,* ed. Robert D. Tomasek (Garden City, N.Y.: Doubleday, 1966).
6. Dieter K. Zschock, et al., "The Education-Work Transition of Venezuelan University Students," *Journal of Inter-American Studies and World Affairs* 16 (February 1974): 96-118.

7. Albert Lauterbach, *Enterprise in Latin America: Business Attitudes in a Developing Economy* (Ithaca, N.Y.: Cornell University Press, 1966).
8. Constantine Menges, "Public Policy and Organized Business in Chile," *Journal of International Affairs* 20 (1966): 343-65.

Suggested Readings

Adie, Robert F. and Guy E. Poitras. *Latin America: The Politics of Immobility*. Englewood Cliffs, N.J.: Prentice-Hall, 1974.
Alexander, Robert J. *Organized Labor in Latin America*. New York: The Free Press, 1965.
Astiz, Carlos. *Pressure Groups and Power Elites in Peruvian Politics*. Ithaca, N.Y.: Cornell University Press, 1969.
Bruneau, Thomas C. "Power and Influence: Analysis of the Church in Latin America and the Case of Brazil," *Latin America Research Review* 8 (Summer 1973): 25-44.
Horowitz, Irving Louis. *Masses in Latin America*. New York: Oxford University Press, 1970.
Lipset, Seymour Martin and Aldo Solari. *Elites in Latin America*. New York: Oxford University Press, 1967.
Pike, Frederick B. *The Conflict between Church and State in Latin America*. New York: Knopf, 1964.
Stavenhagen, Rodolfo. *Agrarian Problems and Peasant Movements in Latin America*. Garden City, N.Y.: Doubleday, 1970.
Suchlicki, Jaime. *University Students and Revolutions in Cuba, 1920-1968*. Coral Gables, Fla.: University of Miami Press, 1968.
Thurber, Clarence E. and Lawrence S. Graham. *Development Administration in Latin America*. Durham, N.C.: Duke University Press, 1973.
Turner, Frederick C. *Catholicism and Political Development in Latin America*. Durham, N.C.: University of North Carolina Press, 1971.
Wiarda, Howard J., et al. "The New Corporatism," *The Review of Politics* 36 (January 1970).

Ten

Political
Parties

Politics in the Western World today typically involves political parties in one form or another. Such parties have gained a strong foothold in the United States and Western Europe and can be traced back to the seventeenth and eighteenth centuries in England and France. States coming to independence after World War II, as well as in those Latin American countries of longer-standing independence, similarly generated political parties during their early statehood. Parties come in various ideological, numerical, and organizational forms. They perform a variety of functions and operate in many ways within diverse cultural settings.

The literature on political development highlights political parties as a key to modernization. "The distinctive institution of the modern polity," writes Samuel P. Huntington, "is the political party."[1] The party, for Huntington and other students of political development, is *the* essential institution that organizes mass participation in politics. The party, in short, is a basic means of institution building, where institutions are defined as "stable, valued, recurring, patterns of behavior,"[2] that perform a number of vital political functions. Political parties, for example, help to organize the state's political processes into a rational body of procedures, rules, and regulations that peacefully express various group demands and integrate them into the government system.[3] This, in effect, means pulling together diverse political communities into broad agreement and consensus, and providing a channel for rational, peaceful political participation.

Other party functions can also be identified. They include building a broad community ideal promoting development goals, and establishing legitimate authority through organized institutions that live beyond the life of a single leader.[4] Having the party as the basis for legitimacy helps to mobilize support for political activities on a more permanent basis, and to provide for the peaceful transition of political power.[5] Political parties are also deemed to be a channel for political recruitment—producing political leaders who are viewed as legitimate and who will be able to make critical decisions. Finally, parties are key governmental mechanisms that formulate policy, designate candidates, provide effective opposition, educate the public politically, maintain government unity, and mediate between government and public.

The problem of assessing political parties in Latin America in a "developmental" sense is to separate appearance from reality. Parties dot the political horizons of most Latin American countries, and they have multiplied in number during the twentieth century. They operate in many legislative arenas, proliferate around election time, and seem to be performing political-development roles.

The presence of political parties, however, can be deceiving. First, they are often not discrete, tightly organized, well disciplined, unique entities in the political system.[6] They often are coalitions of elites loosely tied together by personal interests and immediate short-run goals (spoils, patronage) rather than by discipline and organized institutions with long-range objectives. Elitism and personalism—operative in so many other aspects of Latin American politics—condition political parties as well.

Political parties, secondly, tend to rise at election time and fade between elections. This is largely due to their personal basis and narrow short-range goals. Third, parties are only infrequently relevant in some countries (Haiti, Nicaragua, Panama, and Paraguay), and only occasionally relevant in others (Peru, Ecuador, Guatemala, El Salvador, Honduras, the Dominican Republic).[7] Finally, the military elites pose a constant challenge to political parties, given the basic military distrust of competing party organizations. Even in countries where parties are normally relevant (Uruguay, Argentina, Chile, Colombia, Costa Rica, Cuba, Venezuela, Brazil, and Mexico) the military may intervene and declare them null and void as they did in Chile and Uruguay in 1973. In other countries, as in Brazil after 1964, the parties simply reflect the wishes of military political leaders.

Parties, to be sure, are viable institutions in some Latin American countries. In Colombia, Chile (before the 1973 coup), Costa Rica, Cuba, Mexico, and Venezuela, parties serve as a means of political recruitment, help articulate political goals, become channels for political communication and socialization, and, in some cases, help in the administration of government policies. As one Latin American scholar notes, it is not strange that the primary source of fertilizer in some rural areas is the dominant party headquarters.[8] The stronger the party, the more likely it is that these functions will be performed, as in the case in Mexico's *Partido Revolucionario Institucional* (PRI), Cuba's *Partido Communista Cubano* (PCC), Venezuela's *Acción Democrática* (AD) or its Christian Democratic COPEI.

This chapter discusses political parties in terms of types of systems; ideologies and programs; and organization and functions. What should emerge is the conclusion that Latin America has changed greatly in the twentieth century in terms of the growing numbers of parties, party aspirations, and, in some cases, the positive functions parties perform. In other cases the potential for party-led development is growing, but is constantly permeated by traditional divisive forces.

TYPES OF SYSTEMS

It is safe to say that no party system in Latin America is exactly like another. This makes classification difficult. Parties vary in terms of leadership, ideology, programs, and strength. These specific factors also change within specific countries over time, so any classification really depends upon what year one is discussing. It is also difficult to establish the effective number of political parties in some Latin American countries because a single party may dominate, although others exist, or because parties, although present, are legally barred from electoral competition.

The most helpful typology of party systems is that based on the results of party competition and elections, or legislative representation.[9] Using this criteria, four types of party systems can be identified: single-party dominant; two-party competitive; multiparty dominant; and multiparty loose.

In describing these party systems, the caution against seeing them as uniformly tightly organized, independent institutions is again made. We should also avoid the assumption that a two-party system is better or more democratic than other systems, or that a multiparty system is more democratic than a two-party or single-party system. A party's legislative power, moreover, should not be overestimated, given the limited political role of most Latin American legislatures compared to executives.

Single-Party Dominant

A single-party dominant system is simply one where a party wins 60 percent or more of the seats in the legislative body, with the other 40 percent or less divided among the remaining parties. The one-party dominant system may or may not contain other parties, even though the single party regularly dominates the legislature.

Wide variations of the single-party-dominant system exist. Mexico's PRI clearly controls the legislature and is in effect the government party. While its name, leadership, and structure have changed since its conception in 1929 as the National Revolutionary Party (PNR), it remains the largest party in Mexico.* The PRI, for example, won all but 5 of the 194 seats in the Chamber of Deputies in the July, 1974, elections; it won all 178 seats contested in the 1970 elections. The PRI, incidentally, gave free time on radio and television to the opposition party, PAN, for the first time in the July, 1973, elections. Cuba is another example of a single-party-dominant system. The Cuban Communist Party operates without opposition and is closely integrated with military and other organizations in Cuba. It is led by Fidel Castro, and most of its other leading figures are members of Castro's July 26 Movement, dating back to the first insurrection attempt to overthrow the Batista Government in 1953.[10] No parliament exists in Cuba, marking another key difference between the PCC and other dominant single parties of other countries.

Nicaragua and Paraguay are other examples of single-party-dominant systems, but must be assessed with caution. The parties are in effect little more than extensions of single-family rule, aligned with other conservative elites. They are not the institutional organizations found in Cuba and Mexico. Paraguay's president, General Alfredo Stroessner, has been president of Paraguay since 1954 when he assumed power in a coup d'etat. He was reelected for a fifth five-year term in February, 1973. His ruling Colorado Party then polled more than six hundred thousand votes (or 84 percent of the total) compared to the Liberal Radical Party's approximately hundred thousand (or 12 percent) and the Liberal Party's twenty-six thousand (about 3 percent). Nicaragua is also a single-party-dominant system where the *Partido Liberal Nacionalista* (PLN, National Liberal Party), the mechanism

---

*Opposition parties include the Catholic-oriented right wing *Partido de Acción Nacional* (PAN, National Action Party), the conservative *Partido Auténtico de la Revolución* (PARM, Authentic Party of the Mexican Revolution) and the *Partido Popular Socialista* (PPS, Socialist Party).

of the Somoza family that has ruled in Nicaragua for nearly forty years, is king. Although personalist regimes dominate the single parties of Nicaragua and Paraguay, they do provide patronage for followers and support for the leadership.[11]

Two-Party Competitive

Two-party-competitive systems are those in which two parties each receive not less than 40 percent nor more than 60 percent of the total seats. Examples of this type of system include Colombia and Uruguay (before the Army coup of February, 1973).

Colombia's two-party-competitive system is truly unique. The "Bogotazo" incident of 1948, when liberal leader Jorge Eliécer Gaitán was murdered in downtown Bogota, the subsequent violence of the late 1940s and early 1950s (over three hundred thousand killed), and the military rule under General Rojas Pinilla, prompted the heads of the Liberal and Conservative parties to agree on a means to restore constitutional government. The two parties determined to share power equally and to allow the presidency to rotate between them through elections. This "National Front" government operated between 1958 and 1974. The elections of April, 1974, brought a partial end to the sixteen-year-old National Front coalition pact, when Dr. Alfonso López Michelsen (Liberal) won more than half of the votes cast. Certain parts of the National Front were to continue—particularly the provision to continue the equal distribution of ministries and other administrative posts between the two parties no matter which presidential candidate won. The representative aspects of Colombia's two-party system, however, are undermined by voter abstention. Nearly half of the electorate failed to vote in the 1974 elections. During the sixteen-year National Front agreement, nearly two-thirds of the electorate sometimes failed to vote.

Uruguay traditionally has a two-party competitive system. The dominant party is the *Partido Colorado* (PC, Red Party). The opposition party is the *Partido Nacional* (PN, National Party), sometimes known as the *Blancos* or Whites. These parties will likely return to traditional opposition, but were sharply curtailed by the military in February, 1973, when it intervened directly in the government for the first time in the history of Uruguay, where democratic government dates back to the first elections in 1830. Behind the military intervention lay the armed forces suppression of the left-wing *Tupamaro* guerrilla movement, which had escalated sharply in April, 1972. From that date forward, Uruguay was under a state of internal war that virtually suspended civil rights and allowed the army to round up suspected

Tupamaro leaders. In doing so, the armed forces found widespread "malpractices" and "injustices" in the country, leading to its own investigation of corruption. This resulted in pressures on President Juan Bordaberry, who agreed to their demands for far-reaching reforms and to their own active participation in the country's government. The parliamentary system was suspended in June, 1973.

Multiparty Dominant

The multiparty-dominant system exists where three or more parties receive not less than 40 percent or more than 60 percent of the seats in the legislative body, and where no additional party receives more than 40 percent of the seats. Chile before the coup of September, 1973, and Argentina are cases in point.

Chile's multiparty system is well known to Latin American watchers. Although the parties became defunct after the coup, they should reappear somewhat along their traditional lines when the military regime moves out. With this caveat in mind, the Chilean party system can be viewed as a broad spectrum from the far right to the far left.* The far right is comprised of the National Party (PN), a combination of the old Conservative and Liberal parties which merged in 1966 in order to strengthen their electoral position. These parties endorsed Eduardo Frei in the 1964 presidential elections as the lesser of two evils (Salvador Allende—Frei's pro-Marxist opponent—being the greater evil) and contributed substantially to the Christian Democratic victory. But in the 1970 presidential elections the PN relied on its own organization and identity to try to capture the election. This split them away from the Christian Democratic Party, which also ran its own candidate, Radomiro Tomic. This move split the center and right vote, leaving the leftist coalition of Socialist, Communist, and other small parties—called Popular Unity (UP)—in a stronger position.

The center parties are made up of the Radicals (PR) and the Christian Democrats (PDC). The Radical Party has recently moved steadily toward the left in a movement to increase its votes, although many Chileans continue to regard it as centrist. The PDC, formed in the mid-1930s, became the dominant party in Chile under President Frei (1964-70) and President Allende (1970-73). Although plagued by factions, this party is strongly reform-oriented and led the movement

* The political scene until the coup, involved the following key parties: *Partido Nacional* (PN, National Party), *Partido Radical* (PR, Radical Party), *Partido Democratico Cristiano* (PDC, Christian Democratic Party), *Partido Socialista* (PS, Socialist Party), *Partido Communista de Chile* (PCCh, the Chilean Communist Party), and a number of smaller parties.

for land and housing reform, as well as for increased Chilean ownership of the mining industry, during the Frei years. President Allende
continued these policies, although in a far more radical version.[12]

Traditional leftist parties are the Communists (PCCh) and the Socialists (PS). The Communists are pro-Soviet, well-organized, and
closely aligned to the Central Union of Chilean workers. With an estimated membership of more than sixty thousand, the Chilean Communist party ranked as one of the strongest in Latin America before
Allende's fall. The Socialist Party, extremely divided over doctrine,
leadership, and policy, is far more independent and militant than the
Communist Party.

This multiplicity of parties typically leads to the formation of coalitions at election time.* The PCCh, the PS, and the PR supported
Allende in the leftist electoral alliance, *Unidad Popular* (UP), in the
1970 elections that won him the presidency. Leftist parties had earlier
formed the *Frente de Acción Popular* (FRAP, Popular Action Front)
in 1956. The National Party is similarly an amalgamation of the old
Liberal and Conservative parties created in 1965 to gain electoral
strength. These coalitions symbolize what Ronald McDonald describes
as the principal recent trend in Chile: increased party consolidation
and competition. Where fifteen parties received congressional representation in 1949, only six received it in 1969. Table 5 depicts this trend
in congressional voting patterns for Chilean parties between 1965 and
1973. It shows a continuation of the trend toward consolidation in
party politics. The 1973 congressional elections found the PDC, Conservatives and Liberals united in the Federation of Democratic Parties
(CODE), opposed to the *Unidad Popular*, made up of old Socialists,
Communists, and Radicals.[13]

Argentina is another case of a multiparty-dominant system, although
with strong qualifications. Argentine party history has been periodically
interrupted by military intervention, which permitted no political parties, or for long periods of time was under the authoritarian leadership
of Juan D. Perón (1943-55). The March, 1973, general elections appeared to have returned Argentina, at least temporarily, to a multiparty-dominant system. The elections produced a turnout in which
one group, the Perónist *Frente Justicialista de Liberación* (Frejuli,
Justicialist Liberation Front), received between 40 and 60 percent of
the vote, while the remaining parties together received not less than
40 percent. This election, in this sense, compared to the March, 1965,

---

* Minor parties include the National Democratic Party (PADENA), the *Movimiento de Acción Popular Unitaria* (MAPU, United Movement of Popular Action),
the *Partido Social Democratico* (PSD, Social Democratic Party) and the *Acción
Popular Independiente* (API, Independent Popular Action).

TABLE 5 CONGRESSIONAL VOTING FOR MAJOR CHILEAN PARTIES, 1965-73 (In percent)

Year	PDC	Con.	PL	PR	PS	PCCh
1965	43.6	5.3	7.5	13.7	10.6	12.8
1969	31.1	20.9		13.4	15.1*	16.6
1973		CODE†			Unidad Popular	
		54.7			43	

* Includes both Socialist and Popular Socialist Parties.

† The Unidad Popular coalition was opposed in the March, 1973, elections by an alliance of opposition parties known as the Federation of Democratic Parties (CODE). The latter comprised the National Party, the Christian Democrats, Radical Democrats, National Democrats, and a small group called the Radical Left. A socialist splinter group, the Socialist Popular Union (USOPO), maintained an independent stand. The object of CODE was to obtain a two-thirds majority in the combined congress.

Source: *Keesing's Contemporary Archives*, 1973; McDonald, p. 134.

elections in Chile, both being classic examples of the multiparty-dominant system at work.

From 1955 until 1966, multiparty-dominant representation flourished in Argentina. It centered around the *Unión Cívica Radical del Pueblo* (UCRP), the *Unión Cívica Radical Intransigente* (UCRI), and the frequently illegal Perónistas. The UCRP typically won better than 40 percent of the deputies and senators, but the Perónista's strength was real if dormant, as shown in the March, 1973, elections. Underlying the Argentine multiparty-dominant system were consistent personalist splits within parties, great instability, factionalism, and regionalism. These forces also permeated the Perónistas as Perón's later presidential rule (1973-74) so vividly showed. The Argentine experience challenges the assertion that a multiparty-dominant system provides stable forms of government, or a comparatively high level of institutionalization and political development.

Multiparty Loose

When no single party receives more than 40 percent of the legislative seats in a country where three or more parties are competing, we have a multiparty-loose system. Venezuela and Brazil are traditional examples of this type, although military rule in Brazil since 1964 naturally qualifies our assessment of that country. A number of other countries periodically fall into this category, especially Guatemala, Ecuador, and Panama.

Venezuela, a country that has seen its share of dictators (General Antonio Páez, 1830-48; Antonio Guzmán Blanco, 1870-88; Juan Vicente Gómez, 1908-35; General Marcos Pérez Jiménez, 1952-58), began to become a multiparty country during the 1940s and 1950s. The most important party was known as *Acción Democrática* (AD, Democratic Action), which early included Venezuela's liberals, socialists, intellectuals, and labor leaders. A second strong party of contemporary Venezuela is COPEI or *Comite de Organización Política Electoral Independiente*, a socialist Christian party led by Rafael Caldera.*

Venezuela began its experience in representative government after the fall of Pérez Jiménez as a multiparty-dominant system, but moved toward the loose model after that era. Table 6 shows party representation in the Venezuelan legislature, reflecting this trend. The March, 1974, general elections suggest that, if only temporarily, AD has broken the less than 40 percent rule of the loose-multiparty system by obtaining more than 40 percent representation in the legislature, and thus returning to its earlier, dominant position.

Behind the party scene in Venezuela, as in other countries, are strong personalist forces, elitism, poor organization, lack of party discipline, and struggle for coalitions and patronage. But it should also be said that AD and COPEI, the two leading parties in Venezuela, are strongly reform-oriented. Carlos Andrés Peréz, AD's president in 1974, particularly fits this mold.

The multiparty-loose systems are not necessarily more unstable than multiparty-dominant types, as a comparison with Argentina shows, any more than they are inherently more unstable than countries with histories of one-party rule. Haiti, the Dominican Republic, and Paraguay, for example, are also unstable. The proliferation of parties, however, does contribute to difficulties in building a firm consensus about policy formation and execution. Party proliferation is typically a function of electoral laws permitting the participation of small parties in elections, personalism, narrow parochial interests, and other social factors discussed in Chapters 5 and 6.

IDEOLOGIES AND PROGRAMS

Latin America's political parties fall into two broad classifications: traditional and modern. Traditional parties are the oldest political

---

* Other parties include the *Unión Republicana Democrática* (URD, Republican Democratic Union), the *Partido Comunista Venezolano* (PCV, Venezuelan Communist Party), and the *Frente Democrática Popular* (FDP, Popular Democratic Front).

TABLE 6 PARTY REPRESENTATION IN VENEZUELAN LEGISLATURE, 1969-79

	Senate		Deputies	
	1969-74	1974-79	1969-74	1974-79
AD	38	60	31	50
COPEI	30	28	28	31
MEP	10	4	11	3
URD	6	2	7	2
FDP	2	–	4	3
CCN	8	2	10	2
PCV	2	–	2	1
MAS	–	4		3

MEP = People's Electoral Movement; FDP = Popular Democratic Front; CCN = National Civic Crusade; MAS = Movement Toward Socialism. Other parties in the election which fared less well were: National Integrationist Party (PNI); Left Revolutionary Movement (MIR); Progressive Independents (IP); National Opinion (OPINA).

Source: *Keesing's Contemporary Archives*, 1974 (January 21-27, 1974).

groupings in Latin America; they emerged during the nineteenth-century struggles between Church and state and between those individuals who favored federalism against supporters of a centralized government. Out of this political competition came the Conservatives, favoring centralized government and the entrenched legal position of the Church and its religious property rights and central role in education. The Liberals, the second traditional party, were generally anti-clerical and in favor of federalism.

The key point to remember is that during the nineteenth century, both Conservatives and Liberals drew support from landholding and commercial aristocratic interests. Middle and lower sectors of the population were virtually excluded from direct political participation, and government remained oligarchic. This situation led to the emergence of a third traditional party, the Radicals, an offshoot of the Liberals. Making their appearance in the middle and late nineteenth century as a reaction against both Liberal and Conservative parties, they represented the interests of the growing middle sectors, particularly in Argentina and Chile. They advocated an extension of the franchise, welfare legislation, and social security.

The modern parties are twentieth-century phenomena, arising out of the forces advocating change in Latin America. European immigration, urbanization, closer contact with more advanced states, the rise of labor as a political force all had the impact of shifting party orientations increasingly toward the left. As new parties were born, they appealed to working classes, peasants, intellectuals, and middle sectors. They emphasized social and economic reforms designed to improve the living conditions for middle- and lower-class groups.

On the Ideologies of Modern Parties

At the risk of vastly oversimplifying a truly complex situation, the catalogue of modern reform parties can be broken down into five major groups.[14] They are the Christian Democrat, Communist, Socialist, Jacobin, and National Revolutionary parties. The first three are European in inspiration; the Jacobin and National Revolutionary parties are more indigenous.

Most of the Christian Democratic parties were established after World War II with the exception of those in Chile and Uruguay. The most famous of the Christian Democratic groups are those of Chile (winning in 1964 against a combination of leftist parties) and Venezuela (COPEI). Christian Democratic parties also exist in Argentina, Bolivia, Ecuador, Paraguay, and Peru. The Christian Democrats were also the party of Venezuela's recent president, Rafael Caldera, who turned the presidency over to Carlos Andrés Peréz, Democratic Action candidate, in late 1973. These parties are associated with the Roman Catholic Church insofar as they operate upon the liberal social principles of three well-known Papal Encyclicals.

Pope Leo XIII's 1891 Encyclical, *Rerum Novarum* (in English, *On the Condition of the Workers*), among other things advanced the idea of mutual duties and obligations of workers and employers. It maintained that workers should be treated with dignity, should not be overworked, and were entitled to a just salary. In 1931, Pope Pius XI issued his Encyclical, *Quadragesimo Anno* (*Reconstructing the Social Order*), emphasizing the oppressed status of the poor, especially the urban proletariat, and the need to achieve social justice through Christian ethics and the redistribution of concentrated wealth. Pope John XXIII's 1961 Encyclical, *Mater et Magistra* (*Mother and Teacher*), again stresses Christian social ethics in conducting economic activity in accordance with the common good and individual dignity. His is a call for renewed dedication to the work of transforming the world, motivated by Christian charity.

Christian Democrats, following these Encyclicals, stress individual dignity, social welfare, and worker participation in national life. These goals are to be attained through enlightened state intervention in the private sector to break up disproportionate concentration of economic wealth and to redistribute national income on a socially just basis. The

Christian Democratic Party of Chile (PDC), the first of its kind to hold office in Latin America (1964-70) stressed, during its rule, greater governmental control over the North American copper holdings, agrarian reform to allocate land to landless peasants, a new government housing and education program, expanded social services, increased trade-union power, and administrative decentralization.

Communist Parties

The Communist party picture is more complicated than that of the Christian Democrats, due to a much wider and more diversified theoretical basis. The Sino-Soviet split of the late 1950s produced Peking-oriented counterparts that emphasized violent change compared to the more traditional pro-Soviet Communist parties whose stress was on peaceful parliamentary cooperation.[15] Fidel Castro's turn away from the Soviet position to a more militant and independent line in 1966-68 produced additional variants of Communism in Latin America and imposed even more severe strains on the Communist family.[16]

Ernesto "Che" Guevera's heroic exploits and death (1967) in Bolivia continued to stimulate a cult of militancy within the Communist camp as well as a further fragmentation in its ideological unity.

A variety of Marxist-Leninist parties resulted from the competing ideological crosscurrents. While precise categorization is difficult, they appear to fall into four groups: pro-Soviet, pro-Chinese, Trotskyite, and Communist-Nationalist. The pro-Soviet parties, approximately twenty-four in 1970, typically endorsed the Soviet line and tended to have been dominated by the same leaders for decades.[17] These groups are larger than the pro-Chinese Communist parties, which are quite small and tend to be split into two or three rival factions. They tend to have their greatest influence among young and student groups, especially in Ecuador and Peru. Trotskyite groups have not had much influence in Latin America, largely because of the extremely wide variety of their domestic and international views. The Communist-Nationalist groups are dissident Communists who have broken away from the pro-Soviet parties. The first institutionalized group of this category was the Movement Toward Socialism (MAS), established in December, 1970, following a split in the Venezuelan Communist Party. Communist party strength and status in Latin America are shown in Table 7.

Marxist-Leninist parties have experienced mixed results. The Communist party of Chile joined the successful presidential campaign of 1969 in supporting the victor, Salvador Allende. But when the military overthrew Allende in 1973, they declared political parties null and void. The Cuban Communist party, now the largest in Latin America, is run by men loyal to Fidel Castro. These fidelistas supplanted old-line Com-

TABLE 7 COMMUNIST PARTY STRENGTH AND STATUS IN
LATIN AMERICA

Country	Party Membership		Number of Parties	Legal Status
	1960	1972		
Argentina	70-80,000	70,000 (E)	1	Illegal
Bolivia	4,000	3,200 (E)	3	Illegal
Brazil	50,000	7,000 (E)	2	Illegal
Chile	20-25,000	120,000 (E)	1	Illegal (1973)
Colombia	5,000	11,000 (E)	2	Legal
Costa Rica	300	1,000 (E)	1	Illegal
Cuba	12,000	125,000 (C)	1	Legal and in power
Dominican Republic	Negligible	1,200 (E)	6	Illegal
Ecuador	1,000	1,200 (E)	3	Illegal
El Salvador	500	125 (E)	1	Illegal
Guatemala	1,000	750 (E)	1	Illegal
Haiti	Negligible	Negligible	—	Illegal
Honduras	500	300 (E)	2	Illegal
Mexico	5,000	5,000 (E)	1	Legal
Nicaragua	200	100 (E)	1	Illegal
Panama	Negligible	500 (E)	1	Illegal
Paraguay	500	3,500 (E)	2	Illegal
Peru	6,000	3,200 (E)	2	Illegal
Uruguay	3,000	22,000 (E)	1	Illegal (1973)
Venezuela	30-35,000	8,000 (E)	2	Legal

Note: "E" refers to estimated figures; "C" to claimed figures.

Source: U.S. Department of State, Bureau of Intelligence and Research, *World Strength of the Communist Party Organizations*, 25th Annual Report, 1973 edition.

munists in the top leadership of the party as Castro consolidated his strength during the 1960s. The Uruguayan military coup of 1974 brought an end to Communist-party legality in that state. Legal in Venezuela, the PCV received only 1.19 percent of the votes in the presidential election of 1973.

With the exceptions of Chile and Cuba, most observers believe that Marxist-Leninists will continue to prove unable to compete successfully with other political and social groups. The reasons for this prognosis include the growth of other modern, and stronger, reform-oriented parties, such as Mexico's PRI, Venezuela's AD and COPEI; the illegality of Communist parties in many countries; the individualism, personalism, and hostility to regimentation endemic in Latin America; the lack of a revolutionary tradition in many of Latin America's Communist parties; and the fragmentation of the Communist parties themselves.

Socialist Parties

The Socialist parties are very difficult to describe and enumerate, given the forces that operate within them. These pressures—personality differences, disagreements on strategy, and ideological differences—result in doctrinal fragmentation and shifting policy positions. The Socialist parties, as a general rule, tend to be more militant and nationalistic than the Communists, which makes cooperation between the two groups extremely difficult.

Jacobin Groups

Jacobin parties include a wide variety of radicals and social revolutionaries who advocate immediate, violent, and revolutionary change in the status quo. Disillusioned and impatient with the democratic process, these groups seek to overthrow the present system and completely reorganize a new tomorrow along more socialist lines. The precise dimensions of the future are far less clear than the goal of destroying the old order through immediate and militant action.

The best examples of the Jacobin left are Fidel Castro's 26th of July Movement, which later merged with the Communist party, Venezuela's Armed Forces of National Liberation (FALN), and the various movements of the revolutionary left (MIR) in Venezuela, Chile, the Dominican Republic, and Ecuador. Chile's MIR continued to insist on illegal factory- and land-seizures against President Allende's admonitions during 1970-73. It was a pervasive force that escalated the ideological polarization in Chile, bringing on military intervention. With the exception of this group, the MIR political parties have not been politically strong in Latin America.

National Revolutionary Parties

The National Revolutionary parties are indigenous groups. They include a number of parties whose objectives are ostensibly to convert the country into full nationhood by martialing workers, *campesinos,* Indians, and rural masses through common sources of national identity. They attempt to utilize their country's traditions as a basis for cohesion and ideology, highlighting the goals of political democracy, agrarian reform, government control over economic development, social security, and educational advancement. The prototype of this kind of party is the American Popular Revolutionary Alliance (APRA) founded by the Peruvian Víctor Raúl Haya de la Torre in Mexico in May, 1924.

Other National Revolutionary parties, generated by unique conditions in specific countries, were formed throughout Latin America, each seeking to cope with the conditions in its own country. They included the PRI of Mexico, the National Revolutionary Movement of Bolivia (MNR), and the National Liberation Party (PLN) of Costa Rica. One scholar lists the National Revolutionary Parties as follows:[18]

Bolivia: The National Revolutionary Movement (MNR)
Costa Rica: The National Liberation Party (PLN)
Cuba: The Authentic Cuban Revolutionary Party and the Orthodox Popular Cuban Party (Autenticos and the Ortodoxos)
The Dominican Republic: The Dominican Revolutionary Party (PRD)
El Salvador: The Authentic Revolutionary Party of Democratic Unification (PRUD Autentico) and the National Conciliation Party (PCN)
Guatemala: The Revolutionary Party (PR)
Haiti: The Workers and Peasants Movement (MOP)
Mexico: The Institutional Revolutionary Party (PRI) and the Authentic Mexican Revolutionary Party (PARM)
Paraguay: The Febrerista Party
Peru: The American Revolutionary Popular Alliance (APRA)
Uruguay: The Colorado Party
Venezuela: The Democratic Action Party (ED)

The history of national revolutionary parties shows in some cases a strong shift toward nation-building and political development, at least compared to their nineteenth-century backgrounds. Mexico's PRI emphasizes a Mexican identity in sharp contrast to the nineteenth-century intellectual fascination with all things European. Peru's APRA also moved in this direction in the 1920s, with its stress on Indianism. The PRI also served to focus interest on things Mexican, as does the Democratic Action Party in Venezuela.

The National Revolutionary movements, however, have not consistently lived up to their hopes in many cases. They face opposition from large landowners and merchant classes, traditional Catholic groups, and such traditional interest associations as chambers of commerce and industry, the commercial export sector, bankers' and employers' associations, and other corporate interests.[19] Among the criticisms levied against the National Revolutionary parties are their lack of coherent ideology; lack of change in political leadership combined with excessive personalism in their leadership; lack of a clear line of action; and the tendency not to reconsider policy decisions that may have been overtaken by events. The potential for leadership is strong in the National Revolutionary parties, but they are often unable to overcome those traditional forces that plague other political parties in Latin America.

ORGANIZATION AND FUNCTION OF LATIN AMERICAN POLITICAL PARTIES

A general statement about Latin American political parties is hazardous, given the great variations in party performance. Party systems are underdeveloped in some countries (Haiti and Guatemala). In others they not only are present, but play important roles in integrating the political community, providing less personal organizations (institutionalization) than in earlier times, and strengthening the government's capacity to execute public policy (as in Colombia, Cuba, Mexico, and Venezuela). In still other countries they are sometimes relevant, sometimes irrelevant (Argentina after 1966, Brazil after 1964, Chile and Uruguay after 1973), or play a role only insofar as the military allows. Finally, parties, on balance, are not relevant in terms of automatically producing democracy, given the authoritarian cultural context in which they operate.

More helpful than a general statement about Latin American political parties is a pro and con balance sheet focused on their organization and functions, using the criteria of political party performance in developed countries. The organization and function of political parties in developed countries, closely associated with nation-building and political development, are typically cited as follows. Political parties (1) formulate effective policy; (2) designate candidates; (3) criticize and offer effective opposition and alternate policies; (4) educate the public politically; (5) mediate between government and public; and (6) maintain governmental unity.

To what extent do the Latin American political parties evidence these characteristics?

The Case against the Latin American Political Parties

The case against Latin American party organization and functions in terms of these criteria is strong. It centers in the simple fact that most parties south of the Rio Grande simply do not perform those functions typically associated with political parties in western democracies.

Formulate Effective Policy. As far as parties being effective nonpersonal organizations through which effective policy formation occurs, the truth is that formulation typically rests with the party founder or central leader, not with its institutional system. It is most often men, not programs, that hold a party together. This personalist force is translated into elitist control of internal decision-making *personalismo,* factionalism, and enormous difficulties in organizing for long-range policy development.

Examples of these cultural effects are plentiful. Juan D. Perón remained a strong personalist leader of the Argentine Perónists after his return to that country, yet the Perónistas were bitterly divided. Castro remains an enormously charismatic force within Cuba's Communist Party. Many observers view him, rather than the new political-party structure and other institutions he created after 1959, as the central force in Cuba's revolution. Rómulo Betancourt's influence on Venezuela's *Acción Democrática* remained strong long after the party was formed as did that of José Figueres' power over Costa Rica's *Partido de la Liberación.*

Designate Candidates. Designating candidates also falls frequently to the powerful leader rather than party organization. Candidates often designate a party in Latin America rather than the reverse. This helps explain the profusion of splits by old parties into new parties formed by a dissident leader. Chile is notorious for this, as are Argentina, Brazil, and Venezuela.

Other Effective Opposition and Alternate Policies. Effective opposition and alternate policies are not easily generated by Latin America's political parties. This is due not only to their structural weaknesses, but also to the political setting in which they operate. Basic authority typically rests with the executive; furthermore corporate interests are strong and have little sense of responsibility toward society at large. Many corporate interests do not trust political parties and even view them as illegitimate—as does the military. Even political parties in some cases view each other as illegitimate, particularly in the case of Conservatives and Liberals viewing their rivals and sometimes of Radicals viewing the Labor parties.

Other facets of the operational setting limit party performance. Loyalty at the local level is typically to family, village, or *cacique* rather than to party organization. Little sustained party participation occurs between elections in many cases. The general nature of Latin America's segmented societies makes cohesive party organization difficult, undermining the base of consensus on which effective opposition and alternative policies might be forged.

Educating the Public. Political education of the Latin American public is not accomplished by political parties. Appeals to the public are commonly in demagogic and emotional form, which is not surprising in a culture where emotion and personalism run strong. When the office of presidency is viewed as a public prize, as it is in some countries, control of the press and radio is not long in coming—which does not stimulate any broad public education in objective issues or balanced options.

Mediate between the Government and Public. Mediation between government and public occurs more often through personal connection than through political parties. The anterooms of Latin America's public officials are filled daily with people seeking personal entrées to "the Man." Who one knows is even more important in Latin America than it is in other regions of the world.

Maintain Government Unity. The party is not the key source of governmental unity in most Latin American countries. The power to maintain unity can rather be attributed to the President; the spokesmen for corporate interests; the governmental bureaucracy; the military; or a combination of these and others. The parties—as cohesive and efficient organizations—do not figure strongly in this power equation.

The case against Latin American political parties, in terms of their capacity to perform nation-building and state-building functions, is strong. They are riddled with personalism and instability. They generate political conflict that erodes the political system, rather than integrating it. Small parties multiply while large parties splinter. And all parties lack programmatic content, a broad consensus on policy norms, and an ability to organize for political action.

THE CASE FOR LATIN AMERICAN POLITICAL PARTIES

It is also true that parties and party systems in some countries are rather advanced according to the criteria used here. While they are subject to the above trends, they nevertheless have progressed in their capacity to play policy roles in nation- and state-building, especially when their present status is measured against past conditions.

On the positive side, then, some parties demonstrate a remarkable ability to perform the six functions outlined above, even if modified somewhat by traditional forces. This means that in effect they help to integrate new groups into the political process and stimulate a re sponsibility on the part of those in power toward the population of the country; contribute to the recruitment of modernizing elites; and provide support for executives and administrators who are attempting to carry out new and innovative policies.

Certain specific political parties fall into this category of promise for the future. They are Mexico's PRI, notwithstanding the recent sharp criticism of that party; Cuba's Communist Party, with its strongly nationalist overtones under Fidel Castro's leadership; Venezuela's Democratic Action and COPEI; Chile's Christian Democratic Party under Eduardo Frei, even though it split into three factions between 1964 and 1970. The modification of the National Front in Colombia in 1974 may indicate a new role for political parties there, particularly under the influence of the reform-oriented Liberal Party. The picture of political-party performance, then, is mixed in Latin America, and one's interpretation depends upon the country. But the overall image by far is not totally bleak.

NOTES

1. Samuel P. Huntington, *Political Order in Changing Societies* (New Haven: Yale University Press, 1968), p. 89.
2. *Ibid.*, p. 12.
3. Gabriel Almond and G. Bingham Powell, Jr., *Comparative Politics: A Developmental Approach* (Boston: Little, Brown, 1966), ch. 5; Joseph La Palombara and Myron Weiner (eds.), *Political Parties and Political Development* (Princeton, N.J.: Princeton University Press, 1966), p. 3; and Ronald H. McDonald, *Party Systems and Elections in Latin America* (Chicago: Markham, 1971), p. vii.
4. Huntington, *op. cit.*, pp. 387-89.
5. Almond and Powell, *op. cit.*, p. 16; McDonald, *op. cit.*, p. 7.
6. This problem of viewing political parties, or bureaucracies, interest groups, the military, as discrete organizational entities in Third World political systems is discussed by Gerald A. Heeger, *The Politics of Underdevelopment* (New York: St. Martin's Press, 1973), p. 9.
7. McDonald, *op. cit.*, pp. 2-7. See also John D. Martz, "The Place of Latin America in the Study of Comparative Politics," *Journal of Politics* 28 (February 1966): 71-73; and John D. Martz, "Dilemmas in the Study of Latin American Political Parties," *The Journal of Politics* (August 1964).
8. McDonald, *op. cit.*, p. 7.
9. This method is adopted by McDonald in his *Party Systems and Elections in Latin America*.
10. Castro organized a group of students who attacked the Moncada Army Post at Santiago de Cuba on July 26, 1953. Most of the 165 students were killed. Castro and a few others escaped, but they surrendered

later and were sentenced to fifteen-year prison terms. Batista pardoned all of his political prisoners, including Castro, eleven months later.

11. On the dominant *Partido Liberal Nacionalista* in Nicaragua, see McDonald, *op cit.*, pp. 228-35. It should be pointed out that although the PLN is supreme in Nicaragua, and the opposition parties have little chance of winning elections, they do provide a basis for injecting popular demands into the governmental process at election time. As Eduardo Chamorro, a leader of the opposition Conservative Party, said in 1974, when presidential elections approached, "We know if he [General Somoza] is going to win, but for us it is not a question of win or lose but how much change we can bring to Nicaragua through constant prodding." *New York Times,* February 17, 1974.

12. Michel J. Francis and Hernan Vera-Godoy, "Chile: Christian Democracy to Marxism," *The Review of Politics* 33 (July 1971): 232-41.

13. Chile, characterized historically by a multiparty-loose system, moved tentatively toward a multiparty-dominant system after 1947, and appeared to have been moving toward some new kind of system by 1973 with the two major party blocks in opposition.

14. This particular classification is adopted from Russell H. Fitzgibbon, "Seven Dilemmas of Latin America's National Revolutionary Parties," *Orbis* 14 (Summer 1970): 443-62.

15. On the impact of Communist China in Latin America, see Cecil Johnson, *Communist China and Latin America, 1959-1967* (New York and London: Columbia University Press, 1970). Soviet influence on Latin American political parties may be found in Stephen Clissold, *Soviet Relations with Latin America, 1918-1968* (London: Oxford University Press, 1970). See also Herbert Dinerstein, "Soviet Policy in Latin America," *The American Political Science Review* (March 1967): 80-90.

16. See W. Raymond Duncan, "Soviet Policy in Latin America Since Khrushchev," *Orbis* (Summer 1971): 643-69; and D. Bruce Jackson, *Castro, the Kremlin, and Communism in Latin America* (Baltimore, Md.: Johns Hopkins Press, 1969).

17. William E. Ratliff, *1971 Yearbook on Latin American Communist Affairs* (Stanford, Calif.: Hoover Institution Press, 1971), p. 10.

18. Fitzgibbon, *op. cit.*

19. On these and other problems that face Latin American revolutionary parties, see Robert E. Scott, "Political Parties and Policy Making in Latin America" in La Palombara and Weiner, *op. cit.*, ch. 12.

Suggested Readings

Alexander, Robert J. *The Venezuelan Democratic Revolution: A Profile of the Regime of Rómulo Betancourt.* New Brunswick, N.J.: Rutgers University Press, 1964.

Fitzgibbon, Russell H. "Seven Dilemmas of Latin America's National Revolutionary Parties," *Orbis* 14 (Summer 1970): 443-62.

Halperin, Ernest. *Proletarian Class Parties in Europe and America: A Comparison.* Cambridge: M.I.T. Monograph, Center for International Studies, August 1967.

Martz, John D. *Acción Democrática; Evolution of a Modern Party in Venezuela.* Princeton, N.J.: Princeton University Press, 1966.

————. "Dilemmas in the Study of Latin American Political Parties," *The Journal of Politics* 26 (August 1964): 509-31.

————. "The Place of Latin America in the Study of Comparative Politics," *Journal of Politics* 28 (February 1966): 57-80.

McDonald, Ronald H. *Party Systems and Elections in Latin America.* Chicago: Markham, 1971.

Ratliff, William E. *1971 Yearbook on Latin American Communists Affairs.* Stanford, Calif.: Hoover Institution Press, 1971.

Sigmund, Paul. "Chile: Two Years of 'Popular Unity'," *Problems of Communism* 21 (November–December 1972): 38-50.

Eleven

The
Military

Military politics—the control or take-over of civil regimes—is endemic to Latin America. It dates to the nineteenth century, an era of strong militarism except in Chile and Costa Rica, and it continues to condition the politics of development today. Thirteen of the twenty republics conformed to a military-political model by mid-1974.*

These countries included, much to the surprise of many observers, Chile and Uruguay, frequently cited as showcases of political democracy and a nonpolitical military. A coup d'etat (September, 1973) ended forty-six years of civilian control in Chile. Earlier, in June, 1973, President Juan Bordaberry of Uruguay acquiesced to military rule, dissolving the congress, instituting censorship, and ending municipal councils. Chile and Uruguay indicate that a long period of civilian rule is not evidence of weak military establishment. Civilian governments often remain in power only by placating military interests, particularly by giving them a healthy proportion of the country's budget. An example was the tank mutiny in Chile on October 26, 1969. It resulted in an increase in officers' pay, in some cases 100 percent, but in no case less than 70 percent.[1]

* Bolivia, Brazil, Chile, the Dominican Republic, Ecuador, El Salvador, Guatemala, Honduras, Nicaragua, Panama, Paraguay, Peru, and Uruguay.

While surprising in Chile and Uruguay, military intervention in politics is less astounding elsewhere in Latin America. One author computes three hundred and fifty extraconstitutional assumptions of power in Latin America between 1923 and 1966.[2] States especially subject to coups d'etat between 1823 and 1966 include Haiti (58), the Dominican Republic (56), Ecuador (54), Peru (54), Bolivia (52), El Salvador (42), Paraguay (42), and Guatemala (42). The early 1970s saw a continuation of military coups in Latin America, with Bolivia, Chile, Ecuador, Honduras, and Uruguay providing specific cases in point.

Rates of military spending are high in many Latin American states although lower than in other Third World countries. Latin American purchase of military equipment was approximately 1.7 billion dollars between 1967 and 1972, or five times the previous peak for the comparable era in the late 1950s.[3] The principal purchasers were Argentina, Brazil, Chile, Colombia, Peru, and Venezuela. They accounted for 97 percent of all Latin American arms purchases abroad and approximately 85 percent of total Latin American defense appropriations in 1971 (or 2.5 billion dollars of the total 2.5 billion-dollar defense appropriation).[4] Because the military establishments see themselves as guardians of the country, a role clearly recognized in several Latin American constitutions, they are likely to intervene in the political process whenever the government is perceived as paralyzed, operating in defiance of the constitution, faced with a populist threat, or lagging in economic development.

The armed forces are not unified, which increases their overall role in politics. Different branches of the armed forces frequently disagree over political issues, such as the extent of civilian rule. Examples include an Ecuadorian Air Force dispute with (and victory over) the Army in 1962, Venezuelan Army and Air Force victory over its Marine Corps in 1962, and interservice wars in Argentina (1963), the Dominican Republic (1965), and Bolivia (1970). Different service branches frequently recruit from different sectors of society, which provides another source of interservice rivalry. Navies are known for their landowning and wealthy family background, while armies are recruited from lower classes than the navy, air force, or marines. In all countries the army is numerically superior. Finally, the separation of branches stimulates duplication of arms, and escalates military expenditures. This is especially true since some navies and armies have air divisions, as in Brazil and Peru.

An understanding of Latin American politics requires a look into the background, changing aspects, and political outcomes of military involvement. The following discussion of the military centers on its historical roots; changes in military training and perceptions; explanations for military intervention; and the cases for and against the military as an agent of political, social, and economic development. The latter section is particularly important, given the continuing intervention of the military in civilian affairs and the evolution of political and economic development throughout Latin America.

THE BACKGROUND OF MILITARY RULE

The historical causes for military intervention are varied. Their deep historical roots lie in the seven hundred years of intermittent fighting against the Moors in Spain, which gave a military career high prestige in Hispanic culture. The reconquest of Spain continued, and even heightened, the status of the armed forces before the conquest of the new world. The conquest of the new world in turn continued to maintain that status.[5]

Other roots of militarism date from the colonial period and the struggle for independence. Spanish colonialism helped set the scene for later military politics. Eligibility for military commissions, for example, were restricted to the Spanish and Creole (New World white American) elites, which led the Creoles to identify with the upper classes.[6] Military privileges (*fueros*) also exempted armed-forces personnel from the jurisdiction of civil courts. The new effect was, in the words of one observer, to create "a privileged caste exempt from public liability and civil responsibility."[7] The long struggle for Independence (1810-26), virtually between Creole and *peninsulare* (Spanish-born) elites, again enhanced the military through the leadership of such heroes as Simón Bolívar and José de San Martín.

The military dominated the political scene during much of the nineteenth century. Given the absence of other legitimate institutions and organizations to enforce or command men's loyalties, the military became the natural vehicle to mobilize power. It provided a basis of organized strength, played upon *machismo,* emotions, and *personalismo,* and could be used by middle- or lower-sector individuals as a route to attain wealth and power not available by other means.

Given the otherwise closed, ascriptive, and elite social structure, the military career (possibly ending in the presidency) meant social and political mobility. When the more talented and wealthy professionals of the army who had engaged in the independence movements disappeared from the scene, ambitious and less-patriotic types took to military careers. The upshot was struggle for government power through the military, frequent coups d'etat, predatory military politics, and military dictatorships. As Edwin Lieuwen puts it, the struggle centered around the presidential office, and involved a "plethora of ambitious, opportunistic military men" who made politics in almost every country "little more than an endless procession of dissension, intrigue, and revolutionary turmoil."[8]

The historic roots of military politics, in summary, lie in a number of sources. They include the high prestige accorded a military career and the continued ennobled status of the military through the colonial, insurrectionary, and post-Independence periods. The absence of a self-government tradition during colonialism, the destruction of colonial institutions unreplaced by other statewide legitimate institutions, and the limited bases of organized power outside the military must also be cited. The military, as an organization stressing force, violence, and *machismo*, of political and social mobility, is also closely associated with Hispanic cultural values.

CHANGE IN MILITARY TRAINING AND PERCEPTIONS

The military since World War II shows two distinct changes, compared to the nineteenth century. These changes are toward increased professionalism and a concern for economic development.

Increased Professionalism

A significant aspect of contemporary military politics is the accent it places on professionalism.[9] By professionalism is meant increased education, an emphasis on examinations to rise through the ranks, regularized salary schedules comparable to civilians of similar age and training, and attractive retirement plans. Increased professionalism means that military careers become formally institutionalized, and more technological approaches to problems come from within the military branches. This professionalism contrasts with the heroic, personalist, single-man *caudillo* of nineteenth-century vintage. The military leaders of today operate more from a foundation of a well-trained officer corps and a significantly higher level of technical-military skills.

The emphasis on military professionalism is shown by the type of education required for advancement to higher ranks. Promotion to the rank of general in Brazil, for example, requires that an officer be a graduate of the military academy, the junior officer school, and the three-year command and general staff school. High-achievement officers strive hard to gain admittance to the latter, which involves months of preparation for anyone taking the rigorous qualifying examinations.

Three-quarters of the applicants do not make it, and underachievers are dropped from the course at the end of each year. Peruvian senior officers similarly show comparable educational attainments: 80 percent of all division generals on active duty between 1940 and 1965 graduated in the top quarter of their military-academy class.[10] The curriculum at command and general staff schools covers military organization, administration and tactics, theories of revolutionary warfare, psychology, sociology, economics, political theory, and military history. The officer may attend, in addition, graduate and post-graduate training in universities or in foreign missions, such as the National War College in Washington, D.C.

Professionalism is marked by liaisons and common experiences with civilian counterparts in the higher institutions of learning. Schools at the War College level particularly enhance these connections. Civilian students attend the Brazilian Superior War School (Escola Superior de Guerra, ESG) as they do at the Peruvian center of military studies (Centro de Altos Estudios Militares, CAEM), and the national war colleges in Argentina, Bolivia, and Paraguay.[11] Professionalism is reflected in the concerns evinced by many of today's Latin American military organizations. Instead of using political power as a means to get rich through the spoils of office, a distinct nineteenth-century phenomenon, since World War II these units have shown several new orientations.[12] They now identify themselves with industrialization, are no longer associated purely with the conservative, landed elites and Catholic Church, and are more concerned with economic development.

A corporate identity, pride, and unity with other military branches accompanies increased professional training. This newer outlook can, of course, be a two-edged sword as far as the military's role in politics is concerned—using its élan to promote national development, as in Peru, or protecting its corporate unity from populist threats, as in Chile under Allende. But whatever the political outcomes, the corporate self-identity is strengthened by professionalism. One thing *is* certain: the new professionalism has not lessened the inclination of the military to intervene in politics, as some observers predicted earlier in the 1960s.[13]

A major impact of increased military professionalism is seen in the replacement of the man on horseback with a board or committee—the junta—when military intervention occurs. This does not mean the end of individualism, personalism, and political conflicts in military politics.[14] It does however point to a trend toward joint efforts by key groups within military branches to attempt to unify their efforts toward common goals. The rise of the junta also reflects the new technological-military training and corporate identity of recent years.

Concern with Economic Development

Perhaps the biggest change within the military services is its orientation toward economic development. In more than one country, particularly Argentina, Brazil, and Peru, military officers have come to perceive the importance of economic and social development as part of internal security, rather than concentrating upon a simple maintenance of the status quo, as in earlier times. This perception is undoubtedly due to the training received in formal classes, as well as the emphasis placed on national development during the 1960s by such world organizations as the UN, World Bank, Inter-American Development Bank, OAS, meetings of Latin American foreign ministers, and writings in the foreign press.

Military politics turned increasingly toward development in Brazil (1964), Argentina (1966), Peru (1968), and Bolivia (1969). The Brazilian and Peruvian militaries assumed a basically new and dominant role in their political systems, whereas the Argentine and Bolivian militaries had less success. The Argentine military started a coup in June, 1966, seeking to modernize Argentine society and economy. Unlike Brazil and Peru, the Argentine junta soon broke into competing factions over what specific policies to pursue. When General Alfredo Ovando came to power in Bolivia, following the death of President René Barrientos (April, 1969), he pursued a radical style of politics by nationalizing the Gulf Oil Company, annulling the old petroleum code, and establishing diplomatic relations with the Soviet Union. Divisions within the officer corps led to Ovando's resignation (October, 1970), and General Juan José Torres emerged as the new leader. General Torres expelled the Peace Corps and allowed a "Popular Assembly" to meet in the old congressional building to plan for more radical policies. But Torres was in turn overthrown in August, 1971, by another coalition of officers and political leaders. It was led by Colonel Hugo Bánzer Suárez. The Suárez regime became less development-oriented than its predecessors, but far more so than its nineteenth-century counterparts.

The war colleges in Argentina, Brazil, and Peru stress economic development. Many of the civilian instructors, particularly the economists, are Marxist in orientation. Others are revisionist historians who place an emphasis on xenophobic nationalism and authoritarianism. Both tend to stress the enlarged role of the government in guiding and regulating the development process, in contrast to earlier officers who intervened without charting a new course.

The political socialization of officers in many Latin American countries, to summarize, is now toward the politics of development and the connections between economic progress and national security.[15] The effects of increased training for the politics of development manifest themselves in other phenomena than the coups in Argentina, Brazil, Bolivia, and Peru. The training coincides with the expansion of civilian-sponsored economic and social welfare programs, and this creates more opportunities for officers to participate in such key ministerial positions as those of ministries of transport, communication, and power.

EXPLANATIONS FOR CONTEMPORARY
MILITARY INTERVENTION

A number of scholars turned their attention during the 1960s to explaining the frequency of coups in Latin America. Among the key propositions were interclass conflict; the weakness of electoral mechanisms; and governmental ineffectiveness and illegitimacy.[16] Military corporate interests, low levels of military professionalism, United States and foreign influence, and the personal interests of military leaders were also identified.

Interclass Conflict

Interclass conflict refers primarily to the middle classes, who some observers feel are antidemocratic, authoritarian, and elitist. They tend, in this view, to idealize and seek upper-class values, which leads them in many cases to defend their interests against the working classes on the left or the oligarchy on the far right. Since the army in effect represents the middle sectors in the majority of the Latin American countries, it typically comes to their defense. Elections, political movements, and political parties are the prime instruments of the threat, in this analysis, stimulating what is termed the middle-class military coup and control of government.[17] This interclass argument is supported in part by two American scholars. Martin Needler has shown that military coups between 1935 and 1964 increasingly took the form of the possessing classes (the middle and upper-middle classes) trying to maintain the status quo and were increasingly directed against presidents heading reform-oriented constitutional regimes.[18] This is spelled out more in Table 9. Samuel P. Huntington emphasizes that if increased social mobilization and participation by middle and lower sectors is left uninstitutionalized in legitimate political parties and associations, a greater possibility of military intervention results.[19] Thus, the military, in both of these views, becomes the protector of middle-class interests as opposed to the lower classes, where the middle class is viewed as essentially conservative and resistive to long-run changes threatening their status.

The interclass argument is closely related to the question of socioeconomic reforms and subsequent changes in class relationships. Some explanations therefore stress the question of socioeconomic development as causes of, or conditions for, military intervention or abstention. Samuel Finer, for example, maintains that economic development, industrialization, and social mobilization reduce the propensity for military intervention.[20] Economic development and industrialization, by this thesis spread political resources to wider numbers of people, groups, and associations. This ultimately is supposed to diminish military and strengthen civilian institutions.[21] The interclass and economic development-based arguments show a lack of agreement among scholars on the causes of military intervention.

The Level of Political Development

Ineffective and illegitimate government are associated with other theses about military intervention that highlight the level of political development. Here one encounters a variety of explanations. It has been argued, for example, that low levels of political development mean high degrees of military intervention, and that increasing political development means decreasing likelihood of military intervention. As Samuel Finer puts it, "where public attachment to civilian institutions is strong, military intervention in politics will be weakened. . . ."[22] Finer, John J. Johnson, and Victor Alba maintain that increased participation in politics tends to decrease the propensity for military intervention.[23] Samuel P. Huntington stresses that the increasing strength of legitimate political parties, political interest groups, and civilian governmental institutions (summarized as "political institutionalization") reduces the likelihood of military intervention.[24] So political development appears to be linked closely to decreasing military intervention, a thesis that in fact is substantially undermined by the cases of Chile and Uruguay in 1973. Political development undoubtedly deters military politics, but in Latin America is no guarantee against it.

One hypothesis about military intervention joins political development with economic modernity. Needler, it will be recalled, argues that increased participation and political institutionalization requires increased economic development to provide a higher level of welfare. If not, politicized sectors of society will conflict strongly over the allocation of scarce resources, leading to instability and military intervention, as is often the case.[25]

The Military's Internal Dynamics

The internal character of the military, some students feel, is the real culprit. Military corporate interests, low degrees of professionalism, U.S. and foreign influence, and the personal interests of military leaders fall within this category. The most discussed issue is *professionalization* and its impact on military intervention. Johnson's thesis is that increased professionalization urges the military to withdraw from direct control of government in favor of exercising indirect influence. Edwin Lieuwin sees the continuation of military intervention notwithstanding the growth of professionalization. Einaudi and Stepan show that increased professionalization in Peru and Brazil led to more, not less, military intervention. The military intervened there to bar subversion and stimulate economic development, which they perceived as the basis for internal security. Huntington associates professionalization of the military with decreased intervention and Finer with an increased military role. The corporate identity of the military is also believed to be a stimulus to military coups. Edwin Lieuwen argues that the desire to preserve military institutions is the prime reason for the coup.[26]

Personal interests of military leaders and the influence of the United States are other factors frequently acknowledged as causes of military intervention. The first is associated with the continuing role of *personalismo* and power politics in Latin America, and the route to material benefits provided by the presidential office. Fulgencio Batista of Cuba, Rafael Trujillo of the Dominican Republic, and other strong men come immediately to mind. This force cannot be underestimated in many parts of Latin America today. U.S. training and influence—with the stimulation of an anti-Communist ideology in the military plus the belief that actions legitimized by anti-Communism will be well accepted by the United States—are seen by some observers as potential sources of military coups.[27]

One study attempts to put these explanations into more quantifiable dimensions by using correlation coefficients.[28] Robert Putnam found that "social mobilization seems to encourage the prospects for civilian rule"; "widespread participation in elections, strong parties and pressure groups, and freedom from political violence are neither necessary nor sufficient conditions for military abstention"; "high military spending and high military intervention are closely related"; and "neither foreign training missions nor foreign examples of successful intervention seem to have any impact" on military intervention. Putnam concludes that traditions of militarism are key inputs into contemporary military intervention.

THE CASES FOR AND AGAINST
THE MILITARY IN DEVELOPMENT

What role can the military play in a state's overall development? An openly hostile case against military intervention can be made, based upon its general negative impact.[29] A positive case is also possible.[30] Whatever the position taken, the military is going to be a major political factor for some time to come in Latin America and its role in development therefore merits attention.

The Case for the Military in Development

The case for the military in guiding development has three aspects. First, the military can be viewed as a political factor leading toward long-run economic and political development. Second, the military branches perform economic functions conducive to capital formation and economic growth. Third, the military performs social functions that are related to both economic and political development. These add up to what might be called the case for the military as a dynamic in the politics of development.

The Political Realm

The political force of the military in stimulating political and economic development is based upon its role as a modern organization, an agent for change, and a catalyst for nation-building.

The Army as a Modern Organization

The army, typically the largest branch of the military in Latin America, can be viewed as a modern organization, perhaps *the* most modern organization in some Latin American countries. By modern organizations is meant that it is disciplined, hierarchically structured, and based upon the specialization of functions and skills as other industrial-based organizations. Its modernity, in terms of training, skills, and specialized functions, has been enhanced during the recent years of increased professional training. The armies' personnel are in turn highly achievement-oriented, and promotion within the modern military organization is based upon merit instead of ascriptive, traditional values (see Chapters 2 and 6). Two authors write of the military in Peru that its members are "perhaps the most merit-oriented within the state bureaucracy."[31]

As a modern organization, specific attributes of the military can be identified. The most highly skilled individuals reach the top positions. The organization trains people to perform specific skills and has a command structure to place those skills where they are needed within society. The military, as a disciplined and hierarchically structured organization, can make rational and authoritative decisions. This decision-making system can effectively mobilize a country's human and material resources, allocating them most efficiently in the development process. Since the capacity to develop requires a government able to administer and coordinate diverse activities throughout the country's territory, the military, according to this thesis, is the best political organization suited to the vast tasks involved.

Not only officers are involved in this modern training organization. Conscripts and enlisted men form another category. They receive vocational training, self-discipline in meeting the requisites of a modern bureaucracy, such as promptness, live by rational rules and regulations, and are exposed to an achievement-oriented lifestyle. These new experiences theoretically equip the rank and file, once discharged from the army, to perform useful services within society. Studies of the Latin American military do not, unfortunately, examine this point, so it remains theory only.

The modern military organization is not only equipped to lead in the economic development processes. It also performs functions encouraging long-run political development. It inducts part of the country's population into a modern structure that trains large numbers of enlisted men to be participating citizens once their military career is over. The rank-and-file soldiers learn to be citizens of a country and become aware of the state's constitution and of their rights under it and under the law. The military is thus the training ground for civic consciousness.

Political socialization occurs in other ways through military training. The military teaches its conscripts to read and write. The literate later become more likely political participants because literacy leads toward increased awareness and participation in politics.[32] Finally, to the extent the military can in fact promote industrialization, the latter should have the effect of creating other political groups based on the functional specialization of labor. As an agrarian-based society moves toward industrialization, new political participation based upon new interest-group ties are formed.

The Military as an Agent of Change

The military can also be an agent of political and economic change, as illustrated by several cases. Young officers overthrew the old regime in Bolivia in 1936 and created a socialist republic headed by Colonel David Toro. A civilian-military junta also came to power in Guatemala in 1944, after young officers overthrew the *ancien régime*. They picked as their reformist president Juan Arevalo, who promoted industrialization, social welfare, and an emphasis on military professionalism. Chile and Brazil experienced military-led reforms as early as the 1920s. The military became dramatically involved in the economic projects launched in Cuba, Brazil, and Peru during the 1960s and 1970s.

These military-inspired reforms suggest that in some cases the military is more development-oriented than is the rest of society.[33] The armed forces, increasingly middle class in their social structure, identify with industrialization, increased education, social reform, and national development according to some analysts.[34] They increasingly perceive national-security problems as something beyond purely conventional military operations and extending into existing social and economic structures. The guerrilla battles they experienced in the 1950s and 1960s highlighted this concern internally. Externally, the revolution in military technology enhanced the officers' awareness of the extent to which their countries were economically and technologically underdeveloped.[35] Most of the military's development concern also stems from its professional training and exposure to the general worldwide emphasis on development beginning in the 1960s.

The army is development-oriented and able to make long-range decisions uncomplicated by any need to compromise. When an authoritative command structure is linked to development motivations, the results can be positive for change and reform. Even when the military is not directly interested in development, some observers feel that it contributes to development. Economic growth, for example, requires civic stability. Countries torn by civil war and violence are not those likely to be undergoing high rates of investment and capital formation (investment in land, labor, and capital goods that expand the state's productive capacity). Severe violence often means the destruction rather than construction of such capital-forming goods as roads, railroads, factories, and dams. Domestic and foreign investors, moreover, are not likely to be attracted toward those areas where severe unrest threatens public and private capital. A big argument for military control, then, is the simple point that it is the most likely organization capable of maintaining a degree of political order in which economic growth can occur. Brazil after 1964 is a good case in point. Political freedoms and liberties were held in check, but the country experienced rapid and dynamic economic growth. Mexico is another case. During the dictatorship of Porfirio Díaz (1876-1910), the country underwent a process of incipient industrialization. Foreign capitalists invested large amounts in railroad construction, public utilities, textiles, beer, cigarettes, and other industries—all made possible by a politically repressive regime.

The Military as Nation-Builder

The military can be viewed as a force in nation-building, a relevant point because national perceptions stimulate political and economic change.

How might nation-building operate within the military? Different ethnic and racial members are inducted into the modern and professional military structure. Here they are exposed to status and promotion by merit rather than by ascriptive bloodline considerations. They are taught civic awareness and responsibility. They are at least theoretically equal in terms of opportunity for advancement. They learn, in some cases, that such a thing as Peru and Bolivia, Peruvians and Bolivians exists—which is a beginning step in nation-building. These experiences can have the total long-range impact of reducing racial distinctions, integrating diverse sectors of the population coming from different ethnic and geographic regions of the country, and building a base of common national perceptions.

Some indications suggest that nation-building is slowly beginning to occur. As Johnson's work indicates, the "whites" will not "indefinitely continue to exercise their traditional influence."[36] Johnson argues that everywhere "the tendency is to dip deeper into the social strata for officers, and it is in the lower social strata that the *mestizos*, Indians, Negroes, and mulattoes are most often found."[37] Some evidence, moreover, suggests that Indian and cholo experiences in the military during the Chaco War (1932-35) produced a new awareness of being Bolivian. This new awareness in turn helped to stimulate agrarian political syndicates in the Bolivian countryside and demands for agrarian reform.

Economic Performance

It can be argued that the military performs specific economic functions conducive to economic development. Much of this case is highlighted above, but one additional argument must be made.

The military is of vital importance in constructing economic and social overhead capital. Economic overhead capital refers to public utilities, such as transport, ports, roads, railroads, electricity, gas-production capacity, pipelines, transmission lines, and communication networks. Social-overhead capital consists of the plant and equipment required for shelter, education, and public health.

The military is active in the construction of economic and social-overhead capital. It possesses the trained manpower, the equipment, and administrative capacity to engage in these projects, so vital to long-run economic growth. The domestic know-how to produce social-overhead capital is simply nonexistent, other than in the military, in some Latin American countries.

The military in fact performed this role in Colombia, Paraguay, Peru, and Brazil during the 1960s. Argentine and Mexican military units were active in hospital, road, and school construction during the 1920s. Brazil's military built telegraph and other public utilities in the early 1900s. Economic and social-overhead capital formation require the capacity to mobilize resources, and to operate by schedules, logistics, and supply lines. The military possesses these attributes as demonstrated in concrete projects.

The Case against the Military

The case against the military is strong. It centers upon parasitic economic growth; the difficulty of institutionalizing military goals; and the limits to which the military will lead in development.

Parasitic Economic Growth

The military consumes large amounts of money in nonproductive goods and services. This is the essence of parasitic economic growth. Tanks, weapons, capital ships, and modern aircraft do not increase the state's productive capacity; military weapons are not capital forming. The large percentage of the state's budgets—as reflected in Table 8 below—mean that potential investment funds are not going toward economic development. The purchase of expensive weapons, moreover, means that manpower is tied up in servicing these weapons, money must be spent on foreign training to use them, and spare parts must be purchased abroad. The money spent on these weapons could therefore be more useful if invested in economic and social capital, factories, or even heavy industry. One can see the maldistribution of scarce resources by comparing percentages of budgetary allocations to defense, compared to education or public health in some countries. Table 8 reflects this.

Difficulties in Institutionalizing Goals

Military regimes (or "pretorian politics" as it is sometimes called) can experience great difficulty in institutionalizing their goals, or in motivating a substantial number of the population to work actively for national ends.[38] They do not have an easy task in creating political institutions that assume active participation without relying on physical coercive force. They cannot, in short, guarantee that their goals

TABLE 8 PERCENTAGE OF TOTAL NATIONAL BUDGETS ALLOCATED
TO EDUCATION, PUBLIC HEALTH, AND DEFENSE

Country	Year	Education	Public Health	Defense
Argentina	1961	10	7	16
	1969	14	11	14
Brazil	1961	6	3	17
	1970	7	2	17
Chile	1962	13	–	11
	1968	17	–	9
Colombia	1959	10	12	17
	1972	16	8	20
Costa Rica	1960	27	3	9
	1967	29	2	6
Dominican Republic	1962	7	7	20
	1970	14	7	12
Ecuador	1962	16	3	19
	1970	17	2	14
El Salvador	1965	22[1]	9	10
	1971	26	10	9
Guatemala	1961	22[2]	–	9
	1970	27	–	15
Haiti	1962	10	11	21
	1972	11	13	26
Honduras	1961	19	9	18
	1970	21	9	8
Mexico	1962	16	4	8
	1970	26	5	9
Panama	1961	19	–	–
	1970	26	–	–
Paraguay	1966	14	4	17
	1971	14	4	16
Peru	1960	15	8	16
	1967	27	6	19
Venezuela	1960	11	10	9
	1971	13	13	9

[1] These figures include *all* aspects of culture, thus reducing the amount allocated to education alone (same for the 1971 figure).

[2] *All social services* are included in this figure, rather than education only (same for the 1970 figure).

Source: *Statistical Abstract of Latin America,* ed. Kenneth Ruddle and Donald Ubermann (Los Angeles: University of California Press, 1972), pp. 338-56.

will be institutionalized in ways that encourage the masses to actively pursue the common end sought by the military.

Why does the military experience this problem? One difficulty is its built-in inability to trust and use a mass political party as the instrument of institutionalization. This arises from the military's problem in formulating a symbolic ideology that can be manipulated, or in creating a mass political party that might threaten the military's long-range appeal and power. This makes it difficult to create committed followers.

Peru has faced this problem with innovative attempts at ideology-building, institutionalization, and increased popular participation in the military's reform. But it also faces real problems in achieving these goals. The military government advocates a revolutionary ideology that endorses popular participation, but restricts it to "the regulated, localized, interaction between established government contact points and the local participating units."[39]

Other background forces impede the institutionalization of military-directed development. As Martin Needler correctly indicates, the modernizing tendency is typically only one element in the coalitions that organize reform-minded coups.[40] Consensus on specific programs within the military is often missing, frequently leading to conservative countercoups. The reform-oriented coup in Bolivia led by General Torres in 1970, for example, was in turn overthrown by the more conservative Colonel Hugo Bánzer in 1971. The Argentine military which toppled President Arturo Illia's regime in 1966 fell into competing, irreconcilable factions. These factions continued to plague Juan D. Perón when he returned to become president in 1973.

Secondly, military elites often turn to civilian technicians who are conservatives inherited from past regimes and who may exaggerate the difficulties in stimulating reform. Other civilians are likely to join in this opposition, particularly threatened corporate interests, such as the traditional Church or the landed oligarchy. Some military officers joined Allende (1970-73) in trying to bring about reform, but they were strongly attacked by civilian landed elites and middle-class interests. Public attack on the military in turn strengthened conservative interests within the army, navy, and air force who overthrew Allende in September, 1973. Needler's work on military intervention, emphasizing modern coups as means to typically oppose reforms, supported these two points.[41] Table 9 indicates the type of successful insurrections that occurred between 1935 and 1964.

Dilemmas of Military Leadership

The military in power raises great obstacles to short-run political development whether the country is small and underdeveloped, or large

TABLE 9 THE NEEDLER ANALYSIS:
MILITARY INTERVENTION IN LATIN AMERICA

Martin Needler analyzed the fifty-six successful insurrections that occurred in the twenty countries of Latin America during the thirty-year period 1935-64 and found that they tended to confirm his hypotheses. He found during this period:
  a. the *decline* in reformation of social and economic status quo as goal of the military conspiratorial group.
  b. a low level of violence (e.g., bloodless coup without street-fighting or popular involvement) *decreases* (meaning more violence in latest coups).
  c. an *increase* in overthrow of constitutional governments (as opposed to de facto governments).
  d. an *increase* in overthrows that occurred during the twelve months prior to scheduled presidential elections, or in the four months immediately following.

	1935-44		1945-54		1955-64	
	Number	Percent	Number	Percent	Number	Percent
Total	16	100	22	100	18	100
a. Reformist *(declines)*	8	50	5	23	3	17
b. Low in violence *(declines)*	13	81	15	68	6	33
c. Overthrow of constitutional governments *(increase)*	2	12	7	32	9	50
d. Around election time *(increase)* twelve months before or four months after	2	12	7	32	10	56

Source: Martin C. Needler, "Political Development and Military Intervention in Latin America," *The American Political Science Review* 60 (September 1966): 620.

and relatively developed. Military government often blocks legitimate access to political power through parties, unions, and the public media. It may, moreover, act as an obstacle to long-run institution-building by perpetuating itself in power rather than returning to civilian rule.

These trends are clear in contemporary military politics. The military in Chile dissolved the national congress, declared the mandate of all the congressmen to be ended, and terminated all political parties, groups, movements, and factions soon after taking power in September, 1973. The Honduran military coup of late 1972 led to a similar curtailment of political and union activities running counter to the goals established by the new government. President Juan María Bordaberry of Uruguay, under military pressure, tightly controlled the radio and television networks beginning in December, 1972. He also began to dissolve political parties in July, 1973, and simultaneously set about to regulate trade union activities. Bordaberry closed the country's only university in October, 1973. Meanwhile, General Hugo Bánzer postponed the 1974 elections until 1975 in Bolivia. Earlier, he deported labor-union leaders with whom he did not agree. These acts raised serious questions about the military as an agent of short-run political development.

Long-run political and economic change is another issue. The Huntington thesis, discussed earlier, suggests that the more backward the society is, the more progressive the role of the military; the more advanced societies produce more conservative and reactionary militaries.[42] Peru and Brazil would be the two classic cases to illustrate this Huntington thesis. But in contrast to Huntington's thesis, several of Latin America's smaller underdeveloped countries have not produced a reform-oriented military that stays in power long enough to do much. Bolivia, Guatemala, Haiti, Honduras, Ecuador, El Salvador, and Paraguay show this tendency. The Huntington thesis therefore requires qualification.

Two additional arguments merit attention: that coups tend to be middle-class efforts to protect the status quo[43]; and that professionalism has raised the level of corporate identity. Both arguments suggest a limited role that the military will play in sponsoring political development and economic reform. Finally, the problem of the military mind is another negative argument. Military training can be viewed as essentially authoritarian rather than equalitarian. The military is concerned primarily with discipline and command. This does not tend to prepare enlisted men for the democratic life outlined in the constitutions, but merely reinforces traditional authoritarianism within the society.

CONCLUSION

The role of the military in political and economic development clearly varies in style from country to country. The military, like other organizations in Latin American societies, reflects both traditional and modernizing trends. Some military organizations began to play extremely progressive economic roles during the 1960s, as in Brazil and Peru.

Of those two countries, more political freedom is allowed in the latter than the former. But the economic growth of Brazil is truly spectacular, ranking it with Japan and Germany as leaders in gross-national-product increases during the late 1960s and early 1970s. Certainly the basic organizational and training configurations of the military since World War II are far different from their mid-nineteenth-century counterparts. As such they offer more potential for development than ever before. But with these positive remarks, it should be recalled that military politics seem to have an outer limit as to economic reform. In discussing the Latin American military, we therefore come up against the issue outlined in Chapter 1: that every country is indeed unique and making a general prediction about the military in Latin America is extremely hazardous.

NOTES

1. *The Arms Trade with the Third World* (Stockholm: Stokholm International Peace Research Institute, Almqvist and Wilksell, 1971), p. 53.
2. Warren Dean, "Latin American *Golpes* and Economic Fluctuations, 1823-1966," *Social Science Quarterly* 51 (June 1970): 70-80. These figures are subject to debate; other authors indicate different numbers. Bolivia, for example, is frequently cited as a country where 179 military coups erupted between 1826 and 1952. See Charles D. Corbett, "Politics and Professionalism; The South American Military," *Orbis* 16 (Winter 1973): 944.
3. U.S. Department of State, Bureau of Public Affairs, *Arms Sales in Latin America* (July 1973): 1.
4. These expenditures were to replace old equipment and purchase new, and they reflected the rate of inflation for these years. *The Arms Trade with the Third World*, p. 2.
5. See William F. Stokes, *Latin American Politics* (New York: Thomas Y. Crowell, 1959), pp. 106ff.
6. Edwin Lieuwen, *Arms and Politics in Latin America* (New York: Praeger, 1961), p. 18.
7. *Ibid.*, p. 18; see also Lyle N. McAlister, *The "Fuero Militar" in New Spain* (Gainesville: University of Florida Press, 1957), p. 15.
8. Lieuwen, *op. cit.*, p. 20.
9. John J. Johnson, *The Military and Society in Latin America* (Stanford, Calif.: Stanford University Press, 1964); Corbett, *op. cit.;* Robert F. Adie and Guy E. Poitras, *Latin America: The Politics of Immobility* (Englewood Cliffs, N.J.: Prentice-Hall, 1974); Luigi Einaudi, *Beyond Cuba: Latin America Takes Charge* (New York: Crane, Russak, 1974); Luigi Einaudi and Alfred C. Stepan III, *Latin American Institutional Development: Changing Military Perspectives in Peru and Brazil* (a

report prepared for the office of external research, Department of State, Rand Corporation, Santa Monica, Calif., 1971).

10. Einaudi and Stepan, *op. cit.*, p. 1; Corbett, *op. cit.*, p. 934.

11. The ESG of Brazil had graduated men from many of the key sectors of the political and economic power structure by 1966; 599 were military officers, while 224 came from private industry and commerce, 200 from the major ministries, 97 from decentralized government agencies, and 39 from the federal congress. Federal and state judges comprised 23 of the graduates, and 107 included a variety of professionals such as professors, economists, writers, medical doctors, and Catholic clergy. Einaudi and Stepan, *op. cit.*, p. 18.

12. On the origins of these newer trends, see Alberto Sepulveda, "El Militarismo Desarrollista en America Latina," *Foro Internacional* 13 (July–September 1972): 45-65.

13. Victor Alba, "The Stages of Militarism in Latin America," in *The Role of the Military in Underdeveloped Countries*, ed. John J. Johnson (Princeton, N.J.: Princeton University Press, 1962), p. 165, where Alba states, "Thus Latin American militarism has arrived at the penultimate phase of its history. In its final stage it will disappear. That epoch may be near." Others argue that professionalism has in fact increased the tendency to intervene in politics (Adie and Poitras, *op. cit.*, p. 197; Einaudi and Stepan, *op. cit.*, p. 2.) Brazil, Chile, Peru, and Uruguay illustrate this fact.

14. Richard Rankin, "The Expanding Institutional Concerns of the Latin American Military Establishments: A Review Article," *Latin American Research Review* IX (Spring 1974): 81-108.

15. On the training Peruvian military officers receive at CAEM, see Einaudi and Stepan, *op. cit.*, pp. 22-25; and Carlos A. Astiz and José Z. Garcia, "The Peruvian Military: Achievement Orientation, Training and Political Tendencies," *Western Political Quarterly* 25 (December 1972): 667-85. Einaudi and Stepan argue that the emphasis on professional training and education in the promotion process makes its members "perhaps the most merit-oriented within the state bureaucracy, if not the entire society" (p. 23). Astiz and Garcia disagree, believing that discipline is equally a key to promotion (p. 69).

16. Mauricio Solaún and Michael A. Quinn, *Sinners and Heretics: The Politics of Military Intervention in Latin America* (Urbana: University of Illinois Press, Illinois Studies in the Social Sciences, No. 58, 1973). See also Lyle N. McAlister, "Recent Research and Writings on the Role of the Military in Latin America," *Latin American Research Review* 2 (Fall 1966): 5-36; and Robert D. Putnam, "Toward Explaining Military Intervention in Latin American Politics," *World Politics* 20 (October 1967): 83-110.

17. See José Nun, "A Latin American Phenomenon: The Middle Class Military Coup," in *Latin America: Reform or Revolution?*, ed. James Petras and Maurice Zeitlin (New York: Fawcett, 1968), pp. 145-85.

18. Martin C. Needler, "Political Development and Military Intervention

in Latin America," *The American Political Science Review* 60 (September 1966): 616-26.

19. Samuel P. Huntington, "Political Development and Political Decay," *World Politics* 17 (April 1965): 386-430.

20. Samuel Finer, *The Man on Horseback: The Role of the Military in Politics* (New York: Praeger, 1962), pp. 87-88.

21. Putnam, *op. cit.*, pp. 85-86; and Gino Germani and Kalman Silvert, "Politics, Social Structure, and Military Intervention in Latin America," *Archives Europeennes de Sociologie* 2 (Spring 1961): 62-81.

22. Finer, *op. cit.*, p. 21.

23. *Ibid.*, p. 87; John J. Johnson, "The Latin American Military as a Politically Competing Group in Transitional Society," in Johnson, *The Role of the Military in Underdeveloped Countries*, p. 127.

24. Huntington, *op. cit.*, pp. 386-430.

25. Martin C. Needler, "Political Development and Socioeconomic Development: The Case of Latin America," *The American Political Science Review* 62 (September 1968): 889-98.

26. *Generals versus Presidents*, 1964. Needler in part supports this argument in his essay "The Latin American Military: Predatory Reactionaries or Modernizing Patriots?" *Journal of Inter-American Studies* (April 1969): 237-43. This argument is implicitly strong in Wiarda's study of corporate interests within the Iberic-Latin tradition. Wiarda, "Toward a Framework for the Study of Political Change in the Iberic-Latin Tradition: The Corporative Model," *World Politics* 25 (January 1973): 206-35.

27. Needler, "The Latin American Military," p. 240. See also Alexander T. Edelmann, *Latin American Government and Politics* (Homewood, Ill.: Dorsey Press, 1965), p. 189.

28. Putnam, *op. cit.*, pp. 100-6. A correlation coefficient is the mathematical expression of the degree of covariation that exists for any two variable items. The key point is that when there is no similarity between variables, the correlation is zero; when there is perfect similarity, the correlation is plus one; and when there is perfect dissimilarity, the correlation is minus one. Correlation coefficients allow the investigator to gain information on the relationship between two basic variables.

29. Lieuwen, *Generals versus Presidents;* Edwin Lieuwen, "Militarism in Latin America," in Johnson, *The Role of the Military in Underdeveloped Countries;* and Edwin Lieuwen, "The Military: A Force for Continuity or Change," in *Explosive Forces in Latin America*, ed. John Te Paske and Sidney N. Fisher (Columbus: Ohio State University Press, 1964). See also Irving Louis Horowitz, "The Military Elites," in Seymour Martin Lipset and Aldo Solari, *Elites in Latin America* (New York: Oxford University Press, 1967), pp. 146-89.

30. John J. Johnson, "The Latin American Military as a Politically Competing Group," and Lucien Pye, "Armies in the Process of Political Modernization," in Johnson, *The Role of the Military in Underdeveloped Countries;* Lyle N. McAlister, "Civil-Military Relations in Latin Amer-

ica," *Journal of Inter-American Studies* 3 (July 1961): 341-50; Lyle N. McAlister, "Recent Research and Writings on the Role of the Military in Latin America"; Einaudi and Stepan, *Latin American Institutional Development: Changing Military Perspectives in Peru and Brazil;* David Apter, *The Politics of Modernization* (Chicago: University of Chicago Press, 1965), pp. 36-37, 135-71; and Samuel P. Huntington, *Political Order in Changing Societies* (New Haven: Yale University Press, 1968), ch. 4.

31. Einaudi and Stepan, *op. cit.,* p. 23.
32. See Gabriel A. Almond and Sidney Verba, *The Civic Culture* (Princeton, N.J.: Princeton University Press, 1963), pp. 379ff.
33. Monte Palmer, *Dilemmas of Political Development* (Itasca, Ill.: Peacock, 1973), p. 153.
34. Johnson, "The Latin American Military as a Competing Political Group in Transitional Societies," pp. 121-22; Einaudi and Stepan, *op. cit.,* p. 19.
35. Pye, *op. cit.,* p. 78.
36. Johnson, *The Military and Society in Latin America,* p. 33.
37. *Ibid.*
38. See Edward Feit's incisive essay, "Hand, Sword and People: Military Regimes in the Formation of Political Institutions," *World Politics* 25 (January 1973): 251-73.
39. David Scott Palmer and Kevin J. Middlebrook, in *Peru: A Corporative Revolution,* ed. David Chaplin (New Brunswick, N.J.: Transaction Books, 1973), p. 31. On the problems faced by the Peruvians, see also Jane S. Jaquette, "Revolution by Fiat, the Context of Policy-Making in Peru," *The Western Political Quarterly* 25 (December 1972): 648-85.
40. Needler, "The Latin American Military: Predatory Reactionaries or Modernizing Patriots?," p. 242.
41. Martin C. Needler, "Political Development and Military Intervention in Latin America," *American Political Science Review* 60 (September 1966): 616-26.
42. Huntington, *Political Order and Changing Societies,* p. 221.
43. Nun, *op. cit.*

Suggested Readings

Astiz, Carlos A. and José Z. Garcia. "The Peruvian Military: Achievement Orientation, Training, and Political Tendencies," *Western Political Quarterly* 25 (December 1972): 667-85.

Corbett, Charles D. "Politics and Professionalism: The South American Military," *Orbis* 16 (Winter 1973): 927-51.

Dean, Warren. "Latin American *Golpes* and Economic Fluctuations, 1823-1966," *Social Science Quarterly* 51 (June 1970): 70-80.

Einaudi, Luigi R. and Alfred C. Stepan III. *Latin American Institutional De-*

velopment: Changing Military Perspectives in Peru and Brazil. A Report prepared for Office of External Research, Department of State. Rand Corporation, Santa Monica, Calif., April, 1971.

Johnson, John J. *The Military and Society in Latin America.* Stanford, Calif.: Stanford University Press, 1964.

Lieuwen, Edwin. *Generals versus Presidents.* New York: Praeger, 1964.

Lowenthal, Abraham F. "Armies and Politics in Latin America," *World Politics* 27 (October 1974): 107-30.

McAlister, Lyle N. "Civil-Military Relations in Latin America," *Journal of Inter-American Studies* 3 (July 1961): 341-50.

Needler, Martin C. "Political Development and Military Intervention in Latin America," *The American Political Science Review* 60 (September 1966): 616-26.

Putnam, Robert D. "Toward Explaining Military Intervention in Latin American Politics," *World Politics* 20 (October 1967): 83-110.

Rankin, Richard. "The Expanding Institutional Concerns of the Latin American Military Establishments: A Review Article," *Latin American Research Review* 9 (Spring 1974): 81-108.

Solaún, Mauricio and Michael A. Quinn. *Sinners and Heretics: The Politics of Military Intervention in Latin America.* Urbana: University of Illinois Press, Illinois Studies in the Social Sciences, No. 58, 1973.

Prime
Development
Problems

Twelve

Economic Development

Latin American leaders today face two conflicting realities. First, most, but not all, are committed to economic development within their country as a high-priority goal. Second, they are plagued by obstacles to change, both of a domestic and international dimension. The question of the 1970s and the 1980s is not *whether*, but *how*, to change the economic status quo. The politics of economic development is the central relationship to understand in resolving the issue of how to change.

How will Latin American governments seek to orchestrate economic change? How will they use the political resources at their disposal, their law-making power, prestige, leadership capacity, organizational ability, coordination of interest-group demands, coercive power, financial strength, and so on? Latin America has experienced strong state intervention in the economy in a number of countries, dating especially from the period of the Great Depression onward,[1] but what is new about the 1960s, '70s, and '80s, is the specific commitment to broad-scale economic change to affect many aspects of the economic structure, including land, labor, capital, income distribution, and, consequently, the overall standards of living for masses of people.

The literature on Latin American studies is filled with essays on government planning, bureaucratic structures, land reform, nationalization of foreign industries, dependency on foreign capital, and structuralist versus monetarist studies of economic underdevelopment—all areas where the state's political system and economics interact in the development process. The commitment to economic development is clearly demonstrated in the radical policies of Cuba, of Chile (under Frei and Allende), of the military in Peru and Brazil during the 1960s and '70s, and of the unique policies of Mexico dating back to its constitution of 1917, which incorporated socioeconomic guarantees. This commitment to economic growth is backed by political decisions affecting regional economic unions (The Latin American Free Trade Area, LAFTA; The Central American Common Market, CACM; the Andean Pact, and the Caribbean Free Trade Association, CARIFTA), inter-regional technical cooperation, foreign trade, and aid.

The ultimate success of development intentions depends on how power and influence is shaped within government circles, who influences whom, what decisions are made, and the political constraints in implementing them. All affect the state's economic life. Political power and influence come to bear on a range of the central issues, such as who gets what income (and how it is spent), to capital formation, agrarian reform, and the entire range of legal-institutional forms within which economic life occurs: taxation policies, monopoly control, property and inheritance laws, banking regulations, monetary and fiscal policies, and credit facilities.

The role of government in economic life is clear, as various examples illustrate. Political stability is a basis for investment; great civil unrest is not. The flow of currency and credit is affected by government, as are attempts to regulate inflation, providing social-overhead capital (for example, roads, dams, schools, health facilities, housing), wage policies, restrictions or encouragement of labor unions, and a host of other issues. Government may be successful in fighting inflation through various means, including wage controls, or it may not; but it must convince or coerce different interest groups in whatever it does. Labor unions, as in Argentina and Chile, often resist government efforts at wage control, which partly accounts for continuing inflation, especially if productivity lags. Government can play a role in nation-building, trying to forge a common identity as a people, with common perceptions of the present and future. The Cuban and Mexican governments have done this, with clear implications for political unity and crystallized commitments to economic change. The government can also select and inculcate ideologies of development, as in Cuba's Marxism-Leninism (1959-present), Chile's Christian Democracy (1964-70), Getulio Vargas' earlier *estado novo* (1937-45) in Brazil, or Perón's *Justicialismo* (1949-forward) in Argentina. The point is that political and government life is critical to a state's economic performance.

By "economic development" we refer to a *process* of change. It refers to the growth and more equitable distribution of national income over a period of time.[2] This in effect means a growth in a country's national income and a change in its distribution toward greater equality. The processes involved are those designed to increase the productivity of land, labor, and capital. These include changes in technology, the scale of output, and resource allocation. Economic development, then, means more than simply industrialization or an increase in national income. Its stress is upon improving the general standards of living for a country's population. This chapter briefly approaches the crucial issues of economic development in Latin America by focusing upon capital formation; agrarian reform; and private foreign investment, with stress upon the so-called dependency argument.

CAPITAL FORMATION

Capital formation means increasing the development of goods and services that further increase the overall productivity of the state's economic system. This requires investments to increase the productivity of land, natural resources, machines, and the labor force. These in turn depend greatly upon the rate of domestic savings from which investments in capital formation flow. Capital formation involves a variety of options that can be selected by a political leader. Each one produces certain costs and benefits between what is gained and lost politically and economically in the decision. Whatever option, or combination of options, is selected, the relationship and interdependence of politics and economics is extremely close.

For example, capital may be invested directly in the construction or expansion of industrial plants to increase production, modernize machinery, etc., in order to produce more goods for domestic or export consumption. Or capital may be invested in the infrastructure necessary to support industrial expansion, such as roads, bridges, communications equipment. Or it may be invested in social overhead to provide education, health, and welfare services so that the country's population is better educated and healthier and thus more able to contribute as workers to economic development. Because political leaders have limited resources at their disposal, they must routinely choose among these alternatives. Furthermore, because of the often constitutional requirements requiring provision of social services, they are expected to spend scarce capital in ways that will pay off only in the future.

Capital-forming alternatives, which also entail political decisions, can be easily identified. Political leaders can borrow abroad (foreign aid), encourage or discourage foreign private investment, nationalize foreign property and place it under state direction, and tax local and foreign individuals as a means of forced savings for investment. These funds can then be invested in social-overhead capital or in other economic capital areas, such as agriculture, industry, manufacturing, commerce, or mining.

Capital formation is a necessary, albeit not sufficient, condition for economic development. Other related aspects include, at minimum, introducing more efficient forms of production, mobilization and training of a productive labor force (Japan has been highly successful at this), efficient allocation of resources, and effective planning and coordination of development decisions. Still other aspects include income redistribution to expand consumption capacity in the lower sectors of the population, and reduce demand for luxury goods (non-capital-forming) goods in the high-income brackets, and somehow holding down inflation. These are easy enough to identify, but extremely difficult to produce.

The cost-versus-benefits of capital-forming projects is illustrated in recent Latin American politics. Chile under Allende embarked on nationalization of foreign businesses, including copper, to help increase Chile's percent of revenues from copper sales and to establish more control over copper-production decisions. Allende also pushed through a speeded-up land-reform program, as noted earlier. These perceived benefits were outweighed by resulting inefficiency in copper management, worker strikes in copper mines and elsewhere, and a decline in copper production by early 1973.[3] Meanwhile, Chile experienced a run on consumer goods, short food supplies, a 50 percent drop in industrial production, and a rate of inflation that climbed to 283 percent by June, 1973, shortly before Allende's deposition and death.

These problems were exacerbated by hostile external influences. The United States played the unfortunate role of stimulating a decline of credits to Chile from foreign private and international banks by interfering in domestic politics through the CIA and restricting Chile's copper exports by North American companies affected by Chile's nationalization who felt they had not been justly compensated.[4] Allende's attempt to break the perceived dependency of Chile on outside business interests, then, as one route to capital formation, ran headlong against internal and external foreign influence. This raises the issue of what role private foreign investment plays in constraining capital formation, but it also shows the negative costs that may outweigh the benefits of political decisions made in the capital forming process.

Other countries' recent history illustrates the cost-benefit problems of capital formation. Cuba turned away from the U.S. and toward the

Soviet Union for external aid and export markets in its development process. But by 1937 it was estimated that Cuba was at least four billion dollars in debt to the U.S.S.R.[5] Cuba's failure to reach the ten-billion-ton sugar harvest in 1970 also led to reports of growing apathy by workers, lagging worker productivity, increased criticism at home and abroad of excessive power concentrated in Castro's hands, and of Castro's own emphasis on moral rather than material incentives to spur worker production.[6] These criticisms, with clear economic implications, can be viewed as costs resulting from earlier political decisions.

Capital-formation issues permeate Latin American politics and society. Presidents can recommend, and congresses pass, taxation laws, as most have, but implementing them is another issue, given the nature of dominant corporate-group politics. Governments can borrow, but the burden of debt servicing is great, often debilitating to economic growth, and a key cost to be considered. Latin America's external debt doubled during the 1960s, while the economic performance of most countries did not increase sufficiently to meet the debt-servicing burden.

Private foreign investment can be encouraged to operate in some sectors of the economy, bringing expertise, profits to be taxed, risk capital, and thus a potential source of capital formation. These benefits are offset by the amount of profit outflow and a potential incompatibility with the state's development goals. Basic decisions, then, must be made on what enterprises to nationalize and how to compensate the owner as against what businesses to leave but under what state controls. Some countries lean strongly toward nationalization of foreign investment. They include Cuba, Chile under Allende, Mexico, and Peru under Velasco Alvarado. Others, such as Argentina and Brazil, are far less restrictive. Another option is devising a common approach to private foreign investment; the December, 1970, Decision Number 24 of the Andean Pact countries (Bolivia, Chile, Colombia, Ecuador, Peru, and Venezuela) outlined just such specific conditions for investment of foreign capital.[7] The conditions of Article 24 include uniform rules concerning those areas that historically attracted the most foreign capital, such as mineral resources, public services, banking and finance, and manufacturing. The agreement ended the granting of depletion allowances in natural resources and prohibited establishment of new foreign-owned companies in public services, insurance, and banking and finance. Restrictions also were placed on the transfer of profits out of the region by manufacturing industries, and new guidelines were established for increasing domestic ownership and management of foreign companies. Panama adopted still another policy in April, 1974: a one-dollar export tax on every forty-two-pound box of bananas exported by the United Brands Company, a policy that was not enthusiastically received by that foreign concern.

Other forms of using political power to achieve capital formation through public funding can be identified. State planning for internal policy coordination is one approach that has been around for some time in several Latin American states. Development planning agencies, such as Chile's Development Corporation (CORFO, Corporation de Fomento de la Producción, 1939) and Venezuela's Central Office of Coordination and Planning (CORDIPLAN, 1958), show that the idea of state leadership in guiding capital formation is not new. On the international side are a host of domestic-foreign political linkages, as through the international banks (Central American Bank for Economic Integration, The Inter-American Development Bank, and The World Bank) and regional economic organizations (The Latin American Free Trade Area, LAFTA; The Central American Common Market, CACM; and the Andean Pact).

Latin America's leaders face a host of problems in long-range capital formation. Building social-overhead capital is an expensive process and raises real problems of how and where to allocate scarce investment capital. Problems are exacerbated by the scarcity and remote location of resources in Latin America, which contributes to the high cost of their exploration and development. Resources are not often found together, thus undermining the economies of location. Considering the other geographic problems noted at the outset of this book, such as huge and empty spaces in the hinterland, difficulty of feeder-road construction, ports separated by side-spaced and topographic impediments vis-à-vis natural-resource outlets, the limits to river utilization, and the like, the magnitude of the scarcity of resources and their development loom even larger.

Of the commitment to develop, there can be little doubt. Recent declarations at Punta del Este (1967), Viña del Mar (1969), and Lima (1971) drive this point home. The issue for tomorrow is how to back up this philosophy with coordinated domestic and foreign decisions based upon a rational economic policy and supported by sufficient political influence to make the policy work. The key point is that politics and economics interact on primary issues leading or not leading to capital formation in Latin America. These are summarized in Table 10.

These issues of capital formation only scratch the surface of the Latin American scene. Another major area of concern is the basic question of coordinating labor policies to increase labor productivity. Perón courted the labor sector, but the economy declined; Castro mobilized labor through controlled labor unions and economic incentives with better results than Perón, but with continuing problems of productivity, apathy, and organization. What workers do or do not do on

TABLE 10   CAPITAL FORMATION: POLITICAL AND ECONOMIC LINKS

Agrarian reform: break up the land or not? tax the owners or not? how to sustain training and provide market outlets for the new occupants?

Social-overhead capital formation: how much to invest in health, education, and welfare?

What policy to follow towards private foreign investment: nationalize or not? which investments should be nationalized? how to run them after nationalization?

What policies to follow for domestic savings: taxation? wage-and-price controls?

What policies to adopt in borrowing or not borrowing: from foreign governments? from international lending agencies? how to handle debt servicing?

How to mobilize labor and increase its productivity: moral incentives, as in Cuba? increased participation in industrial decision-making, as in Peru? politicization of migrants and workers as in Chile?

Where and how to diversify the country's trade relations?

What ideology, if any, to stress as a means of building common commitments: Christian democracy, as in Chile under Frei? Marxism-Leninism as in Chile under Allende and in Cuba under Castro? *Mexicanidad* in Mexico? Cubanidad in Cuba?

How much to invest in forging a common national image?

How to hold inflation down?

---

the job is critical to capital formation, and given labor's close relationship to the state, what the state can or cannot do with labor becomes a key piece in the development puzzle. Another whole range of issues involves the policies pursued by the developed countries vis-à-vis Latin America. The developed country's import policies (tariffs, quotas), private foreign-investment practices (multinational corporatist policies), and interference in domestic politics (as with the CIA in Chile) naturally shape the effectiveness of Latin America's style of capital formation. They must be considered as basic parts of the problem, and like the domestic issues they have both costs and benefits.[8] We return to these external problems in probing the "dependency" model later in this chapter.

WHAT TO DO WITH AGRICULTURE

The crucial role of agriculture in economic development is frankly admitted by economists.[9] The problem is how to raise the level of agricultural productivity. Several issues are involved. More and more food is needed to feed an expanding population. Producing more food domestically reduces the need for food imports, which are a heavy drain on scarce development resources. Increased agricultural output also can be sold abroad to earn the foreign exchange needed to import capital goods and other resources required to develop. Agriculture, then—meaning land cultivation, crop raising, farming, and stock raising—is a keystone in the development process; how to improve its productivity is a major problem.

Accelerating agricultural productivity is particularly important in Latin America. Exports of agricultural products are the basic source of foreign earnings in Latin America, thereby affecting Latin America's capacity to import manufactured goods as Table 11 shows. The size of the agricultural sector relative to the whole economy, moreover, makes its rate of growth basic to the overall growth of the whole economy. It affects living conditions, income levels, rates of migration to cities, and levels of employment in rural and urban settings. Many countries rely upon agricultural imports to feed their people, and these imports were running about six hundred million dollars a year during the late 1960s. While total agricultural production has increased moderately during the postwar period in most Latin American countries, the per capita output remained low due in large measure to the alarming annual increases in population.

What lies behind these bleak trends in the overall picture of agricultural productivity in Latin America? The prime target of political economists is the system of landholding, especially the possession of extremely large, multifamily, land units by a very wealthy few, and very small units by the rest of the rural masses. The large units, or *latifundias,* dominate rural life in traditional Latin America. They are notorious for their low productivity, low wages, inefficient use of the factors of production, and monopoly control. Much of the *latifundia* land, the most fertile land available, is held simply for prestige, rather than for production, and is labor-intensive, economically inefficient, and wasteful. Many *minifundias*—the small plots—coexist with *latifundias* and typically employ fewer than two people. Their scale of operation is too small to be viewed as a source of greatly increased agricultural productivity.

Approaches to the Agricultural Problem

Economic development in Latin America's postwar period turned partly on land reforms, particularly, but not exclusively, from the early 1960s on, when Alliance for Progress' and United Nations' goals stressed increased agricultural productivity as a necessity for development. The overall record, as indicated above, has not been especially

TABLE 11 MONOPRODUCT DOMINANCE IN EXPORT EARNINGS, 1965-67

	Principal exports as percentages of total exports
19 Latin American republics	petroleum and petroleum products, 25; coffee, 14
Central American Common Market countries	coffee, 34; cotton, 16; bananas, 13
Argentina	wheat and corn, 30; meat and meat products, 24; wool, 8
Bolivia	tin, 62; lead and zinc, 7
Brazil	coffee, 44; cotton, 6
Chile	copper bars, ores, and concentrates, 74; iron ore, 9
Colombia	coffee, 62; petroleum, 15
Costa Rica	coffee, 39; bananas, 24
Dominican Republic	sugar, 55; coffee, 14; cocoa, 7
Ecuador	bananas, 54; coffee, 19; cocoa, 11
El Salvador	coffee, 49; cotton, 14
Guatemala	coffee, 43; cotton, 18
Haiti	coffee, 49; bauxite, 10; sugar, 9
Honduras	bananas, 47; coffee, 14; wood, 8
Jamaica	bauxite and alumina, 47; sugar, 21
Mexico	cotton, 17; coffee, 6
Nicaragua	cotton, 42; coffee, 16
Panama	bananas, 51; refined petroleum, 28
Paraguay	meat, 32; lumber, 18; cotton, 6; sugar, 6
Peru	fish and fish products, 27; copper, 23; cotton, 10; sugar, 6
Trinidad and Tobago	petroleum and petroleum products, 79
Uruguay	wool, 47; meat, 27; hides, 9
Venezuela	petroleum and petroleum products, 92; iron ore, 5

Source: U.S. Department of State, Agency for International Development, *Latin American Economic Growth Trends,* 1969.

strong due to the continuation in many areas of the old land-tenure system, technological backwardness, and low levels of investment.

Several countries, however, pushed forward dramatic land reforms aimed at both a more equitable distribution of land among the people and increased agricultural productivity. Mexico continued its land-redistribution policy, dating back to its 1910 revolution. Between 1915 and 1967, 147.7 million acres were redistributed to 2.6 million farmers.

Much land, however, where the preponderant amount of crop sales was produced, remained in private hands, and many agricultural problems remained to be solved by 1965. They included lack of irrigation, low technology, low livestock protection, managerial inexperience, illiteracy, weak credit and marketing procedures, and overpopulation on the *ejidos* (of cooperatives). But great strides were made, for Mexico became practically self-sufficient in food (less than 2 percent imported) and was exporting corn and wheat to earn foreign exchange for other needed imports. The Mexican revolution, with its nationalist ideology (*Mexicanidad*), strong institutionalized presidential rule, integrated single-party political system, and commitments to major social and economic development lay behind this remarkable twentieth-century transformation.

Cuba is another case in point. The revolution led by Fidel Castro introduced a total transformation of the agriculture sector. After an abortive attempt to diversify the economy in the early 1960s, Castro began to concentrate on sugar production, traditionally the dominating factor in the economy, shooting for a ten-million-ton sugar harvest by the new state farms in 1970. Investment priorities went to sugar production, and Castro expanded the land under cultivation, at the same time increasing irrigation, mechanization, and fertilization programs. The U.S.S.R. agreed to purchase the sugar exports, since by then the United States had severed relations with Cuba and was consequently no longer an export market. Although the 1970 sugar harvest failed to reach ten million tons (the total output that year was eight and a half million tons), progress had been made in the sugar-production process.[10] As the state consolidated its control over agriculture, new innovations in cattle raising, fishing, and forestry were also launched.

Chile provides an example of the difficulties that can occur when agricultural reforms are attempted. Presidents Eduardo Frei (1964-70) and Salvador Allende (1970-73) started the state's takeover of *latifundias* and the settlement of families on these as communal farms. Frei's policies affected about 30,000 peasants on approximately 3,433,000 hectares of land, taken over from 1,364 estates. Allende accelerated this policy early, taking over 227 estates totaling 1,075,000 hectares. The rapidity of Allende's program stimulated widespread illegal land seizures by poor peasants, polarized political opposition between the far left and the far right, produced enormous discontent among the middle sectors due to a food crisis, and increased the need to import food. Wheat production, for example, fell from 1,360,000 tons in 1971 to under 700,000 tons in 1972, and the cost of food imports grew from $180,000,000 in 1970 to $313,000,000 in 1971 and $400,000,000 in 1972. Behind these figures lay low productivity and enormous difficulties in running the centralized state farms set up under Allende. Difficulties in training the occupants of the newly organized land, and tensions between the old *campesinos,* who had always lived on the land (now under new organization), and the newer *inquilinos* (migrants) who were moved on it by the government were constant constraints on productivity. Like decisions on capital formation, then, agricultural-reform decisions also entail costs and benefits.

The general problems of increasing agricultural productivity that must be faced in the future by Latin America's innovating governments and political leaders can be summarized. Whether or not the *latifundia* system is completely or only moderately changed, several key requirements must be met. These are increased manpower skills; increased levels of technological inputs, as fertilizers (which will cost more as oil shortages become greater, because oil by-products go into fertilizer production), seeds, machinery, irrigation, electrification, and transport; economic incentives to produce more, whether on the part of the *latifundia* owner, or on the part of nearly settled *campesinos* in land reform programs; credit extension to the small, as well as the large, farm owners; and more training of agricultural experts—an enormous problem, given the low prestige of agricultural training and career goals at the university level in Latin America.[11] While the rhetoric of development is strong in Latin America today, very small percentages of national projects go to the agricultural sector. Agricultural budget allocations averaged 5 percent in 1963-67, while military spending, for example, averaged 12.3 percent. The interaction of politics and economics, relative to agrarian reform, is outlined in Table 12.

PRIVATE FOREIGN INVESTMENT: THE "DEPENDENCY" ARGUMENT

One approach to the politics of economic development in Latin America is the "dependency" model adopted by a number of Marxist and non-Marxist United States and Latin American scholars.[12] This model attributes underdevelopment to the economic expansion of developed capitalist countries, especially the United States. The central thesis is that the Latin American economies are dependent on the dominant capitalist economies whose policies determine and limit them. Dependency is viewed as the result of expanded capitalism, where private foreign investments are invariably exploitative and detrimental to Latin American development.[13]

A number of key relationships are involved in the dependency model. Foreign ownership of the industrial sector and heavy involvement of foreign interest in banking and commerce result from dependency.

TABLE 12   AGRARIAN REFORM: POLITICAL AND ECONOMIC
INTERACTION

---

1. Should the large landed estates be broken up or left intact?
   —if left intact, how can agricultural productivity be stimulated? through
   taxation on unused land or some other means?
2. If land is redivided, how should it be reorganized and redistributed? Size?
   Occupants? Owners?
   —state farms? communal farms? private farms?
3. How can the government guarantee that newly organized and redistributed land will stimulate greater productivity?
   —community development programs?
   —rural schools, health programs?
   —agricultural extension services?
4. What will be the nature and extent of investments in irrigation, fertilizers,
   seeds, transportation links, and credit facilities?
   —how does the government get old and new farmers to accept new
   innovations?
5. How does the government encourage specialized university careers in
   agriculture and a basic interest in manual labor, now viewed as demean-
   ing in Latin America?
   —Latin Americans tend to be generalists rather than specialists; how
   can this problem be approached?
6. How can the internal markets for agricultural products be widened?

Latin America, moreover, becomes an exporter of primary products
and raw materials and an importer of the capitalist world's manufactured goods. Since the price of manufactured goods has typically
increased more rapidly in the past than the income from sales of primary products in raw materials, the Latin American economies are
viewed as unfavorably affected. That a number of countries have attempted to break their dependent status is clear in the amount of nationalization of private foreign industry that occurred during the
1960s and early 1970s.

Associated with the external aspects of the dependency model are
certain internal patterns of economic, social, and political relations.
Chile is an excellent example of these patterns, where Frei and, more
dramatically, Allende, sought to break the cycle with their political and
economic programs.[14] Allende, in particular, viewed Chile's problem
of dependency as closely associated with, among other things, severe
internal structural problems and a stalemated political system unable
to change the status quo. The structural factors included low agricultural productivity, a deterioration in the terms of trade, uneven distribution of income, monopolies, and the concentration of power in the
private banking sector. The stalemated political system referred to the

inability of any single political or social force to impose its direction over the state apparatus and enforce and coordinate policy directives to break dependency and structural situations.[15]

Among the steps Allende attempted were nationalization of private foreign and domestic industries and increased control of the state over banking and credit agencies.

There is much to be said for the dependency thesis, for it directs our attention toward the role of external economic and political constraints on Latin American economic development. The dependency argument warns that any analysis of the politics of economic development in Latin America cannot be complete without accounting for the linkages between foreign economic influence and domestic politics, economics, and society. Dependency stresses that the absence of a defined and stable policy for guiding the economic process and channeling it along new paths, prominent characteristics of Latin American policy-making in the postwar period, are linked to powerful foreign economic forces.

The dependency argument, moreover, drives home the point that Latin America's corporate-interest system—noted for its "contradictoriness," "indecisiveness," and "accommodationist" game—is closely linked to external foreign economies. Competing power contenders in the domestic arena are committed not to change in the basic economic system (and thus the dependency relationship), but rather to sharing more favorably in its valued goods. The upshot is frequently a weak state lacking basic consensus on how to direct economic growth. Dependency is thus associated with internal structural obstacles to development, the nature of competing elites in Latin American politics, and political stalemates when it comes to fundamental economic changes in the status quo.

Dependency—with its emphasis on foreign investment, foreign ownership in the industrial, commercial, banking, and manufacturing sectors, and foreign aid—provides an analytic framework to help account for the status of Latin American economic conditions in the 1960s and 1970s. Many economies remain single export in nature, rather than highly diversified. They continue to depend upon the import of capital goods and technology. Economic growth rates generally remain low and indebtedness to the developed countries more than doubled during the 1960s.

Qualifying the Dependency Thesis

While the dependency thesis sharply accentuates the power of private foreign interests within Latin America's states, it has drawn sharp criticism from some scholars. One scholar, for example, argues that different types of foreign investments have different effects on the development process (some are positive), that much (perhaps more) money has been lost in unsuccessful adventures than taken out in profits, and that private foreign interests help Latin America acquire technology.[16] Some private foreign industries also expend huge amounts of risk capital, money that is spent on the exploration of raw materials, which may or may not prove successful. The recipient country need not share in this expense, but may benefit from the product that comes out of the ground later. It should be noted that nondependence may not be a realistic goal, in that dependency/nondependency is in fact one continuous variable; there are always degrees of dependency since most countries require outside markets and the need to trade. The dependency thesis is also offset by restrictions on private foreign investment, as the Andean Pact's Article 24. The shift in power toward oil-rich countries, such as Venezuela, also lessens the dependency argument, since Venezuela is likely to use oil as a weapon to obtain more favorable terms of trade in manufactured goods from the developed countries.

Close inspection of Latin America's internal economic scene suggests that dependency, particularly in its assigning private foreign interests the sole responsibility for Latin America's lagging economies, should be qualified as an explanation. Factors other than foreign and economic power of course debilitate Latin America's present and future economic growth. Many of the cultural, social, and political aspects also responsible were explored in earlier chapters. Other impediments to economic growth can be identified in Latin American business practices. Latin America's domestic businesses tend to be family owned; inside them one finds a notable unwillingness to delegate responsibility or to operate by modern business organization principles.[17] Profit making tends to center on high-markup-per-unit produced rather than emphasizing mass production and low-price-per-unit produced, looking ultimately toward higher profits through volume. Plowing back profits to further growth and expansion is frequently neglected in favor of conspicuous consumption of the business owner. The Latin American businessman often stays out of the business activity unless he anticipates making an extremely high profit—between 20 percent and 40 percent on his investment. This relationship compares with profits that typically run in the 10 percent and 15 percent range in industry and commerce in the United States.[18] Monopoly pricing, oligopolies, and concomitantly high prices are common in Latin America.

When one adds to these unproductive practices the additional difficulties posed by extremely high population-growth rates, the absence of effective trade policies, inefficient domestic production of consumer goods that could be more cheaply imported, low productivity, underutilization of plant capacity, and intense political infighting, then dependency becomes only one of many external and internal impediments to the rapid economic development espoused by many Latin American leaders.

CONCLUSION

The question in Latin America is not so much, in Lenin's words, "What is to be done?," but "how to do it?" New capital and continued capital formation is needed, as is increased agricultural productivity, if national income is to be raised and distributed more equitably. These are terribly difficult tasks, given the whole nature of Latin American politics and, in many cases, the conservative pressures from external sources. Traditional power groups resist change, other interest groups refuse to make needed sacrifices, and the geographical and natural-resource base often form additional impediments. Economic growth, to understate the issue, is a formidable task in these lands where political instability is high and institutionalized problem solving low.

Yet the picture is far from gloomy. Many Latin American leaders are committed to using the state for development, which is consistent with the legacy of government intervention in economies, and many countries are showing innovative economic styles. Cuba, Mexico, Peru, and Brazil are cases in point. They are leaders in the modernizing process, but each country's manner of doing so shows as well the imprint of Latin American culture and traditional politics. It is therefore important to understand that economic development is not only closely linked to politics, but that like politics, it will be along lines consistent with the attitudes and values of the Latin American region.

NOTES

1. Charles W. Anderson, *Politics and Economic Change in Latin America* (New York: Van Nostrand, 1967); Wendell C. Gordon, *The Political Economy of Latin America* (New York: Columbia University Press, 1965).
2. Gerald M. Meier, *Leading Issues in Economic Development; Studies in International Poverty* (New York: Oxford University Press, 1970), p. 7.
3. Norman Gall, "Copper Is the Wage of Chile," *American Universities Field Staff Report* 19 (August 1972): 2.
4. On CIA interference in Chilean politics, the director of the Central Intelligence Agency told the U.S. Congress in September 1974, that the Nixon Administration had authorized more than eight million dollars

for covert activities by the agency in Chile in 1970 and 1973 to make it possible for President Salvador Allende Gossens to govern. See Seymour M. Hersh, *New York Times,* September 8, 1974. See also Elizabeth Farnsworth, "More than Admitted," *Foreign Policy,* no. 16 (Fall 1974): 127-41; Paul E. Sigmund, "Less than Charged," *Foreign Policy,* no. 16 (Fall 1974): 142-56; and Richard Fagen, "The United States and Chile: Roots and Branches," *Foreign Affairs* (January 1975): 297-313.

5. W. Raymond Duncan, "Castroism: From Theory to Practice," *Problems of Communism* 22 (July–August 1973): 85-87.

6. By the early 1970s, Castro appeared to return more toward material incentives, as in the U.S.S.R., perhaps due to increased pressure from that country.

7. On the statement of Decision Number 24, see U.S. Congress, House of Representatives, *Inter-American Relations* (Washington, D.C.: 1973); pp. 383-400.

8. Harold Eugene Davis and Larmon C. Wilson, *Latin American Foreign Policies: An Analysis* (Baltimore, Md.: Johns Hopkins University Press, 1975).

9. Rawle Farley, *The Economics of Latin America: Development Problems in Perspective* (New York: Harper and Row, 1972); Bauer and Yamey, *op. cit.;* and W. W. Rostow, *Stages of Economic Development* (New York: Oxford University Press, 1960).

10. A number of problems lay behind this faliure: bad weather, mechanical breakdowns, difficulties in new feeder-road construction, the earlier exodus of managerial and technical elites as Castro turned to Marxism-Leninism, low productivity per worker, frequent changes in planning, and lack of economic incentives on Castro's transformation of agriculture; see W. Raymond Duncan and James Nelson Goodsell, *The Quest for Change in Latin America: Sources for a Twentieth Century Analysis* (New York: Oxford University Press, 1970), ch. 5; *Revolutionary Change in Cuba,* ed., Carmelo Mesa-Lago (Pittsburgh, Pa.: University of Pittsburg Press, 1971); Jaime Suchlicki, *Cuba, Castro and Revolution* (Coral Gables, Fla.: University of Miami Press, 1972); Richard R. Fagen, *The Transformation of Political Culture in Cuba* (Stanford, Calif.: Stanford University Press, 1969); and Andres Súarez, *Cuba: Castroism and Communism, 1959-1966* (Cambridge: M.I.T. Press, 1967).

11. T. Lynn Smith, *Studies of Latin American Societies* (Garden City, N.Y.: Anchor Books, 1970), ch. 15; and Andrew Pearse, "Agrarian Change Trends in Latin America," in *Agrarian Problems and Peasant Movements in Latin America,* ed. Rodolfo Stavenhagen (Garden City, N.Y.: Doubleday, 1970), pp. 11-40.

12. The Latin American scholars associated with this model are Theotonio Dos Santos, Osvaldo Sunkel, Fernando Henrique Cardoso, Enzo Faletto, Celso Furtado, and Raul Prebisch. United States political scientists known for their emphasis on dependency are James Petras, Susanne Bodenheimer, and Dale L. Johnson. This problem is discussed in

Furtado, *Economic Development of Latin America* (Cambridge: Cambridge University Press, 1970); Andre Gunder Frank, *Latin America: Underdevelopment or Revolution* (New York: Monthly Review Press, 1969); and Albert O. Hirschman, *How to Divest in Latin America and Why*, Essays in International Finance, no. 76 (November 1969), Princeton, N.J., International Finance Section, Department of Economics, Princeton University.

13. David Ray, "The Dependency Model of Latin American Underdevelopment: Three Basic Fallacies," *Journal of Inter-American Studies and World Affairs* 15 (February 1973): 4-20.

14. See the excellent discussion of Chile's dependency perspectives as viewed by Salvador Allende, in Robert L. Ayres, "Economic Stagnation and the Emergence of the Political Ideology of Chilean Underdevelopment," *World Politics* 25 (October 1972): 34-61.

15. *Ibid.*, pp. 39-58.

16. Ray, *op. cit.*

17. Tomas Roberto Fillol, *Social Factors in Economic Development: The Argentine Case* (Cambridge: M.I.T. Press, 1961).

18. Wendell C. Gordon, *Political Economy of Latin America* (New York: Columbia University Press, 1965), pp. 58-59.

Suggested Readings

Anderson, Charles W. *Politics and Economic Change in Latin America*. New York: Van Nostrand, 1967.

Benham, F. and H. A. Holley. *A Short Introduction to the Economy of Latin America*. New York: Oxford University Press, 1961.

Davis, Harold Eugene and Larmon C. Wilson (eds.). *Latin American Foreign Policies*. Baltimore, Md.: Johns Hopkins University Press, 1975.

Farley, Rawle. *The Economics of Latin America: Development Problems in Perspective*. New York: Harper and Row, 1972.

Frank, Andre Gunder. *Latin America: Underdevelopment or Revolution*. New York: Monthly Review Press, 1969.

Furtado, Celso. *Economic Development of Latin America*. Cambridge: Cambridge University Press, 1970.

Gordon, Wendell C. *The Political Economy of Latin America*. New York: Columbia University Press, 1965.

Hirschman, Albert O. *Journeys Toward Progress: Studies of Economic Policy-Making in Latin America*. New York: Twentieth Century Fund, 1963.

————. *How to Divest in Latin America and Why*. Essays in International Finance, no. 76 (November 1969), Princeton, N.J., International Finance Section, Department of Economics, Princeton University.

Jaquette, Jane S. "Revolution by Fiat: The Context of Policy-Making in Peru," *Western Political Quarterly* 25 (December 1972): 648-66.

Johnson, Dale L. (ed.). *The Chilean Road to Socialism*. New York: Double-day, 1973.

Kindleberger, Charles P. *Power and Money: The Politics of International Economics and the Economics of International Politics*. New York: Basic Books, 1970.

Meier, Gerald M. *Leading Issues in Economic Development: Studies in International Poverty*. New York: Oxford University Press, 1970.

Mesa-Lago, Carmelo. *Revolutionary Change in Cuba*. Pittsburgh, Pa.: University of Pittsburgh Press, 1971.

Ray, David. "The Dependency Model of Latin American Underdevelopment: Three Basic Fallacies," *Journal of Inter-American Studies and World Affairs* 15 (February 1973): 4-20.

Rosenstein-Rodan, Paul N. "Allende's Big Failing: Incompetence," *New York Times,* June 16, 1974.

Suchlicki, Jaime. *Cuba, Castro, and Revolution*. Coral Gables, Fla.: University of Miami Press, 1972.

Wionczek, Miguel. "United States Investment and the Development of Middle America." A Warner Modular Publication, Reprint No. 425, from *Studies in Comparative International Development*, Vol. 5 (1969-70).

Thirteen

The Potential for Political Development

This book began with attention to the concept of political development, the integrating of more people within the political system, expressing their demands into government, and the government's responding with a more equitable allocation of such resources as income, housing, education, social welfare. Political development suggests the spawning of a good deal of popular support and compliance among the populace, which is the long-run basis of political stability and peaceful cooperation in government policies for social and economic change. Support is generated not only by attention to social and economic problems, but also through legitimate rule—governance by means acceptable to the people without constant resort to force. Political development, then, entails building authority through legitimate government and strong institutions that mobilize support for government policies.[1]

Key aspects of legitimate rule are concern for human rights, governance by just rather than corrupt policies, and establishment of institutions through which popular demands can be expressed, such as elections. As political development occurs, discontent is registered and conflict resolved more through peaceful problem-solving institutions of the state rather than by imposed coercion by the government, or randomly and chaotically through violence-oriented groups taking matters into their own hands. Political development therefore means less political violence and less physical force by the ruling regime.

The potential for long-run political development along these paths in Latin America is far from easy to judge. On the dark side of the balance sheet, political corruption, violation of human rights, rigged elections, and violence remain high in many parts of the region. What is frightening is their reappearance in countries that had seemed to leave much of such behavior behind—as occurred in Chile and Uruguay in 1973.

Latin American society meanwhile is sharply fragmented. The elements of fragmentation range from old and new corporatist groups to cultural, ethnic, geographic, linguistic, kinship, personality, and personal identity fissures. These tend to produce low levels of national identity with concomitantly low degrees of citizenship. The absence of strong national sentiments by the peoples of most Latin American states is a hallmark of the social-political setting. Fragmented society, defined in political terms, means personalist factions, corporatist interest groups, and patron-client relations—all vying for power to share in the state's valued, but limited, goods and services. Building consensus on how to reconcile differences of opinion on who should participate in these decisions and on who should benefit and by how much is very difficult. If the coordination of domestic policy making is a problem in developed countries, it can be doubly so in lesser-developed regions, where traditionally powerful groups may resist the changes desired by innovating political elites. Trying to mobilize political power sufficient to alter rapidly the *ancien régime* can lead to polarized public opinion and an extremely violent backlash; that is the lesson of Salvador Allende's Chile. Political resources are still divided very unevenly in Latin America, and changing their balance is no easy operation.

On the brighter side, several countries are making substantial strides in combining legitimate authority and popular support with economic growth and social change. Economic growth is occurring at a time when investments are being made to increase literacy, expand social services, reduce poverty, and build the consensus required for long-range development. Mexico, Cuba, Venezuela, Peru, and Brazil are cases in point. Other aspects of the brighter side of development potential are explored later.

The road to development is obviously long and difficult, for even the progressive countries have their notable deficiencies in development. Concern for civil rights is frequently missing, and political instability threatens in much of the region. One thing is certain: political development in Latin America everywhere shows the permanent imprint of traditional culture and authoritarian lifestyles. Future political development will be distinctly Latin American, reflecting the forces discussed in this book. This chapter briefly explores both the negative and positive aspects of future political development, showing the parameters of future change.

THE DARK SIDE OF THE LEDGER

Political development frankly does not appear to be occurring in many parts of Latin America. Corruption, with its emphasis on patron-client relations, frequently appears too entrenched for the development of nonpersonal problem-solving institutions, such as elections, legal aid, or social-welfare agencies. Masses of people without a powerful patron or interest-group association have little or no way of making demands on the polity and are therefore simply left out of sharing in national life and the goods and services provided by the state. Others view the corruption with disdain and show little support for the government and its operations. As Reid Reading, a political scientist, discovered in his research in Tolú, a town of 7,000 on the Colombian Caribbean coast, the residents there showed great cynicism toward politics and both local and national governments were viewed as "dirty and corrupt" and "divorced from the lives of the common person."[2]

Paralleling political corruption is the high level of political violence in Latin America, which illustrates the absence of other outlets to resolve conflict peacefully. Political violence, spawned partly by the traditional political culture of the region, also reinforces the low regard for government and politics. Some forms of violence may of course lead to political development, as with the Mexican, Bolivian, and Cuban revolutions, or the Peruvian military take-over of 1968. But other forms simply result in a game of military musical chairs with little substantive change, or even to the rule of repressive regimes, as in Chile and Uruguay in 1973. Thus, economic and social changes beneficial to the population as a whole can be a by-product of violence, but far from all cases turn out that way.

Closely associated with corruption and violence is the denigration of human rights in many Latin American countries. Jailings without legal cause, curtailment of freedom of speech and press, torture, and suppression of other human rights understandably do not encourage respect for the state's governmental system or its policies. When the government spends more time suppressing dissent than attending to the large problems of economic development, one cannot expect strong feelings of support for the governmental system. And without political support from large numbers of the population, the institutions required for leading economic and social change will not mature.

Political development suggests that more and more of the population come to identify with the state's politics and governmental processes, seeing themselves as citizens of the state in whose goods and services they share and toward which they have responsibilities and obligations. Where a high level of political alienation is found, it indicates the general absence of those positive feelings toward the state's government that could be translated into support for its policies and the feeling that it is the legitimate authority of the land. "Participant citizenship" simply seems to be missing in much of Latin America,[3] as the following discussion illustrates, and will continue to be lacking for many years in some areas.

Political Corruption

Political corruption in the developing world became a subject of growing interest during the 1960s. A great variety of definitions can be used, but broadly it refers to (1) behavior deviating from the formal role (elective or appointive); (2) behavior leading to wealth and status at the private level; and (3) a violation of rules against the exercise of influence in the public domain to promote private interests. Corruption does not favor the public, but more typically a person, close family, kinship group, private clique, or ethnic group.

The causes of corruption are multiple, but are closely associated with the norms of traditional society.[4] The importance of kinship, village, and ethnic ties simply spill over into politics. The network of loyalties does not run from the individual to the state, but includes only the individual to his more parochial ties. The public value is less strong than the parochial value when corruption occurs, and little fear or guilt is associated with promoting personal over public interest. Corruption, then, is a natural counterpart to lingering traditional attitudes and values.

Another reason for corruption is the growth of government in developing areas as a source of goods, service, and employment. As government becomes a producer and consumer, and a taxpayer and spender, a larger share of income passes through its hands. When strong parochial ties exist, it is not strange that government would become a potential resource for nepotism, personal favors, and patronage in the selection and appointment of public officials. However, these practices not only impede participant citizenship, but also lead to overstaffing of public offices and enormous bureaucratic inefficiency.

Cuba, during the first half of the twentieth century, is a classic case of this phenomenon. Politics after 1898 (when independence was won from Spain, but not from the United States) was characterized by irresponsibility, corruption, waste of public funds, and intimidation of the electorate by the military. Since business and commerce were dominated by Spaniards and Americans, many educated Cubans naturally sought governmental positions for themselves and their family and friends. They turned to politics, as one historian wrote in 1924, in order "to earn a living."[5]

Other areas of corruption in Latin America can be cited. Fraudulent elections, discussed below, are closely related to using governmental means to advance private ends and thus become a form of corruption. Police corruption, granting special licenses to construct public projects through public funds, tolerance and exploitation of vice, narcotics, prostitution, and illegal road blocks to the defeat of political reformers have also been identified in Latin America's states.[6]

It is reported that the 1973 earthquake in Nicaragua upset many sources of corruption in General Somoza's system, which included keeping the officers of the National Guard and governmental officials happy. Sources of corruption in Nicaragua include control of brothels, bars, and gambling houses by military officers, and control of documents needed to obtain state or municipal employment, as well as credit.[7] Extensive government corruption is reported by urban slum dwellers in Lima, Peru.[8]

These practices by government officials continue to limit the spread of participant citizenship because they do not inspire faith that the governmental machinery will promote the public's ends. This is true not only for the masses in general, but in some cases for university students who are presumably more politicized.[9] Government's performance, then, does not itself stimulate positive attitudes of support among the population at large.

Violation of Human Rights

Human rights are violated repeatedly in parts of Latin America where detention without charges, torture, and summary executions are used by government leaders to secure narrow private ends. These methods of repressing political dissent are, to say the least, not conducive to building legitimate authority. A number of countries in Latin America can be identified as areas where the use of these practices spread during the 1960s and 1970s. The more publicized of them are Chile, Bolivia, Brazil, and Uruguay.

The military government that came to power upon the overthrow of Salvador Allende in Chile turned toward these activities after September, 1973. Following Allende's overthrow, more than twenty-five hundred people were killed, most of them by summary execution after resistance to the armed forces had ended. By June, 1974, approximately six thousand political prisoners were still held in detention centers, and thousands had passed through those centers during the nine months following the coup.

The military-controlled Uruguayan government of President Juan M. Bordaberry similarly detained several thousand people in jails, military installations, and sports stadiums during its attempts to end the Tupamaro urban-guerrilla movement. Many of these prisoners were held without charges, and church groups publicized allegations of torture. Neil MacDermot, Secretary General of the International Commission of Jurists, reported at the United Nations in June, 1974, after a fact-finding mission, that between thirty-five hundred and four thousand persons had been interrogated in Uruguay since July, 1972, in an effort to stamp out the Tupamaros. At least 50 percent of these are believed to have been tortured. The administrative board of the United State's Catholic Conference issued a public statement of protest against the violation of human and civil rights in Brazil in February, 1973. More than two thousand people have been arrested in Bolivia for political reasons without formal charges since General Hugo Banzer Suarez assumed power through a military coup in August, 1971. The point is that these notorious cases of violating human rights severely undermine long-run political development.

Electional Problems

Political development in democratic political systems is characterized by a heavy turnout of voters at elections. Since Latin American governments provide for elections, and their constitutions suggest democratic government, the conditions linked to voting are a natural area for inquiry. Where effective participant citizenship is stimulated through elections, one might expect to find (1) easy access to the polls; (2) regular and frequent elections; and (3) elections run by fair and established rules.

To what extent do these conditions exist in Latin America? The first point to remember is that Latin American electoral practice often departs from the U.S. concept of constitutional democracy, for the obvious reason that elections occur in different political cultures. Value judgments about U.S. democracy compared to Latin American democracy should be left out here, given the difference in political cultures.

Access to the Polls

Many people are denied access to the polls through pre-electoral and electoral controls of both legal and illegal nature.[10] The situation today is not that of 1873, when Antonio Guzmán Blanco won the presidency of Venezuela by a vote of 239,691 to 18 for the combined opposition! Yet even today access to the polls is limited in many countries.

How is access constrained? The first limit is enfranchisement. Women only gained the right to vote in many Latin American countries during the past twenty-five years. Literacy is required in Brazil, Ecuador, and Peru, where the illiteracy rates are approximately 40 percent, 32 percent, and 39 percent. This bars millions from voting, and since the literate are more apt to be in urban areas, tends to reinforce the electoral importance of urban centers.[11] Chile retained a literacy requirement until 1970. In those countries where literacy is not required, cultural patterns prevent many women, illiterates, and youth from exercising their right to vote.[12]

Access to the polls is curtailed by other procedures. These include complicated registration procedures and other red tape, e.g., requiring one to vote in the district where he first registered, which excludes migrants to capital cities, as in Bogotá, Colombia. Controlling the hours, location, and procedures of local polling stations also occurs in Colombia. Controlling a party's registration is still another method of electoral restriction. Requiring each voter to step up and declare openly before the election board whether or not he favors, say, a new military general in power is not as frequent as in the old days,[13] but effective access to the polls remains a problem.

Regular and Frequent Elections

Elections in Latin America are neither frequent nor always regular in some countries. In place of elections, a coup d'etat is likely to occur just before or, if elections are held, shortly after to nullify the electoral returns. The Chilean and Uruguayan military coups in 1973 affirm this point. In other cases, elections are postponed or delayed in order to assure the continuation in power of a key leader, as with Hugo Banzer Súarez in Bolivia after 1971. The best records of regular and frequent elections are those of Chile, Costa Rica, Mexico, and Uruguay, but the military coups in 1973 in Chile and Uruguay tarnished their records severely.

Opportunity, Established Procedures, Fair Counting

These three aspects of electoral systems are undermined in Latin America by a number of prevailing norms. Arrest or exile of opposing candidates, violence, and control over the communications media restrict democratic elections. The Dominican Republic presidential elections of May, 1974, were accompanied by the customary campaign shootings, arrest of opposition supporters, and general violence. The Guatemalan election of March, 1974, led to charges of fraudulent vote counting. Buying votes, repressing or intimidating voters, and establishing quotas for municipalities and provinces are not uncommon. Elections are constrained by *imposición*, the *candidato único*, and *continuismo* discussed earlier.

Political Violence

Sociopolitical tensions run high in many Latin American countries. Spokesmen of the lower classes are enormously disillusioned with the rate of change in economic and social progress and with the seeming inability of political regimes to institute radical change for the urban and rural poor. These social and political tensions often take the form of guerrilla activity.

The list of complaints by guerrilla leaders runs high, and the specific sources of discontent are many. Lack of land for the landless poor, the effects of inflation on the lower classes, a foreign economic sector draining the country's resources, corruption in government by social and political elites, internal colonialism, random imprisonment of dissident intellectuals, university students, peasant leaders, or Churchmen, insufficient social-welfare, educational, and health facilities for the poor, and general institutionalized political repression are high on all the lists.

Rural and urban guerrilla warfare should not be underestimated as a major expression of anticitizenship. Guerrillas were active in many countries during the 1960s and 1970s, operating in both rural and urban regions. Foreign businesses, for example, paid out over fifty million dollars in total ransoms for kidnapped persons in 1973-74 alone, and one company—Exxon—paid 14.2 million dollars for *one* of its kidnapped executives. But foreign business executives and diplomats were not the only kidnapping targets. Local leaders were abducted, including the father-in-law of Mexico's president, 83-year-old José Guadalupe Zuno Hernandez, for a reported sixteen-million-dollar ransom and the freeing of 100 political prisoners in September, 1974. As the decade of the 1970s began, guerrillas were active in Argentina, Bolivia, Chile, Colombia, Guatemala, Mexico, Peru, Venezuela, and Uruguay. These guerrilla groups included the following:

ARGENTINA
Argentine Anti-Imperialist Alliance (AAA)
Armed Forces of Liberation (FAL)
Monteneros
People's Revolutionary Army (ERP)

Perónist Armed Forces (FAP)
Revolutionary Armed Forces (FAR)
Worker's Revolutionary Party (PRT)

BOLIVIA
Army of National Liberation (ELN)

CHILE
Revolutionary Left Movement (MIR)

COLOMBIA
Army of National Liberation (ELN)
Revolutionary Armed Forces of Colombia (FARC)

DOMINICAN REPUBLIC
Approximately sixteen groups reported to be operating illegally

GUATEMALA
Armed Forces of Rebellion (FAR)
13th of November Movement (MR-13)

MEXICO
23rd September Communist League
Party of the Poor
Revolutionary Armed Front of the People

URUGUAY
Tupamaros (Movement of National Liberation)

VENEZUELA
Armed Forces of National Liberation (FALN)
Revolutionary Left Movement (MIR)
Revolutionary Vanguard

Four militant left-wing organizations from Argentina, Bolivia, Chile, and Uruguay announced in February, 1974, that they would unite in a "junta of revolutionary coordination." These groups were the Argentinian ERP, Bolivian ELN, the Chilean MIR, and the Uruguayan Tupamaros.

Other protests explode from the left in Latin America. Violent strikes and demonstrations in country and city, assassination, and publicized declarations are some of the better-known forms. Widespread illegal acts are frequent in Argentina, such as those in late 1973, when guerrillas and disaffected workers occupied factories and administrative offices. Student, peasant, and worker-led strikes, demonstrations, and clashes with police exploded in Bolivia's Cochabamba province in May, 1974, after government economic measures produced a 100 percent rise in basic food items. Polarized left-right opposition in Chile brought that government to a standstill in September, 1973. These acts, frequently illegal by existing constitutional norms, are open indications of the low sense of citizenship felt by many on the political left.

Government reaction against political dissent is frequently swift and equally militant. These reactions, which further undermine political development, include use of the armed forces, torture, imprisonment for alleged subversive activities, and, at times, political killing.

Right-wing political groups, dedicated to terror and violence, emerged in the late 1960s to combat their left-wing foes. In Guatemala, right-wing terrorist organizations became institutionalized. The French weekly, *Le Monde*, reported in 1971 that for every political assassination in Latin America by a left-wing revolutionary, fifteen murders are committed by right-wing organizations. Many of the political killings from the right were attributed to such officially supported right-wing terrorist organizations as, *Ojo Por Ojo* (An Eye for an Eye) and *Mano Blanca* (White Hand). These groups appear to be operating relatively freely in Guatemala, with little visible attempt by the government to control them. Another publicized right-wing group is the *Patria y Libertad* Movement of Chile, which declared in May, 1973, (before Allende's fall) that the chances of action by the traditional parties were "exhausted" and that "direct action" was necessary against the Allende government. This group was instrumental in bringing down the Allende government. Other right-wing vigilante groups are the "Falcons" of Mexico (paramilitary shock troops), the Christian Nationalist Army of Bolivia (ECN), and the Anti-Communist Alliance (AAA) of Argentina. A wave of right- and left-wing political violence in Argentina—138 killed between July, 1974, when Mrs. Perón assumed the presidency from her late husband, Juan Domingo Perón, and November, 1974—led to a state of siege in that country.

UNDERLYING CAUSES OF LOW
POLITICAL DEVELOPMENT

Many forces account for continuing low political development in Latin America, as we have seen in the foregoing chapters. Special attention should be given to two areas of immediate concern for Latin American policymakers. The first is illiteracy; the second, what might be called the culture of poverty. Both are key aspects of alienated citizenry and low support for political regimes. The persistence of these conditions spells major difficulties ahead for governments concerned with political development.

Illiteracy

Formal education, of all the demographic variables normally studied as sources of political attitudes (sex, place of residence, occupation, income, etc.), appears to be the strongest.[14] Given the high rates of illiteracy in Latin America, the effects of education on political attitudes should be examined.

As Table 13 shows, twelve countries have 35 percent or greater illiteracy. Six countries are 50 percent or greater in illiteracy. These large percentages of illiterate people are not encouraging when one adds to them the very high population-growth figure of more than 3.0 in many countries. It is likely that large numbers of people will be virtually untouched by education in coming years, and this in turn cannot but affect the political process.

Studies show that educated people are likely to play a different role in the political process than uneducated ones. The difference is not due solely to an exclusion of illiterates from the electoral process, obviously an enormous factor where it operates. Brazil, for example, has a literacy requirement for voting, which effectively excludes at minimum approximately 40 percent of the population. Other countries, however, do not have any such requirement, including Chile after 1970, Costa Rica, Colombia, and Venezuela, so the difference in political roles between illiterates and literates, then, often lies elsewhere.

Education appears to have the following general effects on people:[15] It is likely to make them more aware of the impact of government on the individual, indicating that it tends to politicize individuals. The educated person, secondly, is more likely to follow politics, or at least election campaigns, making him or her potentially active in the political process. Thirdly, the educated person tends to have more political information than the uneducated, with opinions on a wider range of

TABLE 13   LITERATE POPULATION: 15 YEARS OF AGE AND OLDER

Country	Percentage of Population	Country	Percentage of Population
Argentina	91	Ecuador	68
Uruguay	91	Dominican Republic	65
Costa Rica	84	Peru	61
Chile	84	Brazil	61
Cuba	80+	Nicaragua	50
Panama	78	El Salvador	49
Mexico	78	Honduras	45
Venezuela	76	Guatemala	38
Paraguay	74	Bolivia	32
Colombia	73	Haiti	10

Source: *Statistical Abstract of Latin America*, ed. Kenneth Ruddle and Mukhtar Hamour (Los Angeles: University of California, Latin American Center), p. 132.

political subjects and more potential willingness to engage in political discussion. He also tends to feel himself more capable of influencing the government and is more likely to be a member of some political organization. Although the person with some education is more susceptible to media exposure, he is also more capable of following political events and potentially more able to play an independent role in the political system. This by no means is to argue that literacy determines how a person is going to participate in the political process. But education makes one a more likely citizen participant, thus contributing to political development.

Increased literacy in Latin America appears to facilitate the growth of political parties. It also seems associated with widened election participation, with fewer insurrections, and with expansion of the middle sector of society whose members desire modernization.[16] These changes in the structure of politics open yet other channels for participation and in some cases establish an institutional framework that can accommodate more peaceful transition of political power on a permanent basis. Table 14 suggests the impact of increased literacy on Latin America's political structures.

As Table 14 indicates, of the ten Latin American countries with 70 percent or more literacy, relatively wide participation in politics occurs through interest groups, elections, and political parties. Argentina is well known for its large labor movement inaugurated by Juan Domingo Perón, and seven republics have modern indigenous parties devoted to social reform, industrialization, and national development: the Colorado Party of Uruguay, the National Liberation Party of Costa Rica, the Christian Democrats (and *Unidad Popular* under Allende) of Chile, the Communist Party of Cuba, the Institutional Revolutionary Party of Mexico, Democratic Action and COPEI of Venezuela, and the Liberals of Colombia. These modernizing parties of the 1960s and 1970s range within individual party systems from the dominant single-party type in Mexico to the two-party system of Uruguay and the multiparty variety in Chile.[17] These parties aggregate diversified interests and help to ensure at least some form of participant citizenship. Countries of under 70 percent literacy have only two modernizing parties, as Table 14 indicates.

Of the nine presidential elections held during 1973-74, all were relatively free of preelectoral or electoral controls, or charges of fraud in the countries of 70 percent and above literacy. These countries included Argentina, Costa Rica, Colombia, and Venezuela. The elections held in countries of less than 70 percent literacy were associated with controls and/or charges of fraud. Those countries were Brazil, the Dominican Republic, Guatemala, and Nicaragua. Chile and Uruguay had excellent records of elections until the military coups of 1973.

TABLE 14 LITERACY, POLITICAL PARTIES, AND COUPS D'ETAT, 1945-73

Country	Literate Percentage of Population	Modern Institutionalized Political Party	Number of Coups
Argentina	91	None[b]	3
Uruguay	91	Colorado	1
Chile	84	Christian Democrats (CD)	1
Costa Rica	84	National Liberation Party (PLN)	1
Cuba	80+[a]	Communist Party (PCC)[c]	2
Mexico	78	Institutional Revolutionary Party (PRI)	0
Panama	78	None	3
Venezuela	76	Acción Democrática (AD)	3
Paraguay	74	None	4
Colombia	73	Liberal	2
Ecuador	68	None	4
Dominican Republic	65	None	1
Brazil	61	None	4
Peru	61	Popular Alliance for Revolutionary Action (APRA)	3
Nicaragua	50	None	0
El Salvador	49	None	3
Honduras	45	None	3
Guatemala	38	None	2
Bolivia	32	National Revolutionary Movement (MNR)	7
Haiti	10	None	3

[a] The literate figure for Cuba is undoubtedly much higher, given the enormous literacy campaigns that began after January, 1959.

[b] "Modern" here means dedicated to social reform, industrialization, and national development. Several institutionalized parties are not included because they are more traditional than modern.

[c] After January, 1959, Revolution.

Sources: Literacy rates from *Statistical Abstract of Latin America*. Number of coups from Martin C. Needler, "Political Development and Military Intervention in Latin America," *American Political Science Review* 50 (September 1966): 616-26; also later coups computed from Keesing's Archives.

High literacy rates and modern party systems also appear to be in some countries related to fewer coups d'etat and slightly less military intervention in civilian political affairs. The total number of coups d'etat (1945-73) in the ten countries of 70 percent or above literacy is twenty. The ten countries of below 70 percent literacy had a total number of thirty coups d'etat (see Table 14). Uruguay had not experienced a successful military intervention during the twentieth century until the coup of 1973, and Chile had a long period of civilian-dominated government, until its military overthrow also in 1973. Mexico and Costa Rica, in terms of the long-range record, are also relatively free of military intervention. The military in Venezuela appears at present content to allow the Democratic Action Party to run the government, and its nonintervention during the tense days of the December, 1963, presidential elections are positive signs for civilian predominance there. The new military of Cuba is well under the control of Fidel Castro, who has defeated military counterrevolution from the old professional army through a rebuilt armed forces, tight party organization, and personal control since January, 1959.

These facts suggest that a high literacy level, though insufficient in itself, is a necessary precondition for reduced military intervention, the development of political parties, effective elections, and a wider range of participant citizenship in general. Literacy has also stimulated the expansion of the middle sectors in Latin America by providing an educational base for semiprofessional and professional status, higher income, and social and political mobility. The ten countries with 70 percent and above literacy have a higher percentage of their labor forces in the intermediate and senior grade of industrial employment than the ten countries of lower than 70 percent literacy; and Argentina, with the highest literacy, has the largest industrial-management group. Not surprisingly, most countries with over 70 percent literacy also have a higher per capita income than those under 70 percent, and they are also more urbanized. To the extent that the middle sectors represent a potential for de facto expansion of participant citizenship, education appears to be playing an important role. On the correlations between a higher literate percentage of the population and (1) a higher GNP per capita, (2) a lower percentage of the labor force in agriculture, and (3) a higher percentage of the population living in cities, see Table 15. Education must be viewed as at least the precondition for expanding citizenship participation, and thus a central variable in government planning for future political development.

The Culture of Poverty

The economic factor is one of the most dominant, if not *the* most dominant, force preventing the transition toward increased citizenship and support of the government. It continues to hold back long-range political development through much of the Latin American region. The strength of this economic factor is found again and again in studies of political attitudes in Latin America which stress separation of the masses from the elite.[18]

TABLE 15 LITERACY AND MIDDLE-SECTOR FORMATION IN LATIN AMERICA, 1970

Country	Literate Percentage of Population	GNP Per Capita (U.S. dollars)	Percentage of Labor Force in Agriculture	Percentage Urban
Argentina	91	1160	20	74
Uruguay	91	820	18	80
Chile	84	720	28	68
Costa Rica	84	560	47	35
Cuba	80+	530	41	53
Panama	78	730	45	47
Mexico	78	670	54	53
Venezuela	76	980	32	72
Paraguay	74	260	55	36
Colombia	73	340	47	52
Ecuador	68	290	55	36
Dominican Republic	65	350	62	33
Peru	61	450	49	47
Brazil	61	420	53	46
Nicaragua	50	430	59	44
El Salvador	49	300	60	39
Honduras	45	280	66	23
Guatemala	38	360	65	34
Bolivia	32	180	48	35
Haiti	10	110	84	12
United States	98	3966	5	70

Sources: *Statistical Abstract of Latin America,* 1970; *A.I.D. Economic Data Book* (Washington, D.C., 1970).

Poverty breeds its own culture of anomie and alienation, places people in a highly disadvantageous social position, and makes them vulnerable to a wide array of sanctions that prevent social advancement and effective expression of political demands. Ignorance, fatalism, and disinterest about government and political processes are common among Latin America's urban and rural poor. The key point is that a person who is informed and interested is also one more likely to participate; the uninformed and apathetic are unlikely to be political participants, and poverty tends to structure this kind of symbiotic relationship.[19] As Alex Inkeles, a student of political development, writes, "a man will not have the inclination or extra energy to take an interest in public life and participate in civic activity until he attains a reasonably decent standard of living."[20]

The fatalism, apathy, and disinterest in politics is captured by a number of scholars who have studied the slum dwellers of urban Latin America's teeming capital cities. Sven Lindqvist, a Swedish observer, provides insight into the culture of poverty through his extensive interviews in the slum areas of Lima, Peru, as the following interview suggests:

Lindqvist: "So the rich will always be rich, and the poor poor?"
Respondent: "That's how it's been all my life and that's how it always
             will be."
Lindqvist: "Have you voted?"
Respondent: "Yes, I voted for the Acción Popular."
Lindqvist: "Why?"
Respondent: "You get fined if you don't vote."
Lindqvist: "Isn't the party any good then?"
Respondent: "If you have relatives and friends, the party will help
             you. I've never had a thing from them."[21]

Jesús Sánchez, the poor urban dweller studied by Oscar Lewis, had this to say about politics in Mexico:

> I don't know potatoes about politics. I read one or two paragraphs in the newspapers, but I don't take it seriously. Nothing in the news is important to me. A few days ago I read something about the Leftists. But I don't know what is the left and what is the right, or what is Communism. I am interested in only one thing . . . to get money to cover my expenses and to see that my family is more or less well.[22]

Urban poor people are highly vulnerable to sanctions that discourage their making demands or organizing any support behind demands. They feel, and are conditioned to be, inferior vis-à-vis those of higher social status. Social-service and political support for a lower-class individual in trouble with the government tends to be minimal in many Latin American countries, because government bureaucracy tends to be staffed by middle-sector people who perceive the lower classes as inferior and treat them accordingly. Labor unions where they exist are not always highly developed and are frequently restricted in their political activities.

The plight of the urban poor, and their potential for acquiring participant citizen attitudes, is underlined by the inability of some Latin American countries to absorb the working population in productive employment. This situation is complicated by the high population-growth rate. About 40 percent of Latin America's economically active labor pool was underemployed or unemployed during the 1960s, not a sound foundation for reducing urban poverty.[23]

If these attitudes and sanctions operate against participant citizenship by the urban poor, the culture of poverty is equally strong in rural areas. Some rural poor are subject to control by the large *latifundistas* who in some countries "vote them" at election time. Others, who live on *minifundias* (small land plots), are isolated from larger groups and society. Dwellers in Colombia rural communities, for example, have been found to be distrustful of institutions, leaders, and people not of their social group.[24] The conditions of internal colonialism, where rural poor are systematically dominated by landowners and thus constrained in developing a participant citizenship attitude, are well-known phenomena in Latin America.[25] These conditions are spawned by lack of occupational skills; abundance of cheap labor; a scattered population; tenant farming; and landlessness.

The number of people subjected to rural poverty in Latin America is extremely large. Approximately 5.7 million rural families were small landholders (*minifundistas*) in 1960. Another 6.9 million families were poor landless workers, who received extremely low wages or were paid in kind. The estimated 12.6 million poor rural families represented about 73 percent of the total of 17.2 million farm families in 1960. The income inequalities between these poor people and the wealthy landowners were great; they form the base of the culture of rural poverty that placed Latin America's peasantry in an extremely weak situation for transition to higher stages of politicization.

THE BRIGHT SIDE

The picture is by no means bleak. Latin America faces tomorrow with a number of political assets, and it should not be assumed that traditional lifestyles are incompatible with development. First, the commitment to development (both politically and economically) is strong on the part of a large number of Latin American leaders. The 1960s accentuated this trend, as did election campaigns in the 1970s. The strength of commitment to development varies from country to country, but on balance sharply contrasts with the nineteenth-century status quo political and economic stalemate by landed oligarchs, the Church, and nonreformist military organizations.

Second, several political systems are relatively stable and, at least by their own past histories if not that of the developed world, seem capable of beginning to mobilize the consensus and power required for economic development. Brazil, Cuba, Mexico, Peru, Panama, and Venezuela illustrate the point. Stability is achieved by various political alternatives: economic-development-minded military rule in Brazil, Panama, and Peru; strong-man, charismatic rule in Cuba; a strong president and dominant single party in Mexico. These regimes are trying in various ways to build support for their policies, and to mobilize the human and material resources for improved standards of living.

Third, a number of the Latin American countries possess those raw materials that are of growing demand in the developed world, such as, oil in Mexico, Peru, and Venezuela, and sugar in Cuba. This raw-material possession may strengthen their capacity to earn the foreign exchange required for capital formation. As President Carlos Andrés Pérez of Venezuela argued in a full page *New York Times* advertisement in September, 1974, higher oil prices could be used to strike a more favorable balance in the cost of manufactured goods from the developed countries—traditionally much higher than the earnings from raw-material exports of the developing countries. Venezuela authorized a total state take-over of the oil industry in August, 1975, paving the way for dynamic new development projects.

Fourth, the Latin American countries—now identifying with the Third World developing areas—show a willingness to experiment with new approaches to development (or to update older approaches). Expropriation and curtailment of foreign businesses in certain sectors (Andean Pact countries, Cuba), encouragement of private foreign investment in others (Argentina, Brazil, Mexico), joining in new regional economic organizations (the Andean Pact, Caribbean Free Trade Area), worker participation in industrial communities (Peru), taxing basic exports (such as bananas in Panama), total mobilization of society (Cuba), and mixed economies (Argentina, Brazil, Mexico) are some of the better-known options.

A new determination to widen their trading outlets is a fifth positive asset. An increasing number of countries began to trade with the Soviet Union, China, and Japan during the 1960s. This trend is likely to continue, as will that of widened trade relations with Cuba, which opened in July, 1975, when the Organization of American States ended its political and economic sanctions against Cuba, thus lifting an eleven-year-old embargo imposed against Cuba for fostering Communist guerrilla activities in the hemisphere. This meant also a lifting of a United States ban on exports to Cuba by foreign subsidiaries of American countries, although the embargo on direct trade between Cuba and the United States remained in force as of August, 1975. These new trade patterns in Latin America reflect the new accent on independent trade lanes, rather than the older one that led to the United States.

These trends suggest that the politics of tomorrow will increasingly turn on the politics of economic development. How is economic development of the country to proceed? What political decisions will be made to encourage it? Who will be affected by the decisions? What conflicts will be generated and how will they be reconciled? How resistent to change will the traditional elites be? Will new policies toward population control be exerted, given the population pressures on rapid urbanization and the parallel issues of how to cope with housing and transportation shortages, squatter settlements, health, and employment? What will be the treatment of private foreign investment, and who will be affected internally by the decisions made? (Conversely, what role will foreign investors, lenders, and traders be playing vis-à-vis the Latin American countries?)

Other political decisions indicate the risks and costs involved, adding to political—and economically related—difficulties. Fidel Castro's decision to adopt a Marxist-Leninist ideology and to throw in his lot with the U.S.S.R. in the early 1960s sparked a mass exodus of highly skilled technicians, managers, and agronomists sorely needed by Castro's plans for development. It meant heavy investments in education to train replacements. Salvador Allende's decision to nationalize the copper industries with relatively low compensation (at least in the eyes of those concerns expropriated) led to severe economic pressures by the foreign companies affected and by their government, especially in light of the U.S. curtailment of public and private loans. The Peruvian military began to have difficulties after 1969, partly due to a raised level of expectations about mass participation, local economic decisions, and better employment, not always matched by performance. The politics of the future, then, will be oriented sharply in the economic domain.

A number of more strictly political questions will face the Latin American governments and people tomorrow. To what extent can institutionalized political procedures be adopted to guarantee against the violation of civil liberties from the left and right? Under what conditions will constitutionally elected governments committed to reform be allowed to remain in power where the military is powerful? Can citizenship identity be strengthened as a basis for evolving more open participatory political regimes? Will increased attention turn to nation-building as in Cuba, Mexico, and Peru?

Emotions and violence run strong in Latin America. The repressive character of many governments, manifested in closing down opposition presses, curtailing political parties, torture, and political arrests in Brazil, Chile, Peru, and Uruguay in the early 1970s, is one aspect of this setting. Radical leftist activities, such as bombings, sabotage, assassinations, and kidnappings in Argentina, Mexico, and elsewhere are another phase of Latin American emotionalism and frustration with institutionalized problem solving. These activities, coupled with growing evidence of right-wing vigilante groups indicate a decline of citizenship identity (or, more accurately, a decline in the *potential* for forming citizenship, since in many cases it is not strong in the first place). The 1973 military overthrows of the long-term democratic systems in Chile and Uruguay are not hopeful signs of the political future. Only the future will reveal the outcomes to Latin America's challenging political questions.

NOTES

1. See Norman Keehn, "Building Authority: A Return to Fundamentals," *World Politics* 26 (April 1974): 329-52; Edward Feit, "Pen, Sword, and People: Military Regimes in the Formation of Political Institutions," *World Politics* 25 (January 1973): 251-73.

2. Reid Reading, "Political Socialization in Colombia and the United States: An Exploratory Study," *Midwest Journal of Political Science* 12 (August 1968): 352-81.

3. Alex Inkeles, "Participant Citizenship in Six Developing Countries," *American Political Science Review* 63 (December 1969): 1120-41.

4. James C. Scott, *Comparative Political Corruption* (Englewood Cliffs, N.J.: Prentice-Hall, 1972), p. 4.

5. Charles E. Chapman, "The Cuban Election Problem," *The American Review of Reviews* 70 (October 1924): 413-19.

6. See Kenneth Johnson, *Mexican Democracy: A Critical View* (Boston: Allyn and Bacon, 1971), pp. 47, 165-66, who discusses these points as they occur in Mexico, one of the more "modern" Latin American states. See also Charles W. Anderson, *Politics and Economic Change in Latin America* (New York: Van Nostrand, 1967), pp. 140-49; and Leo B. Lott, *Venezuela and Paraguay: Political Modernity and Tradition in Conflict* (New York: Holt, Rinehart and Winston, 1972), pp. 101, 129, 298-99.

7. See *Latin America* 7 (February 9, 1973): 42-44.

8. Sven Lindqvist, *The Shadow: Latin America Faced the Seventies* (London: Penguin Books, 1972), chs. 1 and 2.

9. Dieter K. Zschock, et al., "The Education—Work Transition of Venezuelan University Students," *Journal of Inter-American Studies and World Affairs* 16 (February 1974): 96-118; Johnson, *op. cit.*, p. 47; and Almond and Verba, *op. cit.*, pp. 495-96.

10. See Ronald McDonald's perceptive essay, "Electoral Fraud and Regime Controls in Latin America," *Western Political Quarterly* 25 (March 1972): 81-95.

11. On this tendency in Brazil, see Phyllis Peterson, "Brazil: Institutionalized Confusion," in *Political Systems of Latin America*, ed. Martin C. Needler. (New York: Van Nostrand, 1964).

12. Daniel Goldrich, *Sons of the Establishment* (Chicago: Rand McNally, 1966), pp. 105-7.

13. President Carlos Castillo Armas of Guatemala used this procedure in

October, 1954, after he overthrew the Jacobo Arbenz regime. The voter's answer was written down in the election book, and the voter signed "Si" or "No" after his name. The final vote: 485, 531 "Si" and 393, "No." We don't know what happened to the 393 naysayers.

14. Inkeles, op. cit., pp. 1132-33; Almond and Verba, op. cit., p. 379.
15. Almond and Verba, op. cit., pp. 380-81.
16. See W. Raymond Duncan, "Education and Political Development: The Latin American Case," The Journal of Developing Areas 2 (January 1968): 187-210.
17. Party activity in Chile and Uruguay was curtailed by the military intervention of 1973, and it remains to be seen what role political parties will play in the future of these countries. Until 1973 they were dynamic parts of participiant citizenship and development.
18. See Inkeles, op. cit., p. 134; Oscar Lewis, The Children of Sanchez, (New York: Random House, 1961); Irving Louis Horowitz, Masses in Latin America (London and New York: Oxford University Press, 1970); and Lindqvist, op. cit., chs. 1 and 2.
19. Daniel Goldrich, Raymond B. Pratt, and C. R. Schuller, "The Political Integration of Lower-Class Urban Settlements in Chile and Peru," Masses in Latin America, ed. Irving Louis Horowitz (New York: Oxford University Press, 1970), p. 149.
20. Inkeles, op. cit., p. 134.
21. Lindqvist, op. cit., p. 25.
22. Lewis, op. cit., p. 424.
23. Economic Survey of Latin America, 1969 (New York: United Nations, 1970), p. 7.
24. Camillo Torres Restrepo, "Social Change and Rural Violence in Colombia," in Horowitz, op. cit., p. 509.
25. Rodolfo Stavenhagen, "Classes, Colonialism, and Acculturation," in Horowitz, op. cit., pp. 235-88; and Julio Cotler, "The Mechanics of Internal Domination and Social Change in Peru," in ibid., pp. 407-44.

Suggested Readings

Adie, Robert F. and Guy E. Poitras. Latin America: The Politics of Immobility. Englewood Cliffs, N.J.: Prentice-Hall, 1974.

Einaudi, Luigi, et al. Latin American Institutional Development: The Changing Catholic Church. Santa Monica, Calif.: The Rand Corporation, October, 1969.

Inkeles, Alex. "Participant Citizenship in Six Developing Countries," The American Political Science Review 63 (December 1969): 1120-41.

Johnson, Kenneth. Mexican Democracy: A Critical View. Boston: Allyn and Bacon, 1971.

La Belle, Thomas J. Education and Development: Latin America and the Caribbean. Los Angeles: Latin American Center, University of California, 1972.

Lindqvist, Sven. *The Shadow: Latin America Faces the Seventies*. London: Penguin Books, 1972.

Russel, Charles, James A. Miller, and Robert E. Hildner. "The Urban Guerrilla in Latin America: A Select Bibliography," *Latin American Research Review* 9 (Spring 1974): 37-80.

Stokes, William S. "Violence as a Power Factor in Latin American Politics," *Western Political Quarterly* 5 (September 1952).

Williams, Edward J. and Freeman J. Wright. *Latin American Politics: A Developmental Approach*. Palto Alto, Calif.: Mayfield, 1975.

Appendices

APPENDIX A POPULATION AVERAGE ANNUAL GROWTH RATE
(1960-70), GROSS NATIONAL PRODUCT PER CAPITA,
AND AVERAGE ANNUAL GROWTH RATE (1960-70)

Country	Population (thousands)	Growth Rate (percent)	GNP per capita (U.S. dollars)	Growth Rate (percent)
Argentina	23,212	1.5	1,160	2.5
Bolivia	4,931	2.6	180	2.5
Brazil	92,764	2.9	420	2.4
Chile	9,780	2.3	720	1.6
Colombia	21,632	3.2	340	1.7
Costa Rica	1,727	3.3	560	3.2
Cuba	8,390	2.1	530	—0.6
Dominican Republic	4,068	3.0	350	0.5
Ecuador	6,093	3.4	290	1.7
El Salvador	3,534	3.7	300	1.7
Guatemala	5,190	3.1	360	2.0
Haiti	4,867	2.0	110	—0.9
Honduras	2,520	3.3	280	1.8
Mexico	50,670	3.5	670	3.7
Nicaragua	1,984	3.5	430	2.8
Panama	1,464	3.3	730	4.2
Paraguay	2,379	3.1	260	1.3
Peru	13,586	3.1	450	1.4
Uruguay	2,886	1.3	820	—0.4
Venezuela	10,399	3.5	980	2.3
United States	204,800	1.2	4,760	3.2

Source: *Finance and Development* 10 (March 1973): 26-27.

APPENDIX B POPULATION: HEALTH, URBANIZATION, LABOR FORCE
IN AGRICULTURE

Country	Life Expectancy	Inhabitants per Physicians	Percentage Urban	Percentage of Labor Force in Agriculture
Argentina	67	610	74	18
Bolivia	50	3,570	35	48
Brazil	57	2,530	46	52
Chile	61	1,590	68	28
Colombia	60	2,340	52	47
Costa Rica	65	1,860	35	49
Cuba	67	–	53	41
Dominican Republic	58	1,920	33	61
Ecuador	54	3,030	36	53
El Salvador	58	4,110	39	60
Guatemala	49	3,810	34	65
Haiti	47	16,000	12	83
Honduras	49	4,490	23	67
Mexico	60	1,810	53	47
Nicaragua	54	2,350	44	60
Panama	61	1,880	47	46
Paraguay	58	1,870	36	54
Peru	53	2,030	47	50
Uruguay	71	880	80	18
Venezuela	66	1,220	72	32
United States	71	650	70	5

Source: U.S. State Department, Agency for International Development. *Economic Data Book,
Latin America* (February 1970).

APPENDIX C LAND, COMMUNICATIONS, TRANSPORTATION

Country	Agricultural Land (percentage of area)	Telephones (thousands)	Motor Vehicles Registered (thousands)	Roads (improved; miles per 1,000 square miles)
Argentina	61	1,553	1,786	56
Bolivia	13	30	25	30
Brazil	16	1,473	2,487	156
Chile	19	295	233	116
Colombia	17	735	241	60
Costa Rica	30	27	51	194
Cuba	—	—	—	—
Dominican Republic	40	34	20	274
Ecuador	18	45	54	88
El Salvador	59	38	44	314
Guatemala	19	35	57	148
Haiti	31	4.3	16	51
Honduras	38	10	22	33
Mexico	52	1,046	1,524	54
Nicaragua	14	13	33	62
Panama	18	58	47	65
Paraguay	27	16	19	22
Peru	23	152	203	28
Uruguay	86	195	197	7.6
Venezuela	24	327	524	66
United States	47	103,750	99,960	900

Source: U.S. State Department, Agency for International Development. *Economic Data Book, Latin America* (February 1970).

Index

271

National Conference of Brazilian Bishops, 163
National Front (Colombia), 184
nationalism, 84ff.
  in Cuba, 40-43, 74, 94-95
  present in Mexico, 38, 74, 94
  missing in Guatemala, 46
  in Costa Rica, 50
  in Peru, 95, 127
  in Paraguay, 96
  Indian, 127
  in political parties, 197-98
  in military, 213
nationality
  and political consciousness, 75
  and ethnic identity, 84-88
  and political stability, 93-94
  legitimizing state authority, 96-97
  and Ibero-Latin tradition, 97-98
National Liberation Army (ELN, Bolivia), 62
National Liberation Party, 135, 256
National Merchants Federation (FENALCO, Colombia), 174
National Party (Chile), 185
National Revolutionary Movement (MNR, Bolivia), 61, 125
  and landed interests, 158
  agrarian reform, 167
  peasants, 168
National Society of Agriculture (Chile), 160
National War College (Washington, D.C.), 205
Neapolitan, 87, 90
Needler, Martin, 124, 207, 216-17
Nicaragua, 49-50
Nixon, Richard, 60

Odría, Manuel, 106
Oduber Quiros, Daniel, 23, 50
Ojo por Ojo (Guatemala), 254
Organization of American States (OAS), 9-11, 42-43, 49-50, 61, 262
Organization of Central American States, 5
Osorio, Carlos Arana, 47
Ovando Candia, Alfredo, 62, 206

Páez, José Antonio, 188
palanca, 107, 176

Panama, 50-52
  export tax on bananas, 231-32
Panama Canal, 51
Paraguay, 68-69, 214
Paraguayan Bishops Conference, 163
Parsons, Talcott, 101
Partido Colorado (PC, Red Party, Uruguay), 184
Partido Liberal Nacionalista (PLN, National Liberation Party, Nicaragua), 183
Partido Nacional (PN, National Party, Uruguay), 184
Partido Revolucionario Institucional (PRI, Mexico), 38, 94, 106, 135, 146, 158
  and labor, 166
  peasants, 167
  as dominant single party, 183
  and political development, 256
Partido Socialista (PS, Socialist Party, Chile), 185n, 186
Party of National Action (PAN, Mexico), 38
Party of the Poor (Mexico), 253
Patria y Libertad (Chile), 254
patron-client relations, 110
Paz Estenssoro, Víctor, 61, 158
peasants, 167-70
  in Honduras, 168
  in Bolivia, 168
People's Revolutionary Army (ERP, Argentina), 252
Pérez, Carlos Andrés, 9, 23, 54-55, 146
Pérez Jiménez, Marcos, 55, 106, 172, 188
Perón, Isabel, 63, 67, 165, 254
Perón, Juan D., 63, 66-67, 91, 106, 146-47, 186, 216, 254, 256
  return to Argentina, 196
Peronist Armed Forces (FAP), 253
personalismo, 104ff., 172, 203
Peru, 57-58
  reform-oriented movements, 58
  university students, 171
  military in development, 205, 214
Pinilla, Rojas, 56, 106, 184
Platt, Robert S., 78
political culture, 20
  defined, 15-16